ALSO BY WILLIAM DAMON

*Greater Expectations: Overcoming the Culture of Indulgence
in Our Homes and Schools*

*Some Do Care: Contemporary Lives of Moral
Commitment* (with Anne Colby)

The Moral Child

*Self-Understanding in Childhood and
Adolescence* (with Daniel Hart)

The Social World of the Child

THE
YOUTH
CHARTER

How Communities Can

Work Together to

Raise Standards

for All Our Children

———

WILLIAM DAMON

THE FREE PRESS
New York London Toronto Sydney Singapore

*f*P

THE FREE PRESS
A Division of Simon & Schuster Inc.
1230 Avenue of the Americas
New York, NY 10020

Manufactured in the United States of America

10 9 8 7 6 5 4 3 2 1

Library of Congress Cataloging-in-Publication Data

Damon, William, 1944–
    Youth charter : how communities can work together to raise
standards for all our children / William Damon.
        p.   cm.
    Includes bibliographical references and index.
    1. Child rearing—Moral and ethical aspects.   2. Moral
development.   3. Moral education.   4. Community organization.
I. Title.
HQ769.D2253   1997
649'.7—dc21   97-23786
                                                                    CIP

ISBN 0-684-82995-9

TO
JOSEF
AND
MARSY MITTLEMANN

Contents

Preface

When it comes to the hopes and dreams that you hold for your children, you have more in common with the people around you than you may realize. Beneath the sense of isolation that has divided our communities, we all share a deep well of concern for the younger generation. If we can find a way to tap into that well, child rearing can become the secure and fulfilling joy that it should be, rather than the risky and nerve-wracking challenge that it has become for too many parents.

Everywhere I go, parents and teachers complain that the forces influencing children have spun wildly out of their control. How can a parent pass on good values when children are exposed to every imaginable form of sordidness through the mass media? How can a teacher pass on skills and knowledge when the popular and peer cultures discourage serious academic motivation? Other citizens, too, express concerns. How can a pediatrician, seeing her caseload bursting with unnecessary teenage health disasters—suicide attempts, alcoholism and drug abuse, eating disorders, assaults, injuries from driving accidents—do anything effective about preventing the damage when her young patients refuse to take her warning seriously? How can a citizen, seeing his home town wracked by youth vandalism, theft, and other petty crime, stop young people from destroying his town—and their own futures—when neither the police nor the youngsters' families seem able to control the youngsters' behavior?

We must ask ourselves: *Is the world today as wholesome a place to raise children as the places where we ourselves grew up?* If we cannot answer this question with a resounding yes, we must take positive steps to create a better cultural climate for our children. The first step must be to resist feeling helpless about the social forces shaping our children's futures.

This book is about how adults who care about the future of young people—parents, teachers, community members—can regain the control that they need to raise a healthy younger generation. We can regain control by joining together around a shared set of high standards and expectations for the young. Borrowing from some recent work in education and sociology, I am calling this shared vision a "youth charter."[1]

Young people today receive many contradictory messages concerning the standards they are expected to meet, and the multiple voices they hear can create a confusing cacophony of demands. Teachers encourage a student to study hard, but the child's peers think that schoolwork is dorky. A guidance counselor advocates the importance of fair play, while a sports coach insists that his players do whatever it takes to win the big game. Parents expect their child to speak respectfully, but their child's teenage television idols emanate contempt for adults—and why not, since all the storylines make adults out to be clueless nitwits? Some of a child's teachers demand achievement, service, or obedience; others proclaim that youth is a time for playfulness, freedom, avoiding stress, and building self-esteem. Youngsters search in vain to find the coherent and inspiring guidance they need for a successful transition to responsible adulthood.

The youth charter is an approach that brings together all adults who are in positions to influence young people—parents, teachers, town officials, police, clergy, sports coaches, club leaders, counselors, news media, employers—in the quest to define high community standards for youth development. A youth charter focuses on the core features of character and competence that young people need to acquire in order to become responsible citizens.

A community youth charter, written or unwritten, identifies a community's standards and expectations for young people's behavior and creates occasions for imparting these standards and expectations to the young. It guides the younger generation toward fundamental standards of honesty, civility, decency, respect, the pursuit of excellence, courage, skill, and a sense of purpose in work. A youth charter can open new lines of communication and start productive conversations, triggering the cultivation of resources and other opportunities for youth development. Youth charters can be revised as circumstances dictate, and because they reflect each community, they vary.

Youth charters, as powerful communication devices, can help young people understand the reactions of others to their behavior. When a teacher is disappointed in a child's performance or when a police officer calls a parent about a misbehaving teenager, a youth charter can turn the emotional experience into a constructive lesson. Youth charters can provide the basis for rigorous academic standards at school. They also can provide conduits for regular feedback between parent and child and create as well healthy links between young people and the adult community. Youth charters can be critical in dealing with crises, such as a sudden incident of self-destructive behavior or a school cheating scandal. It can help a community overcome the usual blaming and finger-pointing when such crises occur.

In my usage, the youth charter has two distinct but interconnected meanings. The first meaning is the process of building youth charters through town meetings, task forces, and other conversations among parents, teachers, community members, and young people. The second meaning is the product—the actual set of standards and expectations (often unwritten) that comprises a youth charter, providing guidance for young people in all areas of their lives. Both meanings are central to the notion of the youth charter.

The process of building a community youth charter is a method for establishing the core consensus that some places have enjoyed all along, but that has waned in many sectors of our divided society. The process relies on a series of large- and small-group conversations among members of a community—meetings among parents, teachers, police, sports coaches, religious leaders, local news media producers, employers of youth, and other concerned adults. These conversations can take many forms, and their outcomes can be as diverse as our society itself. The ultimate shape of the conversations and subsequent actions must be determined from within the community. It is variable, permeable, and evolving. One community may use a youth charter primarily to promote academic achievement among its young. Another may use it to discourage drug use and drinking at teen parties. A third may focus on spirituality or community service, a fourth on how to make sports, recreation, and part-time employment into character-building activities for young people. Each community takes up its own combination of concerns, and each resolves them in its own way. In this sense, the youth charter is a kind of operating system. It makes youth programs effective, but—within a very broad set of constraints—it does not define the nature of the programs. The youth charter process opens the system up for the work that needs to be done.

A youth charter is not about just any conceivable set of standards and expectations. It reflects the basic standards of civilized living, including respect, compassion, common decency, honesty, fairness, and personal responsibility. It also promotes high standards of achievement in school and other work settings. It is *not* a values-neutral approach. In fact, if there is one thing that we have learned from educational history, it is that neutral approaches—such as extreme moral relativism—do little more than pass on to young people the cynical message that adults have no principles that they care about enough to stand by.

In this sense, the youth charter is literally what it says: a charter of specific principles to guide the raising and education of the young. This does not mean that the youth charter is a formal document, written in stone, imposed from above, or identical in all contexts. It is a set of evolving understandings, some negotiable and some steadfast, that form the basis of deliberation and action. For example, a community from time to time might reconsider the specific sanctions that it imposes to deter cheating in school or vandalism on the streets while still affirming its continuing adherence to standards of honesty and respect for public property. A youth charter arises from within a community, and it reflects the community's experiences and circumstances.

In this book, I describe both the process of building youth charters and some of the core standards and expectations that will play a role in most community charters. Young people encounter standards and expectations in multiple contexts—at home, at school, through the mass media, on sports teams, on jobs, among friends—and so I have devoted chapters to each of these settings. My first purpose is to show how all the major influences on young people in these settings can impart high standards and lofty expectations. My second purpose is to show how all these influences can work together, supporting rather than undermining one another.

I believe that every community has the capacity to establish a useful youth charter. Indeed, every community can do so on its own, without outside experts or a grand movement. This book offers my ideas about how this could take place. I present ideas about how such efforts can be launched, what a successful youth charter might look like, and which conditions in homes, schools, and society need to be changed in order to support such an effort.

The solutions that I offer are action-oriented. They bring together all members of a community to create common standards for young people's behavior, and they offer ways to keep these standards alive in the daily behavior of the young. Key players in this effort are the adults who are in positions to promote healthy development in the young. The main beneficiaries of the effort are the young people, the future of our society. I hope that my proposals will benefit the adults at the same time as the children. By opening new lines of communication around common standards, adults not only can help young people build a sense of purpose, but they can also create a sense of community for themselves. In this way, the youth charter holds the promise of reconstituting fragmented communities around a purpose that practically all people care about: the prospects and well-being of our young.

Acknowledgments

Anne Gregory, my research associate during the past two years, has been a true partner in our fledgling efforts to start youth charter discussions in local communities. Anne's dedication and good sense have contributed greatly to whatever success we have had in the initial attempts at launching this approach. Our research assistant, Lauren Bierbaum, also deserves thanks for her excellent support during youth charter meetings and also for organizing the start of a database on youth charter outcomes.

I am grateful to Lisa Stone and Judy Jones for spearheading the first comprehensive youth charter initiative in Wellesley, Massachusetts. I thank them not only for their help in arranging town meetings and other youth charter events, but also for the encouragement that they offered us. In this regard, I also thank John Whyman, Fred Livezey, and Rita Allen for their leadership of youth charter task forces, and also Jane Davidson and all the members of DAPAC for their vital support.

The town of Wellesley has shown me what is possible when citizens dedicate themselves to the futures of young people. (In order to prevent false inferences, I wish to be clear that I did *not* have Wellesley—or any other particular town, for that matter—in mind when I wrote the fictional account of Windsor for the first two chapters. In fact, the incidents that I invented for the fictional account in Chapters 2 and 3 bear little if any resemblance to *any* specific incidents that I have observed in Wellesley.)

In Rhode Island, Mike Cerullo of Spurwink gave us some welcome encouragement, as well as an opportunity to try out the approach with a number of youth service professionals and community leaders. In New Hampshire, Jim Zeppieri of the Louis Necho Trust hosted a town meeting that provided us with early formative experience in arranging and facilitating discussion groups. I express my appreciation to both of them and to all the others who have shown interest in this approach. Any new approach is most in need of a boost in its early stages, and I am grateful to all parents, teachers, professionals, and newswriters who provided us with such a boost.

For generous personal support and advice, I give special thanks to Joe and Marsy Mittlemann, to whom this book is dedicated. I also offer thanks to Howard Gardner for the continued lift that his friendship and writings have given me and to Nancy and Mike McCaskey for their valued support and the fine examples that they are setting with their work in professional sports and in the Chicago community. Vartan Gregorian's friendship, mentoring, and moral leadership have been a major influence on the direction of my own work, and he also has shown me how an institution can be brought to life by infusing it with a spirit of community.

My intellectual debts in this book are spread across many disciplines. In addition to my usual sources from human development, education and psychology, I also have drawn from sociological theory in the tradition of Emile Durkheim and Robert Bellah. I am grateful to Professor Bellah for the time and advice that he gave Anne Colby and me in our examinations of social responsibility in contemporary society. I have learned a great deal from the writings of sociologist and educator Francis Ianni, who (to the best of my knowledge) coined the phrase "youth charter." I thank Professor Ianni for his splendid 1989 book, *The Structure of Experience,* and for two unpublished reports and manuscripts that he graciously sent to me. Yet I should state plainly that

I have interpreted the notion of youth charter in my own way and that Professor Ianni bears no responsibility for the way in which I use the concept, which I know departs from his own meaning in some significant ways.

Thanks, too, to Susan Arellano, my excellent editor; to Pat Balsofiore; to Kim Witherspoon; to my wife, Anne Colby; and to my three children, Jesse, Maria, and Caroline, who never stop reminding me that I still have a long way to go in understanding the mysteries and constant surprises of child and adolescent development.

PART ONE

THE NEED

1

WINDSOR, 1997/98

The following excerpts are drawn from the diary of Frank Castor, a high school guidance counselor in the pleasant suburban town of Windsor, Ohio. Frank has worked at the high school since the mid-1980s. Before that, he served as a junior officer in the U.S. Navy, and then, for a couple of frustrating years, he tried his hand at journalism and creative writing. Frank began his high school career as an English teacher, then moved up to assistant principal, then became head of the school guidance department. The diary excerpts quoted here cover the school year 1997/98.

These excerpts tell the first part of a before-and-after story from Frank's perspective. Chapter 2 relates the second part of the story from several other perspectives in addition to Frank's. The main story line across the two chapters is as follows: During two turbulent years, a modern suburban town transforms itself from a divided collection of isolated people into a community that comes together in an effort to create a more wholesome environment for the town's young. In the course of the effort, the townsfolk discover and use high common standards for raising their young.

The "before" part of the story, captured in Frank's diary, will seem familiar to anyone who has read the local newspapers or journeyed out into the local streets and schools. Windsor in 1997/1998 is all too typical of many affluent but conflict-ridden towns and cities today. The signs of social isolation, mutual distrust, and cynicism are easy enough to recognize. It is the "after" part of the story in Chapter 2 that may sound far-fetched to readers. The remaining nine chapters of this book are dedicated to making Chapter 2 as plausible as Chapter 1.

The town of Windsor, the dates, the diary, Frank, and all the people in the story are fictional. Yet all the events are actual—or, to be more precise, each event in the diary has some parallel in an actual story. The events resemble incidents that I have observed or learned about through other means. I have changed or invented all identifying information for this fictional account. In fact, many of the events resemble not one but a number of incidents that I have heard about; and so this is the place to say that readers who may believe that they recognize themselves in this fictional account do so because such events are commonplace, not because I am discussing them in particular. In fact, most incidents that I recount have occurred not just a few times but many times, in thousands of places around the world, and with increasing frequency during the past decade or two.

This does not mean that I have seen all these events occurring together in one town, such as the fictive Windsor. Yet incidents of this sort are abundant enough that they could all happen in one spot, and perhaps they have. I am sure that this is true of the "before" part of the story. It is my hope that we will see a time when this can be said just as readily about the "after" part, in Chapter 2.

Frank's diary

29 August 1997. The end of another summer, with school just around the corner. Committee meetings all week, trying to get things ready for the opening day. I'm sorry to see that there is no hope of cleaning off the school walls anytime soon. I have never seen so much graffiti. The designs swirl into one another like angry insects. Where *do* the kids get hold of all these gaudy neon spray paints?

I'm not sure why the graffiti bother me so much. The police consider it such a small matter that they don't bother to patrol for it. Even when they catch kids red-handed (or purple-, white-, or green-handed, as the case may be), they never make much out of it. If the police did, I suppose the parents would have a fit. It's just another matter of "kids will be kids," and the parents here would fight any police action that could lead to their kid getting a record.

Maybe I should take a more cheerful view on this, like the newspaper article last year that celebrated the "folk artists" who paint the stuff. The article quoted a teacher as saying: "These kids are really artists first and foremost . . . they have a lot of talent." Hearing this, of course, the kids openly bragged about their activity. One boy who was caught told the reporter that he would keep on spraying: "A real writer never quits, no matter what," he said. Another boy was quoted as saying, "You walk around your neighborhood, you feel great. Every stop sign, every wall, every surface in my neighborhood has my name on it."[1] Some stores in town are selling magazines dedicated to the hip new "urban/suburban art form" of spray-painting graffiti. The magazines display fancy new methods of splattering walls, mailboxes, and street signs.

2 September 1997. First day of school. We got our union contract ratified in time to avoid any disruptions this year. I'm glad about that, though there are two provisions in the contract that I'm not crazy about: teachers are not allowed to stay after school to do extra work with students, and teachers will meet exactly once with each student's parents during the year—no more and no less.

The union's position is that extra teacher meetings with students or parents are all right, but they should be seen as a negotiable commodity—a bargaining chip. If the town wants teachers to do more, it needs to provide more pay. If you think about this in terms of economics alone, it's a reasonable position. But the district says it can't pay more, so teachers are left without a way to communicate to students and parents as often as they need to. Some teachers aren't happy about this, but there's really nothing they can do. The union threatens to bring them up on work rules violations if they do more on their own. It's odd to think of teachers getting angry over "rate busting." Teaching used to be considered a calling, a career full of personal dedication and satisfaction. Something has gotten lost somewhere along the way.

9 September 1997. Today we tried out a new school institution: Pride in Me and My Family Day. All the students made statements in class about what it was about themselves and their families that made them proud. They really got into it—a very high-energy day. In fact, it got a bit raucous. I wonder if the conversations might have been more reflective if we had allowed them to talk about their parents' work. I understand why teachers decided to rule that out; there's a lot of occupational inequality in our society, and students might feel bad if they found out that some kids' parents have better jobs than their own parents. Still, this didn't leave a whole lot to talk about on the family end. The kids ended up comparing their parents' lifestyles—the clothes, the cars, the clubs, the money—or joking about how their parents act. Some of the imitations that I saw did make me laugh, though I don't think we'll want to go public with this part of the event.

16 September 1997. What are we going to do about the boys' bathroom? I've been given the problem to deal with but, as usual, no resources to provide monitors or guards. I can't believe the things that they have been doing in there. It's one thing to smoke on the sly. We all used to do that. But these kids are wrecking the place. Every day last week they jammed the toilets with paper, bottles, cans—you name it. Yesterday they tore the doors off all the stalls. You would think that they would want the doors on for privacy, considering all the smoking that goes on in there. It's all totally senseless. Meanwhile I'm the person who's supposed to figure out a solution.

17 September 1997. So much for verbal negotiation and the law of reason. Ted Hughes [our new school principal] and I stopped a group of boys in the hall for being loud and disorderly, but the real point was to talk with them about what has been going on in the bathroom. At first, I was glad that Ted was there. As principal, he has some real authority in a school— more than a mere guidance counselor like me. But it turned out to be a pretty embarrassing moment for both of us. We were truly lost for words when one boy said, "What are you guys talking about? It's *our* school, not yours."

22 September 1997. The bathroom problem is solved: the police have assigned a youth officer to patrol the school during the days. Something this youth officer said has made me stop and think, though. He grew up in a pretty rough place, nothing like our own comfortable little town. Still, he says, our kids always manage to take him by surprise with their attitudes and misbehavior. Of course, he thinks that his own home town has turned into a real jungle, so he's certainly not wishing to be there.

30 September 1997. Jason Creely's mom came to see me today, truly outraged. It's one of those situations where I can see both sides. Jason was caught taking lunch money out of other kids' backpacks. (How could Jason think he could get away with that anyway?) Naturally the teacher sent home a note about this. Jason's mom called the teacher and said, "What are we going to do about this? I am not going to have Jason go around stealing things, learning to become a thief!" And our teacher said, "Wait a minute. Please stay out of this. It's a school matter, and we know how to handle it. We've consulted about it. We decided that we are not going to use a word like *stealing* for something like this. It would only embarrass Jason and make him feel bad about himself. He might label himself a thief." The teacher was, in fact, correct: we passed a schoolwide resolution setting a policy to avoid giving students feedback that could lead to negative self-concepts. The teacher then said to Jason's mom, "We told your son that this is uncooperative behavior. He is not going to be very popular with other kids if he keeps acting that way."

That was when Jason's mom called our office. She was upset. Was the teacher saying that it would be all right for Jason to steal if he could get away with it and still be popular? Why didn't the teacher say that stealing is simply wrong? Jason's mom said that this approach had undermined her efforts to discipline Jason. No matter what she said, the boy would not take it seriously. Jason at one point said, "My teacher is cool with it. Why can't you be?"

3 October 1997. As I left work today, there were beautiful sounds coming from the cafeteria. I popped my head in to see what was going on: a new student singing group, called the Spirituals. The kids organized it themselves and arranged for their own volunteer choirmaster (one of our retired music teachers). They are practicing like pros. These kids deserve lots of credit, taking the initiative at just the time when it is most needed. Not only has the district stopped supporting after-school activities, it also has reduced arts and music instruction during school to a perfunctory half-hour per week. But these kids have gone ahead with it anyway, showing wonderful initiative.

13 October 1997. Another star pupil is leaving. We're losing Gregory Pollack to Windsor Country Day. I'm sorry that his parents are transferring him in the middle of the term. What a disruption—plus it's kind of depressing for his classmates to see Greg pulled out of school like that. Greg's parents are by no means rich; they will sacrifice dearly to meet the private school tuition payments. At least this will put an end to their running battle with Greg's teacher. The teacher told Greg to slow down—to stop reading ahead of the class. Our teachers do that all the time; they get uncomfortable when one student stands out from the rest. They figure that a competitive atmosphere in the classroom doesn't do anyone any good. This makes some sense, I guess, but I also understand the parents' point of view on it. Greg was bored, and he wanted more of a challenge than he was getting. I wish that the teacher hadn't actually reprimanded Greg for "showing off" in front of the other kids when he wouldn't stop skipping to more advanced readings ahead of them.

29 October 1997. The year's first ethnic incident. The principal was composed, almost to the point of being dispassionate. I won't repeat the ugly epithet that a student hurled at one of the new Asian students during history class. As for the other students—well, from the reports, a few looked embarrassed, some chuckled with approval, but most sat there impassively. The teacher was frozen, not knowing how to respond. Later she called the principal in. Ted made a deliberate effort to downplay the whole affair. He obviously doesn't want this to blow up any further. Ted simply told the class, "What a ridiculous thing to say," and left it at that.

18 November 1997. A hilarious parody in today's school newspaper: a letter to the editor, protesting the school's Thanksgiving holiday, signed by the Alliance of Vegetarian and Aviary Support Groups (at least I guess that it's a put-on; you can't always tell). The students who signed the letter (fake names) threatened to ignore the holiday and come to school *anyway*. Somehow I'm not worried that this demonstration will materialize, because it would mean that the students would need to come to school an extra day!

12 December 1997. In hindsight, my last note seems prophetic—or perhaps *portentous* is a better word. Of course, there was no vegetarian demonstration on Thanksgiving—the students' letter indeed was a parody. But a few people actually took the letter seriously. The students' parody has been followed by two weeks of real protest about a matter of genuine controversy, and it's all turned into a dismal mess. The only positive thing about the protest is that the town newspaper has finally shown some interest in what's happening in school beyond our sports teams. Still, I'm not sure their coverage has been all that helpful.

It started innocently enough, when Walter Corbitt, the retired music teacher who has been directing the Spirituals, thought it would make sense for the students to give an open rehearsal of the group's holiday show. Practically no one showed up, with a few conspicuous exceptions, notably Mrs. Jackson and Mr. Morris. The next day, the two wrote the following letter, published in both the town and school newspapers:

"To whom it may concern:

"We are sick and tired of the bull-headed insensitivity that continues to go on at the high school, despite innumerable complaints of students and citizens alike. Last week there was a letter in the school paper from a student group opposed to Thanksgiving, and there has been no response whatsoever from the administration. Today we attended a rehearsal of the school choir's holiday program. The program consisted almost entirely of Christmas carols. This is an outrage to the many people in the community who do not share that particular faith. It must be hurtful to many students who feel left out of the performance. We demand a stop to all these unthinking, oppressive activities at the school. We await an answer from Mr. Hughes and his staff."

You can't ignore a letter like this. Ted Hughes arranged a meeting between the students and the two aggrieved parents. The students said that they had not meant to offend anyone, and they offered to include songs from other religious traditions in their repertoire. Mrs. Jackson replied that they would never be able to think of all the religions that people in the district might belong to. Mr. Morris asked, "What about the atheists? They have feelings too." (One interesting thing that came out was that Mrs. Jackson and Mr. Morris are both practicing Christians. Just trying to protect other people's kids, they said.) Ted said very little other than that this would take some more thought in order to work it out to everyone's satisfaction. The students looked baffled and a bit dejected.

Next came the letter from the lawyer, the running debate in the town paper, and the noisy PTA meeting. All this happened in the space of ten days, and by the end of it, Ted Hughes gave up on the idea of getting people to agree on anything. He took the simplest way out by asking the students to skip the holiday performance. There were plenty of other occasions for the students to demonstrate their singing talents, he said. They are better off concentrating their energies on material that is not so charged with controversy.

8 January 1998. Meetings all week with parents over first-term grades. Parents are coming in acting like their children's lawyers and agents. When a child gets a bad grade, it's not the child's fault, they say, but the school's for giving the child a raw deal. What about getting the child to try harder, to do better next time, to learn something? Thankfully, the parents have not singled out one particular teacher like they did last year. I would hate to see a repeat of 1996, when we had to fire poor Miss Donnely for refusing to stop giving failing grades in her class. It seems that the other teachers got the message. With enough complaining, parents do succeed at getting their kids' grades raised at least a notch or two.

21 January 1998. District-wide workshops yesterday and today on how to improve our schools. The superintendent attended an institute at the university last summer, and he has been anxious to bring some of the new ideas home, so he invited leaders of large school reform movements to speak to us about their work. They are charismatic figures, true believers in their own approaches—very impressive. Not much agreement among them, though. Lots of flag waving and drum beating.

It's hard to know what to make of it all. The new ideas seem okay in the abstract but don't provide solutions to one main problem: getting students to apply themselves. Some of our students barely show up. The ones who do usually just go through the motions. The school reformers talk about changing the size and shape of the classroom, the way that teachers teach, the way we test students, the way that we organize the school. But most of our students don't want to be here in the first place. What can a school do about *that*?

It would help, too, if the reformers could spend less time telling us why their own approach is the best and more time telling us about methods that they all are sure will work. Our teachers have been through this "new ideas" thing too many times before. Old Mr. Abrams told me that when he was first starting out, his principal announced in the auditorium one day that the final answer to education now had arrived: audiovisual equipment! When I started, it was going to be computerized instruction. That fizzled as soon as people realized that you still need to teach students to do something intelligent with the machines, and this brings us back to the unsolved riddle of how to teach the kids who aren't interested in anything related to school.

We go from fad to fad, but the old problems remain—or get worse. Every year, fewer and fewer students come to school *eager* to learn. There is no way that a school can reach them, because they are completely closed to the whole idea of schooling. Every influence in their lives— their parents, their friends, the TV shows that they constantly watch— tells them that school is uncool; it's for "dorks" and losers, and it's not where "the life" is to be found. No matter what we do inside the school, no matter how many personalized learning experiences or computer labs we create, these kids still disengage from the place. Everything outside of school has prepared them to disdain it. The school reformers seem oblivious to this unlovely fact, perhaps because they always loved school themselves and are blinded by their passion and pride in their work. The reality has not been lost on our staff, however. None took the workshop seriously. I'm afraid that this effort is going nowhere.

4 February 1998. Some recognition for a couple of our students, though from a rather unexpected source. A Hollywood film company needed some footage of superior roller bladers in action, and they got word of Henry and Luther. Last year's local TV feature on the two boys must have gotten around. Anyway, the boys deserved the honor, considering the amount of time they spend on those blades.

7 February 1998. The roller-blading shoot that I was so excited about didn't work out. The boys turned down the offer—money, glory, and all. One of them told me that they blade for fun and fun alone. It would ruin the experience for them to roller blade under pressure. They would no longer find it relaxing. Everyone else here agreed that the pressure would be too much for them. The school nurse said that these boys have enough trouble getting to school on time, let alone having to meet an early-morning film crew schedule! At first I was sorry that the boys had forgone a juicy opportunity, but now I can see that it's probably for the best. Maybe I let my fascination with Hollywood glamor impair my judgment.

11 February 1998. "Cheating scandal at High School!" The headline says it all—and I'm right in the thick of it. All I know is that one of our seniors got hold of the calculus exam the night before the test and passed it along to twenty-nine of her friends. The teacher became suspicious when so many kids aced the test. One of the girls spilled the beans, and now we're faced with figuring out what to do with the twenty-nine cheaters. The town is in an uproar about this. I wonder how the girls managed to pass along the exam to so many students in one night.

12 February 1998. My last question has been answered: the Internet! The student put the exam out through e-mail. I've got to hand it to her: I would not have thought of that myself. I'm glad that this generation is using its creative abilities to communicate in cyberspace, so all is not lost, intelligence-wise. Why don't they apply the same energies to learning their math? What's so odd about all this is that, according to the teacher, the exam was a snap. But he says he still knew there was something wrong when so many students did so well. In math, he said, there's no way to put the bar low enough these days.

20 February 1998. The school is still in a state of paralysis over the cheating incident. Ted Hughes called a staff meeting to discuss a response. Two members of the school board are demanding that we suspend the students, but there's no policy in place to do so. The school board could never come to an agreement about this, although they have argued long and hard about it on several occasions. It's all in Ted's lap, now that a crisis has occurred.

Ted said that he wants the school to institute a suspension-for-cheating rule, for both this incident and for any future ones. This has led to long, rambling discussions among staff that have covered every social and legal issue under the sun. First, the idea of passing a rule that would apply after the fact to a student in trouble has been summarily rejected. There wasn't even much debate on this one. Everyone could see that this would be a sure loser in all the litigation that was bound to follow. For this reason, the group gave up hope of determining a punishment for the Internet Twenty-Nine (as someone dubbed them). We have turned instead to a general consideration of a new school policy regarding cheating. Now things have started getting really complicated.

Ted's agenda is to have us formulate a clear, firm policy, but this goal doesn't stand a chance. There are too many philosophical differences among the staff. For example, one teacher points out that in cultures that value interdependence over independence, there is no such thing as cheating. Children learn to help one another at an early age. It may seem natural for them to share test answers among themselves. Who is to say that this is not a better way of doing things? Another teacher points out that even our own society is full of cheating. People cheat all the time on their taxes, their jobs, their spouses. Aren't we being hypocritical to demand more of a teenager?

Lots of other mitigating factors have been introduced. The most common theme is student alienation. Students don't see why they shouldn't cheat because they don't know why they are being tested on material that seems useless to them. In one group meeting, a teacher said to a round of applause: "Kids don't see cheating as wrong because they reject the whole system." This was repeated several times in different ways. But then fierce old Joan Hawley objected that "students damn well better find out that *life* is going to test them on how much they know, and they're going to flunk that test if they don't get their rears in gear." That really broke things open. There ensued a chaotic argument about what students need to know. There was so much interrupting that I couldn't keep track of the various positions. The only thing that was clear was that there is virtually no agreement among our staff on this or any other matter. We ended the meeting without getting back to the unsolved problem of student cheating.

What amazed me at the meeting was the lack of any consensus. No one agreed with anyone else about what our students should be doing or why they should be doing it. There wasn't any agreement on why cheating is wrong or even if it *is* wrong. Every time someone spoke, someone else got mad. By the end of the meeting, you could have cut the animosity with a knife. All order in the meeting had broken down. Communication became hopeless. The din was so great that people were just talking and listening to themselves.

It's a good time to get away. Marge and I are eagerly awaiting the London trip next week. It's the first time we've taken advantage of those package deals the union offers. The first time I've been abroad since the service.

2 March 1998. It's amazing how much a week's vacation can renew your energy. Also, I am coming back feeling that we are not alone in the United States with respect to youth problems. I brought back the notes I took from the BBC show on the European football scene (soccer to us). The way young people over there act at sports games makes our kids look tame in comparison. Here are my notes, verbatim:

1. Teenage fans of the opposing teams fight before, during, and after the games. The youngsters use serious weapons, including clubs and knives. Efforts to screen weapons out have failed. The kids hide barbed sticks inside rolled-up newspapers or fill plastic lemons with ammonia to hurl in their opponents' faces.

2. There have been frequent maimings and more than a few deaths. The football clubs have found it necessary to warn women and children away from games between clubs with especially hot rivalries. They have erected barricades between fans and placed limits on attendance. Still the mayhem continues.

3. Skinheads and other youth groups give out neo-Nazi pamphlets and other hate literature at the games. Drugs and drinking are a constant part of the scene, despite occasional attempts to ban them.

4. These are not isolated occurrences. Youth violence at soccer games is common in Great Britain (England, Scotland, Ireland) and throughout North, Central, and Eastern Europe.

I wonder if this kind of thing will spread to this side of the Atlantic. Not that youth sports in our country is problem free by any means, but the trouble is as often caused by the parents and coaches as by the kids. Some of the parents go bananas when they watch their kids play. It's "Win, win, win!" at any cost. And some coaches bend any rule to keep a star athlete on the team. I've seen coaches turn their backs when their players sneak in blows and other dirty stuff on the field. I've seen coaches ignore reports that players are using drugs. And I've been in the middle of a million arguments between coaches and teachers over a star player's poor academic performance at school. The coaches will do anything to keep the kid qualified. Where are all these kinds of messages from adults they respect leading these kids?

4 March 1998. Postscript on the cheating episode. Ted Hughes announced today that the so-called Internet Twenty-Nine (the name stuck) will be assigned to two weeks of community service for their misdeeds. This is not to be considered a punishment but rather a gift to the town for the anxiety that was caused. The distinction sounds confusing to me. I wonder if this will convey any message about cheating. Perhaps we need to bring back Ben Franklin to remind us that honesty is the best policy. Well, at least the crisis seems resolved for now.

11 March 1998. Apathy has killed our tenth-grade spring field trip again this year. We had exactly 8 sign-ups out of 256 students. This year we were planning to go to a ball game in the afternoon and the circus that night—not exactly dull fare. Admittedly, last year's plan to go to a museum and a concert was doomed from the start. But a ball game and a circus?

I must have called forty or fifty parents to see if I could whip up some enthusiasm. Frustrating. The parents couldn't be bothered to speak with their kids, or maybe they realized it was hopeless. Nothing unusual about that. As for the kids, they said it was too much trouble for them, especially on a weekend. They would rather hang out and watch TV, I suppose.

It makes me wonder about how our kids are spending their free time. Are they doing anything that focuses their attention, brings them skills and knowledge, makes them form good habits? I'm not thinking about studious stuff like homework (although that would be nice). I am wondering about the quality of their free time.

My friends and I learned more math by memorizing baseball statistics than we learned at school. Other kids I knew collected coins or stamps, creating a small world of order and learning a bit of history along the way. I had friends who loved jazz but couldn't afford the records. They would rig a radio up to a tape recorder and get the music off the wire during live performances by the great masters—Ellington, Miles, Mingus. My friends would spend hours learning the new riffs months before the recordings were even cut. This was exciting, it took effort, and it gave them a lot of technical skill, musical as well as electronic. Who's doing such things now? What *are* they doing instead?

2 April 1998. All I saw was Mrs. Herman's glasses, face down and broken, on the floor next to the French book. The glasses always looked pathetic anyway. You have to wonder about people who still wear those pointy librarian-style frames. Lying there on the floor like that, the glasses made a statement of their own about the pathos that now has enveloped us.

Who should be believed? Michael admits to throwing the book. But he says two things in his own defense. First, he says that he was aiming at the wall and Mrs. Herman unexpectedly got in the way. Second, he says that he was provoked. The teacher had just called him a "bald-faced liar" for claiming to lose his midterm paper. He threw the book in frustration—but, he says, at the wall and not at her. Michael says that he's sorry that the book struck Mrs. Herman in the head. He's even more sorry about her bruised cheekbone. "Nonsense," Mrs. Herman says, claiming it was a hateful intentional act. Mrs. Herman has insisted that Michael be charged with assault. It looks as if he will be.

Assault is a big word. People use it all the time, but it always frightens me. What Michael did certainly was assault, especially if he intended it. But he's so young. I can't get used to the idea of Michael's going to trial, just like an adult. I know his parents. They probably never sent him to bed without dessert, let alone punished him harshly for anything he'd done. In elementary and middle schools, students get away with throwing temper tantrums all the time. In most cases they are sent down to the nurse's office and given something to settle their nerves. They are asked what set them off, and if they have a complaint, it is taken quite seriously. There may be something at home that warrants looking into. Or the teacher may be asked to try to be more sensitive to the child. Suddenly, when these kids get big enough to be dangerous, we come down on them like a ton of bricks. Yet, this is the same child, a few years older. Without warning, this child's world changed. Now the world takes him seriously, without bothering to prepare him for it.

Assault. The word is used a lot when we talk about children. When they are young, we worry that they are on the receiving end of it. Before you know it, the assaulted has become the assaulter. Or have we created a climate in which everyone is either being assaulted or feels that way?

11 April 1998. Pregnancy number six came to light yesterday—four in the past month alone. None of the girls has been that upset about it. There's certainly no sense of shame that I can detect. Almost the opposite—some of them seem to project a kind of pride in their condition. The girls get together, form "baby clubs" and support groups, trade stories and tips, and act as if everything is all right. Is it?

This is one area in which I feel totally out of touch. I am supposed to meet with these girls and counsel them, but how can I be effective when I am not even sure how to advise them? Nor do I understand what's going on. Each year, we cram more sex education into the curriculum. Each year we make prevention techniques more available, along with full sets of instructions. The girls can read, and they do avail themselves of the materials. Yet, inexorably, the number of girls who get pregnant rises every year. The girls seem to get younger too, although this may be my own advancing age. In any case, most of them drop out of school, possibly to return or possibly not. I worry about what kinds of mothers they will become. Yet I've been told that the official approach now is to support their motherhood and not criticize it. Among the girls, the word is that they can do it at least as well as their own mothers, if not better.

21 April 1998. Special assignment: Investigate why so many students are ignoring their homework. People around here expected that the downward trend would stop last year when we dropped the after-school activities. The idea was that without so many extracurricular activities, students would have more time for their schoolwork. (I always thought that this was a phony justification for the real reason we dropped the programs—to save money in the tight budget—but some parents indeed *had* been complaining that their kids were overloaded with things to do and feeling under too much pressure. Well, whatever students are doing with the time they have saved, it is not going into their homework. Now I'm supposed to find out why not.

14 May 1998. I took off every afternoon last week to drive around town, just observing. I went everywhere that kids hang out. For a couple of days, Jenny Smith and Patrick Davoli showed me around. (More about these two later—great kids getting by under infuriating circumstances.) The week was an eye opener for me. Here's my record of travels and conversations with Jenny and Patrick:

First stop, the mall. Nothing out of the ordinary. Lots of our students there, roaming in small packs, the way teenagers do everywhere. (Of course, the dress style is different. I do find it odd that these kids try so hard to look baggy and scruffy rather than spiffy, but I know that is just my age showing.) Some of them wandered around listlessly, some of them sauntered about with a jive-ish rhythm, but most of them sat or stood around with their friends. They all seemed to be cupping cigarettes in their hands. So many of them smoke! There was some window shopping, and one or two bought a CD from the record store, but mostly they just hung out. How do the merchants make a living off them?

From the mall, I stopped off at three or four of the bigger playgrounds in towns—the ones with the baseball markings laid out and the asphalt tennis courts, complete with nets and cracks in the asphalt. The fields and courts were empty. I know that these playgrounds get a bit of use on weekends, from tennis and Little League (although even Little League is now down to a couple of teams and a very short playing season). But where are the weekday pickup games? And where are the rest of the kids who don't belong to the formal leagues?

Many of the kids, I know, are at home watching TV. I don't need a trip around town to tell me that. Last year I read a survey reporting that, on the average, young people in the United States watch between three and four hours of TV on school days and about seven hours each weekend day. No wonder the playing fields are empty.

At midweek, Jenny and Patrick took me to one place that has become a popular hangout. I wouldn't have known about it on my own. It's under the old railroad bridge, about a quarter of a mile from the high school. It's an out-of-the-way spot, yet on weekday afternoons it bustles with the restless traffic of teenagers on foot and bike. We stood at a distance watching. The kids were too preoccupied with their affairs to notice us. There, under the bridge, the kids were acting out the whole panoply of risky behaviors that we have shown them films, videos, pamphlets, and special programs about. They were smoking, and drinking beer in plain sight. Off to one side, a cluster of eight or nine boys and girls gathered around a card game, holding wads of money. Trash littered the area. Scattered among the trash was some drug paraphernalia.

If I had seen nothing illegal or dangerous going on, I would have kept the scene to myself, out of respect for Jenny and Patrick. But I felt that I needed to report this teenage den of trouble to the police. I assured Jenny and Patrick that I would not reveal the source of my discovery.

As it happened, my reporting was ineffective. First, it took over a week for the officer to return my calls. (This is not unusual; the local police have little use for those of us who work in the schools: they don't bother to hide their disdain. Nor do we usually trust the police enough to cooperate with them, so I guess the feeling goes both ways.) When the officer finally called, he got irritated at what I told him. He said that he knows perfectly well what goes on under the bridge and that he's on top of it. He said that he was waiting for something to happen that he could act on. "Mr. Castor," he said, "if you arrest someone in this society, even a teenager, you've got to have a good reason. You can't stop young people from congregating." He pretty much told me to butt out.

After that conversation, I called the Department of Social Services to see if that might provide a better avenue for action. The social worker was a lot more sympathetic than the police officer, and was especially vocal on the issue of how insensitive and lazy the cops are. But the bottom line was that there is nothing she can do about it. This is not her territory; she is not authorized to deal with it. If one agency encroaches on another's turf, she said, no one wins.

Meanwhile I spoke with Jenny and Patrick. Do they have friends who hang out under the bridge? Sure, some of their friends do, but not all. Shouldn't you say something to those who do? *That* would not be acceptable in the least. What do your other friends do with their time? All the stuff that I know about already: TV, the mall, the fast food shops, driving around with the kids who have cars. Do any of you get together to do homework? Not often. Maybe once or twice before a big test, or when someone has some special [read *secret*] information to share. (The cheating incident earlier this year was not unique, except that it was discovered.) What, I asked, about practicing music together, joint projects, money-making schemes like putting together a baby-sitting club or a snow-shoveling service? Eye rolling over such propositions.

Jenny and Patrick both do well at school, but they have been frequently teased about it. Jenny has been teased more than Patrick, for she's something of a math whiz. This doesn't jibe well with the others' ideas about what girls should be like. Jenny says no big deal, and I think she means it. She's tough despite her soft-spokenness. Maybe the teasing has toughened her up. Also, Jenny likes most of the other kids at school, even when they are giving her a hard time. She doesn't want to go "in their face" with her own interests and ambitions. She plays along with them, keeps her own private thoughts well hidden. It does bother her when they act like jerks—and yet they are fun to spend time with, and Jenny is a sociable kid. She's not going to spoil everyone's fun by complaining. She's certainly not going to make a point of being "serious." She can live with the occasional sniping. She's an avid reader of biography and fiction, and she knows something about human nature, so she suspects that people are always going to be this way.

Patrick is more vulnerable and more discouraged. He has serious goals, but he has trouble sustaining his motivation, especially when his popularity is on the line. He seems to need more support than Jenny. He isn't finding support anywhere in his life other than in his relationship with Jenny, who is a close friend but not a girlfriend. Patrick's parents are not easy to talk with, and they are usually otherwise occupied. The other kids shun him when he gets too serious. One of his teachers told him, "Ease off. You're putting too much pressure on yourself and others around you." When Patrick started coming in to see me, I could see that this was a boy who feels very alone in the world. He's a quiet kid. He wants to be liked, wants to join in. He looks up to the popular kids, the leaders, although he doesn't particularly like the way they are spending their time.

For a while, I hoped that I may be able to provide Patrick with the bolstering that he is obviously looking for, but he doesn't come in often enough. He stops by to see me furtively, as if asking for my guidance is something to be ashamed of. In this, as in other ways, Patrick is different. When most kids want something, they charge in to see me, full of entitlement. When they've done something wrong, they answer with bravado rather than doubt. Patrick thinks twice and looks inward. He's the one who's always feeling intimidated, even when he's clearly in the right.

22 May 1998. The school is abuzz with preparations for the spring prom. Everyone's feeling upbeat, including me. It's been a tough year, but not a whole lot worse than last year or the year before that—just an incremental slide. I hope we will end on an up note, with the prom and graduation. I'll miss the awards ceremony at graduation, but maybe people were right about the whole idea of prizes fostering a too-competitive atmosphere. Grades, of course, are next on the chopping block. At least we managed to postpone the debate about a no-grades policy until the fall. That is going to be a bitter and stormy argument when it comes, and we don't need that right now.

24 May 1998. Patrick stopped in to see me today to announce that he is taking Jenny to the prom. He confided in me that she wasn't his first choice, but she doesn't need to know this. (I'm sure that I won't be the one to tell her!) He originally asked Dorinda Gray, and she accepted, but Dorinda got in trouble on a shoplifting charge last week. Her mother tried to get the matter dropped, but the store insisted on pressing charges. The store's lawyer worked out a settlement that cost Dorinda's parents some money. *That* got Dorinda's mother furious at everyone, and she decided to ground Dorinda. Now Dorinda is feeling "totally wronged" by her mom. Patrick was set loose, so he asked Jenny. It's amusing how even a shy boy like Patrick can feel that he's God's gift to women when it comes to offering someone a prom date. Well, I'm glad it's working out for both of them. I like these two enormously, and it's nice to think of them having fun together.

3 June 1998. I must make a record of a fine act of heroism by three of our students yesterday. Carlos, Lenora, and Thatcher came back into the school after hours to pick up some shoes that Thatch had left in his locker. Lenora stopped into the women's room for a moment. While there, she heard a groan from one of the stalls. The stall was locked from the inside, but Lenora looked under the door and saw Mrs. Peterson collapsed on the floor.

Lenora couldn't get the door open by herself. She found Carlos and Thatcher, the three returned to the women's room, and Thatch jimmied Carlos over the stall door. When they pulled Mrs. Peterson out, they could see that she was having some sort of convulsion. It was a big mess, with vomit, saliva, and so on, but they figured out how to clean her up and resuscitate her. Mrs. Peterson responded a bit but still couldn't move. Lenora stayed with her while the two boys went for help. The only person still in the school at that time was a physical plant man who could barely speak English. None of them could figure out how to use the school phones to place an outside call. The boys split up, one on bike and one on foot. Carlos ran to the nearest store, about a mile away, where the owner let him make a 911 call. Thatcher rode all the way to the emergency room of the local hospital. Unfortunately there was no one available to go over to the school, but in the meantime Carlos's 911 call had done the trick. Within the hour, an ambulance came by the school. (Lenora, who spent the time comforting Mrs. Peterson and praying for her to hold on, calls this "the longest hour of my life.") The medics told the kids that they probably saved the teacher's life.

We are all so proud of them. The three students rose to the occasion as if they were fully responsible adults. They really mobilized themselves. It shows how resourceful and caring these kids can be when the chips are down.

19 June 1998. If I have to meet one more time with the district attorney I may actually break down over this horrible catastrophe. He's grilling me about things that no one could answer. Was there anything troubling Patrick? Is he a kid who would lie to the police? Does he know someone over age who would buy liquor for him? Who might that be? Would he be capable of stealing liquor from a store? From his parents?

After lingering for two days in a coma, Jenny died last Tuesday. Everyone is devastated: Jenny's parents, teachers, classmates, and me right at the top of the list. Lord knows how Patrick is feeling. He is not opening up to anybody. What a crushing burden it must be. The other kids in the car are smashed up pretty badly, but they will recover. Patrick, the driver, got away with minor injuries. Some people are saying that this is because he was drunk and in a relaxed state, but that's nonsense. For one thing, all the other kids had been drinking too—including Jenny, from all reports. For another thing, the driver is often in a more protected position than the other passengers—especially the person next to him.

What a loss for all of us. I wish that we could find a way to comfort one another, to salvage something worthwhile out of this disaster. Instead, there is nothing beyond recrimination in the air. People are casting about for villains, for answers to one overriding question: Who is to blame?

As far as I can tell, everyone who knows these kids is either investigating someone or being investigated, or both at once. Where did they get the booze? Where were the parents, and what did they know? Was there any prior indication of a drinking problem? If not, who was asleep at the switch? (I guess I am on the line for that one, although the social workers, school psychologist, and nursing staff are also targets.) Who monitored the prom? Why didn't the school rent limousines for the kids rather than let them drive? (The town paper and many of the parents have been asking this one with increasing stridency, but I wonder what the school committee and other local politicians would have said if we had requested funds for such a thing *prior* to the accident.) And everything about Patrick, from his habits to his attitudes, has been thrown open to intense, frenzied examination. He is such a private boy. All this must add salt to his wounds, unbearably and unnecessarily too. He is the one ultimately responsible, but he is not denying that.

There must be a more constructive way to handle all of this. We are thrashing about in misery, tearing each other apart, making things worse for ourselves. Will this honor Jenny's memory? What will the investigations and the finger-pointing accomplish? No one is asking those questions.

We are too confused, angry, and isolated from each other to respond with any sense of common purpose. With each new crisis, we tear into each other, bringing ourselves further down into despair. And with each passing year, the crises become more frequent and more devastating. The town responds to each one like a dissolving, dysfunctional family. When the town can get away with it, it will try to ignore any crisis, pretending that it is just an anomaly. But when the disaster is too awful to ignore—poor Jenny!—we find a way of turning it into an expanding mishap rather than trying to resolve it or learn from it.

Meanwhile, we have a schoolful of students who are sick with grief. I am in charge of the mopping-up operation. The prescribed routine is to run a psychologist past Jenny's class and others who consider themselves to be close friends. There will be calls to mount extra alcohol abuse programs next year. No doubt the school will sponsor an alcohol awareness day in Jenny's name. I wonder where I will be by then.

2

WINDSOR, 1998/99

The four hundred people scattered throughout the school auditorium took up less than a third of the seats, but they rustled about with such energy that the room seemed overflowing. Frank came in late and sat toward the rear. He did not know what to think. He had been to his share of town meetings, but this one was different. For one thing, neither Frank nor any other school official had arranged the meeting. Instead, it had been called by a coalition of concerned citizens: parents, church and synagogue leaders, and volunteers from local community agencies. For another thing, the meeting had no agenda beyond a very general charge, publicized in leaflets and handouts, to "discuss problems and prospects of Windsor's young people."

As he looked around the room, Frank could see a few teachers and parents he knew, but many of the people were unfamiliar to him. Onstage was one of the teachers, sitting alongside seven other citizens. Among these seven, Frank recognized a young woman who happened to be his daughter's pediatrician. The remaining six were an assorted lot: a man wearing a business suit, another in a police uniform (was this the town's new youth officer Frank had never met?), two women dressed casually in jeans, and two clergy from local houses of worship.

Frank wondered whether his own actions after the school year may have played some small part in triggering the meeting. Frank had begun the summer of 1998 in a rare state of dejection. He could not remember a time when he had been so uncertain about the work he was doing. What did it mean to counsel young people when everything else in their lives overwhelmed any effect that he might have on them? How could he accomplish any of his goals when all his efforts were constantly being undermined by conflicting advice, uncertain standards, and low expectations from everyone else in his students' lives?

Around midsummer, Frank began speaking about his doubts with some friends and neighbors. These conversations gave rise to a heartening discovery: others in town were feeling the same doubts. Parents and teachers, the police, the church and temple leaders, the coaches, the librarians, and others were worried that things were getting out of control. In many cases, these good people felt undermined not just by "the culture" as a distant abstraction, but by one another. They were all trying their best to guide their young in a positive direction, but they felt as if they were working in opposition to one another rather than in unison. Apart and isolated, they were defeating their own (and each other's) purposes. Frank became convinced that his own frustration and paralysis were widely shared among his fellow townspeople.

Now here was this meeting—coming, from all he could tell, out of nowhere. There was no way for Frank to know whether his summer conversations had played any part in triggering this event. The sea of communal concern that swirled in the auditorium was so large that it absorbed any individual contributions that might have gone into it.

Usually school officials took charge of meetings about youth, but here the school people were just participants, much like everyone else. The first person to speak from the stage was the young pediatrician. The quiet force in her voice grew increasingly intense as she spoke. She said that it was during the summer that she first heard people in town worrying out loud. Many were complaining that their family lives were frantic and unsatisfying, if not in disarray. Her own caseload told her that young people in town were more at risk from the consequences of their behavior (drunk driving, drug use, smoking, fights) than from the old-fashioned biological diseases. She had heard repeated expressions of concern from parents and teachers about children's academic performances, their work habits, their attitudes, their social lives, and the way that they are spending their time. And she had been present at some of the worst crises during the past few years.

Sure, the pediatrician went on to say, the town had always had its share of usual human foibles—petty crimes, local scandals, personal misadventures—but in the past, problems of this sort were quickly buried under the town's forgiving cover of hushed secrecy, casual reassurance, and bustling activity. Whatever the problem, it had always been "business as usual" before too long. But over the past couple of years, the trouble had been bubbling to the surface and staying there. To make matters worse, people seemed intent on keeping it there. A tragedy used to bring people together; now it continued to fester.

Then one of the clergy rose to take the microphone. He said that everyone owed a debt to the pediatrician for taking the initiative to make the first telephone calls on this concern, which they all shared. The churches had been sleepy on this but now were responding to the call. The purpose of the meeting was to start a discussion. The real subjects of the discussion—the town's young people—were not there, he said, but were very much on everyone's minds. The minister hoped that as a result of this and other meetings, discussions could become townwide before long. He pledged the resources of his church and called on those in charge of other public and private agencies to do the same.

In quick succession, others took turns at the podium. Each spoke briefly, expressing dismay at the recent past and determination to organize a response. The last person to speak was a woman who had been active on the school board. Unlike the other speakers, she used notes and carefully emphasized the points she was making. She said: "The eight of us met last week in my family room. None of us are experts, but we could all see that our kids are floundering. Many others in town have been saying the same thing: that our children are just not reaching the potential that we had in mind for them. Some of the kids are getting into trouble, sometimes serious trouble. A lot of kids are hurting—or worse." She looked up and stopped for a moment. Then she went on: "Who can we turn to? The school's a mess these days."

In the front row, Ted Hughes shuffled in his seat, almost ready to interrupt. The woman noticed the obviously uncomfortable school principal: "It's not that you people haven't been trying, Ted, but a lot of these kids are not prepared to listen to you by the time you get them. And it's hard for you to get the help you need with them. Neither the police nor the service agencies have been very effective. They all spend as much time fighting with each other as working together. Meanwhile, the kids are falling between the cracks."

Ted settled back in his chair warily. The woman picked up her notes and finished her statement in a deliberate manner.

Together, the eight of us up here decided to do the following:

1. We will call a town meeting of everyone we can reach: people from all walks of life, anyone who comes in contact with youngsters, or anyone else who could be in a position to influence them in a constructive way.
2. The meeting will be an attempt to see what we agree we should be doing. What expectations should we be holding out for youngsters in town? What can we do to get these standards across?
3. The meeting will be a public event, open to all, and nonconfidential. No one will be excluded. There will be no secrets, and nothing will be kept hidden. The news media will be part of the process and will be asked to report about the event.
4. This will be the start of a townwide process. The main efforts will come from within our town. There are no outsiders who can solve our problems for us. We must work together to solve our own problems.

After the woman from the school board had finished speaking, the pediatrician again took the microphone and said, "These resolutions that we made were just meant to start things off. We aren't intending to dictate rules of engagement for this whole process." Gesturing to the entire auditorium, she added, "That's for all of us to decide. But the one thing that we did feel strongly about was that we can't promise to keep things confidential. If you feel you need that kind of privacy on a problem, we think you should speak about it in a professional setting, for example, counseling or therapy."

"Or confession," a priest in the audience offered.

Onstage, the man in the business suit announced himself to be the owner of a restaurant chain that employed many local teenagers. He stepped up to the podium alongside the pediatrician. He said that the people onstage were a group of concerned citizens, no more and no less. They were delighted that so many had shown up. Now the meeting should be in the hands of everyone who came. He and the others onstage would be happy to lead a discussion or answer any questions.

There were questions. Someone asked what the organizers of the meeting were hoping to accomplish. Several of the panelists responded, saying much the same things in slightly different ways: "We are trying to develop a shared understanding about what our children need in order to grow up well. We are hoping to find a common set of values, the same high standards and expectations for all our children, so that we can count on each other's support. So that we can work together rather than in isolation from one another. So that we can cut through the atmosphere of conflict and mistrust that envelops our town. So that we can open lines of communication that we can use in good times and bad times, during the times of celebration and the times of crisis. So that we can create a wholesome climate for our children, and while we are at it, a healthy community for ourselves."

A spirited discussion ensued until late in the evening. Few people left, many spoke, and those who did not listened attentively. The intensity of the interest was exhilarating. But there were some hard questions and skepticism. "How can you count on people with conflicting interests to support one another?" one person asked. "People in our society don't agree on much of anything. There are always going to be turf wars between schools, sports leagues, police, public agencies, religious groups, volunteers. How are we going to find a common ground? Around what shared belief systems?"

There were many other concerns. Who would be in charge of all this? The panelists responded that any persons or institutions in town could share responsibility for organizing further meetings, task forces, committees, and other projects or plans that arose from this meeting. It would remain an open process, and anyone who wished to take responsibility for some part of it was welcome to do so.

Someone expressed a worry about oppression. Was this a way of bringing collective pressure on individuals to conform to community norms—a twenty-first century version of Big Brother reborn? The thought horrified the members of the panel. No, the panelists answered. The gist of their answers was this: "None of us has any desire to stifle individual freedom of choice. We simply believe that when it comes to our aspirations for our children, we do in fact have more in common than we may realize. We want our children to be happy, healthy, successful, honest, compassionate, decent, intelligent, and much, much more. Of course we don't know the extent of agreement about any of this, but we have never tried to ask. After all, we rarely talk with one another about even the most vital issues. We have great respect for individual choice and freedom. That, in fact, is one of the values that we believe we all have in common. It is a common value that we all want to pass on to our children, and we are sure that there are many other common values among us as well."

The statement proved compelling. It was clear that the audience took it as a case in point. By quiet nods of approval, the people in the auditorium signaled a consensus around the notion of community-wide standards for children in the context of liberty and choice. The agreement in the room had a deliberate though not coerced feel to it. Someone from the audience said as much, adding that disagreement could arise as they got down to detail.

"That certainly seems likely," ventured one of the women on the panel. "We are not expecting to eradicate dissent or ignore differences of opinion. But we do want to have a conversation about the things we agree on. We believe that there may be more of those things than many may suspect. We want to start with the commonalities. Then we will have plenty of chances for discussing our differences. Perhaps we will be able to learn from these differences rather than fighting about them."

As the meeting wound down, the panel introduced a resolution: everyone who was willing and able would return on Saturday morning and continue the discussion, in smaller focus groups. Then they would reassemble as a whole to see where this was leading. If things went well, they would make plans for further action. There was general assent to this idea, without a formal vote of any kind, and the meeting adjourned.

In the days that followed, two occurrences captured the town's attention. A day after the meeting, the town paper printed an op-ed piece written by one of the women on the panel. She described the meeting and announced Saturday morning's follow-up. The column ended with a direct challenge to the town paper itself. According to the woman, the paper had declined to cover the first event because it was not newsworthy. The woman wrote, in protest, "If we are so numbed by sensationalistic news stories that we find a townwide discussion about young people too boring to report, we are really in trouble. The paper could play a constructive role in promoting the discussions by covering them thoughtfully. It could be part of the process, helping us to build our community, rather than further dividing us by appealing to the lowest instincts of its readership." As a postscript to the column, the editor noted that he was publishing the piece, critical statements notwithstanding, and that he was proud to open the town paper to free-ranging discussions of this sort.

The second thing that happened was that Ted Hughes received a stern memo from the school board. The board wanted the school to develop a clear policy regarding student cheating, and they wanted it *now*. Ted showed the memo to Frank Castor in a state of high agitation. This was sure to be a bomb, he said. If he developed a policy on his own, the teachers would be furious that they were not consulted. If he included them in the discussion, they were bound to get nowhere. Every time they had talked about cheating before, they ended up floundering in an obsessive puzzlement about whether students were really doing anything wrong. The most that could come out of such a process would be a wishy-washy statement that the board would reject out of hand. Ted felt stymied, and the clock was ticking.

When people returned to the school auditorium on Saturday morning, it was raining heavily. Perhaps because the rain had waylaid people's weekend plans, or perhaps because the op-ed piece in the newspaper had caught their eye, or perhaps because word of mouth had provoked interest, the turnout had swelled well beyond the original gathering. Those who were new required some repetition of what was said at the prior meeting. The same panel took turns making brief statements that summarized the earlier conversation.

This time there were some sharper questions. People had had a chance to think things over, and they were perhaps more alert in the morning hours, more analytical, and more wary. They raised a number of questions that the panel had no ready answers for. There was a good deal of questioning about the panel's idea of common values. Whose values? Who's to say what they should be? What if the kids don't go along with them? Someone commented, "Shouldn't we be careful about communicating too much with each other about values and other personal business? What about the old saying that tall fences make good neighbors?" The panel found itself venturing into new territory, ad-libbing some responses but also throwing many questions back to the audience. The audience increasingly became active participants in the discussion. It became impossible to keep track of which ideas were originating with the panel and which ones with the audience.

Overall, the discussion was lively, although not quarrelsome, even when doubts were expressed. There is a fine line between belligerence and skepticism, and people seem determined to preserve an overall friendly tone. The reservations were more cautionary than accusatory, as if to say, "We're not really against what you are trying to do, but let's not get carried away with ourselves."

Frank Castor was impressed by the tone, but he started to be concerned that the discussion was too unstructured. The bits of wisdom that he was hearing were in danger of drifting away without adding up to anything definitive. Frank felt the pall of impatience that creeps over administrators whenever they fear that a meeting they are attending might end up to be a waste of time.

"You know, we need someone to keep a record here," Frank said out loud to no one in particular. As people turned around to look at him, Frank realized that this was the first statement that he had made in either of the two meetings. He went on, "So that we can see where we have gotten to by the time we're done. So that we can sort out the ideas worth keeping from the ones that don't make sense or aren't realistic."

"Okay, Frank, wouldn't you be the best person to make such a record?" someone asked. Frank felt another unpleasant sensation that administrators often get: the chill of realizing that he may have stuck himself in an assignment of unwanted and thankless work. More out of reflex than out of conscious determination, he looked around the room for some other volunteer. His eyes fell on Bob Hicks, the reporter the town paper had sent to cover this second meeting. Frank had an inspiration.

"Bob, you would be ideal for this. You know how to keep an accurate record, you're a fine writer, and you're making notes to cover this thing anyway."

"But the story that I'm writing for our paper is a *news* story. It will have my angle on it. I'll be writing up some things from my notes and letting others go by.

"You can still do it. But in the meantime, the rest of the things you jot down could give us a pretty good record of what we did here today. All you need to do is give us the unedited version of the notes that you're going to use for your own story. That way you'll be contributing something to what we're doing. For once, no one will be able to complain that your paper is being irresponsible." Frank said this with a smile, so as not to give offense. Still, his comment had some impact.

"It's not my usual way of doing things. But this isn't exactly a high-stakes assignment. To be honest, I haven't even been counting on getting a publishable story out of it. Okay. I'll go along with what you're asking. I'll organize the complete set of notes that I take so that you can use them as a record of what the group has decided to do."

The meeting proceeded with a discussion about what people wanted to accomplish, how they might go about accomplishing it, and the difficulties that might spring up along the way. In his notes, Bob captured the main themes and decision points in the discussion. Bob's notes took the form of a brief outline that recorded the group's choices, supplemented by fuller explanations of how the group arrived at the choices that required argumentation and resolution.

Bob Hicks's Notes, Windsor High, 10 November 1998

During the introductory statements, the following goals for the meeting were laid out:

> 1. Define our shared expectations and standards for young people's behavior.
> 2. Discuss how the adults in our community can communicate these standards and expectations to young people and how young people can participate in the process.
> 3. Create ways that the adults can support each other's efforts, open stronger lines of communication between themselves and young people. How can we prevent any young people from falling between the cracks?
> 4. Identify organizations and institutions that could help: schools, libraries, sports clubs, churches and synagogues, town agencies (police, social service), mass media (newspapers, entertainment, Internet, TV, and radio).
> 5. Figure out why this isn't already happening. What are the obstacles? Have we lost something in recent years? Is our town a less wholesome place to raise children than it

was when we were growing up? What's gone wrong, and how can we set it right again?

6.   In order to accomplish the specified goals, create problem-focused task forces and plans for action.

7.   In order to avoid wheel-spinning, divisiveness, dead-ends, and wrong turns, leave the following off the table; political debates, hot controversies that people tend to take absolutist positions on, ideological doctrines, and personal problems requiring privacy or confidentiality.

Several speakers hit on a common theme, along the following lines: "We must make a special effort to avoid labeling one another in a way that makes it impossible to work together. We are professionals, laborers, teachers, homemakers, but we are all also human beings trying to raise our children in the best way possible. To offer coherent guidance, we must get past the divisions that have separated us in the recent past. We must set aside our different backgrounds, occupational roles, religious and political beliefs. We must start identifying one another."

After the introductory discussion, members of the panel said that now would be a good time to break out into smaller groups, in order to talk more intensively about problems and possible solutions. The small groups would identify the standards that people in town could expect young people to live up to. At the end of the small-group discussions, everyone would assemble to compile the overall results of the conversations.

Each member of the panel announced a room in the school where he or she would go to lead a conversation. They urged people to stay and participate. About half the audience stayed, dispersing themselves in groups of about twenty or twenty-five each across eight classrooms. I observed one small group that Ann Garrett, a pediatrician from the panel, organized.

She began by asking whether there were any particular issues that had people in the room worried.

"Cheating," said Ed Riley, a local businessman and member of the school board.

"What about cheating, Ed?" asked the pediatrician.

"There's too much of it at school, and we never get around to doing much about it."

"Is this something we ought to be discussing?" the pediatrician asked the group.

It was. There was a lively discussion, with people taking turns expressing their beliefs about whether, how, and why young people were cheating on their schoolwork. The conversation began with some doubts about whether cheating is really so bad.

"How can we hold young people accountable when so many adults in our society cheat?" asked one man. There were several murmurs of agreement.

A young woman, herself a student teacher, went on to say, "Many of the children think that they are just cooperating with their friends when they so-called cheat. I think that in some of the cultures they are coming from, they don't even have this idea of individual achievement and competition. So we are really holding them at a disadvantage when we expect them *not* to cheat."

As the discussion proceeded, such reservations were overridden by general objections embedded in the comments of many who spoke. As the general objections were voiced, the case against youthful cheating began to build, and people in the room gained a sense of urgency about bringing this now-rampant practice to a halt. One by one, members of the group acknowledged that cheating among young people should not be justified. In the course of the conversation, a number of broad principles emerged:

> 1.   Cheating is *unfair* to those who don't cheat because it puts the cheater at an unearned advantage grade-wise.
> 2.   Cheating is *dishonest.*
> 3.   Cheating violates the *trust* between student and teacher.
> 4.   Cheating disrespects the *authority* of the teacher and the school.
> 5.   Cheating contaminates the *feedback* that grades are meant to give, warping the school's mission of providing *teaching and learning.*

These reasons were compiled in a "standards and expectations" log, along with solutions that ranged from clearer messages to students about what constitutes cheating to firmer sanctions for violations. Then people in the room identified other concerns: drug and alcohol use, sexual conduct, rap music, academic performance, attitudes toward work and service, bedtime and curfews, dress codes, hairstyles and tattoos, smoking, violence in school and out, sports, money, cars, friends—the whole risky, unsettling, exhilarating, and brightly promising world of youth. As the concerns were discussed, common standards were quickly identified. As with cheating, a number of core principles made their way into the "standards and expectations" log, along with possible solutions.

Toward the end of the small group meeting, Frank Castor, head guidance counselor at the high school, spoke up on a problem that he declared was his own pet peeve. "What about all the graffiti in town? It's all over the place—on mailboxes, signs, fences, walls, parks. We've given up removing it from the school grounds; it just reappears again the next day. It's the kids who are doing it. And from what I hear around school, it's kids from all over town. Am I the only one who's bothered by this?"

Some of the people in the room nodded in agreement; others looked quizzical. The pediatrician asked no one in particular, "What do folks think? Is this something to be concerned about? Should we be doing more about this?"

"Well, it really bothers me too," said a woman who had nodded her head. "It's so ugly. I want to rub it out every time I see it."

There was a pause. Then one of the men in the room spoke: "I guess I don't see what the big deal is. Kids have always scratched their names on trees. It's a natural impulse to want to make your mark on things, especially when you're an insecure teenager, and God knows all of us were." Some grunts greeted this remark. "It's just that now there's spray paint. That's the only difference."

"Okay," said the pediatrician. "I think we need to decide whether we really care if kids are going around spraying graffiti on everything. I know I don't want my son to do it. But I *have* heard people say that it's just a creative outlet for kids, and obviously some of us here tonight don't think it's much to worry about. Let's hear what some others have to say about this."

One by one, speakers voiced their opinions about why teenagers in their town were making graffiti, about what this meant for the town and the kids who were doing it, and about whether this was acceptable behavior that could be condoned. Many who spoke said that they had never given the subject much thought. Others said that they had felt anger and frustration about the attitudes of youngsters who were spending their time this way. Some expressed concerns about how they wanted their neighborhoods to look, others about the economic value of homes in the neighborhoods, and others about the tendency of minor antisocial acts like vandalism to escalate into serious and even dangerous crimes.

Someone said, "You know, we can do something about this." And someone else added, "Yes, we *should* do something about it." The sense of the group drifted further and further away from the opinion that graffiti were "not a big deal." Even the man who expressed the original doubts had second thoughts. At one point he said, "Well, I suppose graffiti are wrong, not because of what they are but because of what they represent." As for what the graffiti represented to the people in the room, some conclusions were recorded in the log. Graffiti, it was noted:

1. Violate property rights.
2. Are slovenly, in poor taste, offensive, and sometimes obscene.
3. Create a slippery slope to more serious crimes by showing that the town can't control its streets and public places.
4. Can be meant as signs of gang membership and drug dealing.
5. Are not a good way for youngsters to spend their time and energy, when they could be doing something constructive instead.
6. Are depressing to look at.
7. Decrease property values in a neighborhood.
8. Can block out important messages on street signs, causing a safety hazard.
9. Are expensive to remove, draining the town budget.

When the people in the room looked back on their discussion, all of these points seemed obvious enough, yet as the points emerged one by one during the group discussion, they felt like something of a revelation. Cumulatively they had the effect of unchaining the group from a state of paralysis. No longer were people stuck on the question of whether graffiti were worth paying attention to. Here were nine good reasons that graffiti should be curbed. The reasons showed why graffiti are wrong for the town and wrong for the kids who make them. The reasons spelled out the dangers of this seemingly innocuous activity to the community. People felt mobilized to do something effective about it.

The conversation quickly turned to solutions. Within five minutes, a score of responses—some preventive, some punitive, some restorative—had been offered. Someone suggested that the town establish alternative public spaces for young people's artistic expressions, awarding prizes for the best "graffiti-like" drawings. Someone else suggested "graffiti patrols" or other means of surveillance, sponsored by the local police and supported by cooperating townspeople. A number of people endorsed the idea that young people who produced the graffiti and were caught should be required to clean the property that they had defaced and to do something in addition to beautify the town. Someone mentioned a new substance that can be sprayed on surfaces to make them graffiti-proof. That would be a good service for a young "graffiti artist" to contribute to the community.

Our small-group meeting went on for almost two hours, until someone knocked on the door to signal that it was time for all the groups to reassemble in the auditorium. The pediatrician gathered up the log along with other notes that people in the room had taken. Others stood up and stretched, some commenting on how quickly the two hours had flown by. "We must do this again," one man said.

In the auditorium, people took their seats quickly. There was a loud din from energetic conversations among people seated together. The original panel took the stage and waved their hands for silence. After some further rustling and clatter, the meeting came to order. The panel invited the leaders of the small groups to come onstage and report the groups' conclusions. The leaders were given time limits of four minutes each, which they more or less abided by. In fact, those who spoke last were able to wrap up their reports within as little as two minutes because there was so much overlap among the conclusions of the small groups. These last reports simply highlighted the areas of overlap and added a few new ideas that the previous speakers had not covered.

In the end, Bob found that his notes turned out to be the basis of a newsworthy story after all. Indeed, he wrote a long and detailed story out of the notes that he had taken. His editor published the piece unabridged, devoting the entire middle section of the paper to it. The editor said that he knew all along that this would be an important event to cover, and Bob Hicks knew enough not to contradict someone who is in the midst of congratulating himself. Bob thanked his editor for the helpful lesson in how to scout out a good story. The story is too long to reprint here, but portions of it follow:

TOWNSPEOPLE MEET TO WORK OUT YOUTH STANDARDS

On a drizzly Saturday morning last week, over five hundred citizens of Windsor met at the high school to express their frustration with the present environment for raising young people in our society. During five hours of small- and large-group meetings, citizens demonstrated their readiness to address the problem by agreeing on common standards and expectations that all youngsters should live up to. The citizens who attended the meeting pledged their commitment to making Windsor a wholesome place for youth by communicating high standards to young people in homes, in schools, and throughout the community.

The meeting that ended the day was energized and action oriented. Like the rest of the day, the final meeting exuded a positive, constructive, open atmosphere that allowed for both debate and some firm resolutions. Some of the resolutions named the standards and expectations that citizens had agreed on. Other resolutions set forth plans for task forces, standing committees, future meetings, and other activities designed to promote the standards that the group had identified. The standards pertained to activities ranging from schoolwork to sports. Included in the standards were prohibitions against the kinds of youth misconduct that have become all too familiar: drug use, smoking and drinking, vandalism, cheating in school, and violent behavior.

But the discussions did not dwell on only negative behavior. Many focused on expectations for achievement in school and service to the community. Many people expressed the desire to rekindle the flames of aspiration, hope, and idealism in the young.

The conversations covered topics ranging from the mundane to the spiritual. Parents discussed children's early habits, modes of discipline, household chores, guidelines for TV viewing, homework, and their children's friendships. Teachers spoke about students' academic skills. Social workers and police talked about juvenile problem behavior in the community at large. People from the science museum and the town's art and music programs mentioned the importance of fostering creativity at an early age. Young people's need for faith and spirituality was emphasized by leaders of the town's churches and synagogues.

The day-long event also raised questions that remain unresolved. During the meetings, people asked: How can we reach townspeople who are not here? What can we do about powerful forces that influence our children in ways that we do not approve of—for example, the cult of violence, selfishness, and excessive materialism in the popular culture? How can we provide our children with the guidance that they need when our jobs and our busy lives take us away from them for long periods of time? No one in the group had ready-made solutions for these problems. There was a general agreement to attack them in future meetings.

Also left for future meetings was the question of how to coordinate Windsor's multiple resources for raising children better. There was a strong feeling that many of the agencies charged with children's welfare and education too often had acted in conflict with one another as well as with the children's parents. Teachers and school officials complained that parents were not giving them the support they needed to educate or discipline students. One teacher said, "Some parents complain almost as much as the students about how much homework I give out." A parent replied, "My kid doesn't get nearly *enough* homework." Both agreed parents and teachers needed to communicate better on this matter. A task force comprising parents, teachers, and representatives of several agencies in town will look into this problem and report back to the group at its next meeting.

The accomplishments of the day were both specific and general in nature. Many specific ideas for new program development were introduced, and committees were set up to explore the possibilities. On a more general level, common values were identified. Consensus around core standards such as honesty, fairness, trustworthiness, and respect for authority was achieved. New lines of communication among diverse groups of citizens were opened up.

Perhaps most important, the organizers said at the close of the meeting that a forum had been established for discussing the prospects and problems of the town's young people. The forum—a continued series of meetings to be scheduled regularly throughout the year—will be used to create new opportunities for Windsor's young people, prevent predictable risks, and respond to trouble when it occurs. This will give citizens a way to share ideas about guidance, discipline, education, relationships, service, and all the other building blocks of young people's character. It will, according to the organizers, support the efforts of parents and teachers to hold out the greatest possible expectations for youth development.

After the last meeting of the day, Sally Ann Rogers, a teacher from the middle school, said that she came away with a renewed sense of dedication to her work. "There is a clarity of purpose here," she said. "Everyone always worries that teachers have been hamstrung for lack of resources, but what is really paralyzing is all the confusion and the conflict around us. If we can work together with parents and all the others, we have a chance to get through to the kids. That's an exciting prospect." A small cluster of fellow teachers gathered around her as she spoke and voiced similar sentiments.

In this world where doctors no longer remember their patients' names (let alone make house calls!), where businessmen take the money and run, where lawyers disregard all the old conventions of their profession and violate each other's trust without thinking twice, where teachers care more about their union rules than about their students, and where journalists (yes, we too) write cynical and sensational stories without concern for the societal consequences, many believe that we are tearing apart the fabric of our communities. How will we ever be able to sustain a civilized life? What will remain of our society to pass on to the next generation? Who will be qualified to do the passing on? In a small but tangible way, the Saturday meeting at the high school sketched an outline of an answer to these disturbing questions. In that outline, one could see the vital spirit of a newly conceived moral community forming around the developmental needs and prospects of Windsor's children.

Story by Bob Hicks, with the assistance of 502 Windsorites

Odds and Ends from the 1998/99 School Year

By mid-fall, Frank Castor had given up his diary. There was too much else going on and, besides, he felt less of a need to express his thoughts about his work in private. There were plenty of other chances. The town meeting had triggered a succession of follow-up discussions, committee work, and planning activities. Many meetings were held at the high school, and young people themselves began joining the meetings—at first a few youth leaders, then many young-sters in their footsteps. The library, the community center, the churches and synagogues in town, and the local Y also took turns at hosting the meetings. The point was to disperse the locus of the activity in order to reach as many townspeople as possible. Frank took part in several of the planning groups. His job at the high school gave him a lot to say about both the academic and social side of young people's development.

For Frank, the year went by in an unrecorded blur, but a number of things stuck in his mind. First, he had some strong overall impressions. He sensed a renewed vigor all around him—and within himself too. The problems of his students did not go away, nor did the high school or the town turn into blissful utopias. There were still petty crimes, drug and alcohol use, cheating, underachievement, and even a dis-turbing attempted suicide halfway through the year. Frank and his fel-low townspeople still felt that they were fighting a widespread decline of standards, a creeping cultural decadence that always threatened to overwhelm them. But at least they felt that now they were fighting it. And they could fight it on familiar territory, a battleground they could control to some extent. They also now had some weapons and some allies in their struggle. No longer were they passive or powerless. They were working together, with the redeeming awareness of "united we stand, divided we fall."

Frank's capacity to respond to trouble was transformed entirely. In early spring, the police dropped by to tell him that some of his students had been hanging around a neighborhood park after school, smoking, drinking, and harassing passersby. Some neighbors were so upset about this that they were ready to move.

These were some of the same kids who had been gathering under the infamous bridge in previous years. The police had been able to clean that area up, on orders from the town council, but the park was a trickier business. The kids were claiming rights of access, and their parents were defending them on principle.

Frank recognized this as just another version of an old story that in the past had always amounted to a standoff. This time, though, a group of townspeople got some of the kids' parents to come to a meeting. The parents heard the neighbors' complaints firsthand and were horrified. They asked what they could do with surly teenagers who resist parental authority. Someone suggesting grounding and other ways of withholding privileges until the teenager shapes up. One of the parents said that when he tried something like that before, his son threatened to call the social worker and claim abuse. The social worker was there to reassure the man that such a complaint would fall on deaf ears. The police, too, presented themselves at the meeting as no more and no less than a resource—members of a supportive team rather than a threat. The parents' defensiveness melted away. They returned home and implemented the group's suggestions. Some of them even went so far as to contact the parents who had not shown up at the meeting, successfully enlisting them in the cause. Within two weeks, peace and quiet had returned to the park.

Frank could hardly keep track of all the issues that were discussed, debated, and acted on by the end of the school year. Finally they were able to put in place a firm cheating policy for the high school, and soon all the schools in the district followed suit. Parents and teachers came to an understanding over grades, and strident parental complaints about their children's report cards waned. Dress codes were proposed, and although they were rejected in the end, the student participation in the conversation was constructive, intelligent, and respectful. That is exactly how they should learn to win their case, Frank thought. As his personal bonus for the exhilarating year, Frank presided over the cleaning of the graffiti off the school walls. As he reached for a scrub brush to get a small purplish blob that the others had missed, Frank thought to himself, "Nothing's perfect, but we've made a pretty good start."

3

YOUTH CHARTERS

A youth charter is a coherent set of standards and expectations for youth behavior, shared by all the important people in a young person's life. The charter can include moral standards such as honesty, compassion, decency, fairness, respect, and responsibility. It can include work-related standards such as excellence in academic studies or in the vocational crafts. It can include standards of physical safety and fitness, such as refraining from substance abuse, learning good health and hygiene habits, or acquiring athletic prowess. It can include expectations of service to family, friends, and community. And it can include spiritual goals such as the pursuit of transcendent purposes above and beyond the self.

A youth charter represents a rough consensus—or at least an overall congruity—in the directives that adults offer young people for their personal guidance. In practice, the consensus will never be absolute; there will always be variations on even the most consistent themes. Nor does the charter need to be articulated in a formal manner. Rather, a youth charter is generally unwritten, informal, and open-ended. It is expressed in multiple, diverse, everyday transactions between young people and parents, grandparents, teachers, sports coaches, religious leaders, counselors, employers, and other youth mentors.

A youth charter makes itself known when a child comes home from school with a poor report card and the parent, rather than complaining to the teacher, tells the child that she must try to do better. It makes itself known when a manager at the local fast food outlet catches a teenage employee smoking in the bathroom and says, "I'm not going to let you wreck your health around here any more than your parents would let you do that at home." It makes itself known when a sports coach calls church and synagogue leaders to check about scheduling games around the time of important religious holidays. It makes itself known any time a police officer feels that he can work with a delinquent child's family, friends, and teachers to help set the child straight rather than working in opposition to them all. When a youth charter's standards and expectations are expressed consistently by the adults in a young person's life, those standards and expectations will be understood and supported by the young person—and by the young person's peers as well.

Youth charters flourish where people have a strong sense of community and a clear sense of shared belief. They are scarce where people feel estranged from one another and uncertain about their core convictions. Modern society has not been kind to the formation of youth charters. As communities have waned and common standards have faded, youth charters have become increasingly hard to find. They have been endangered by the same withering cultural forces that have turned many communities into mere aggregations of people.

The good news is that where youth charters do not now exist, communities may take positive steps toward establishing them. To build a youth charter, members of a community can start a process of discussion to work out their core standards and expectations. They can then create action plans to convey these standards and expectations to the community's young. Steps in this process include a special meeting sponsored by a local group or institution; local media coverage and publicity on a periodic basis; task forces dedicated to creating new opportunities for youth or resolving a troublesome crisis; and opening up new lines of communication between parents, neighbors, teachers, and the local institutions (civic, professional, religious, business) that serve or come in contact with young people.

Chapter 2 offers one account of what this process could look like in a typical American town. Although the account is fictional, many of its examples are similar to events that I have observed in my own attempts to facilitate a local youth charter. In the final chapter of this book, I describe the procedures that my associates and I have developed for helping citizens of any town or city launch a local youth charter initiative.

The youth charter process begins by bringing together adults in positions to influence the development of young people: parents, teachers, local officials, police, religious leaders, sports team coaches, the news media, employers of young people, and so on. During an initial meeting, participants discuss standards and expectations for young people's behavior. Sometimes they do so with reference to particular problems that have arisen in recent times, sometimes with reference to envisioned opportunities that could promote young people's healthy development. The discussions move from the large-group to small breakout sessions. The goal of the discussions is to determine how the community can help young people acquire the skills, character, and sense of purpose that they need for successful and satisfying lives. After the initial set of discussions, further meetings are arranged to work out the details and to bring in young people from the community. In addition, task forces may be formed to deal with specified problems or opportunities. As a result of the ongoing discussions and task forces, new lines of communications among adults and young people are opened up.

The topics discussed vary with the needs and nature of the community. In one place I visited, participants were concerned about cheating at the local school. In another setting, a pair of teenage suicides and widespread drug use among the town's young people dominated the conversations. In a third, parents were upset about an epidemic of binge drinking, especially at teen parties. Other meetings have taken up issues ranging from racial and ethnic conflict to disrespect of authority in school and work settings. Despite their many differences, each of these discussions identified core standards that could provide the basis for productive responses to a pressing problem or crisis.

For example, after an afternoon of intense discussion, teachers and students in the school with the cheating problem agreed that cheating should be considered unacceptable because it (1) violates trust between teacher and student, (2) makes it impossible for teachers to give students meaningful feedback on their work, (3) gives students who cheat an unfair advantage over those who do not, (4) encourages further dishonest behavior, and (5) undermines the social order and the academic integrity of the school. These agreed-upon principles offered a welcome change from prior sentiments; some teachers and students had been quoted as saying that it would be hypocritical to stop students from cheating when so many adults in society do it. This prior ambivalence about the moral status of cheating had created an atmosphere that was highly resistant to effective prevention or enforcement efforts. In such a case, youth charter discussions can help a community define and implement its core standards, because the discussions produce a shared understanding of why the standards are necessary and valid.

In another community (see the Appendix), a coalition of local institutions and people, originally formed to reduce the use of drugs and alcohol among youth, asked me to help them develop a youth charter. The coalition was made up of representatives from private and public schools, the police force, parents, an interfaith council, local colleges, the business community, human services agencies, the town council, and other concerned citizens. A subcommittee of the larger coalition organized a townwide forum. With the hopes of gathering a substantial cross section of the community, the organizers arranged large-scale publicity for the forum that encompassed articles in the local newspaper, flyers, notices to the parents of students, and presentations to community groups, such as the Rotary Club, the police department, and senior citizen centers. The three-and-a-half-hour forum was held in the local high school auditorium on a Sunday afternoon.

The large- and small-group discussions covered a series of topics centering on how young people were spending their time after school. From this initial forum arose resolutions, action plans, and task forces dedicated to the following issues: (1) the need for more town settings that provide safe and wholesome places where young people can spend their time (for example, a youth activities task force has created a coffee house where young people now congregate in the evenings), (2) promoting the benefits of youth sports and reducing the costs (for example, efforts are being made to avoid scheduling conflicts between sports and religious services on weekends, to allay the pressures of competitive sports on young people, and to raise the ethical standards held by coaches, players, and referees), (3) preventing the use of drugs and alcohol by young people, and (4) fostering spiritual awareness and community service among young people.

As this town continues to build networks and implement its action plans, there will be new dialogues across new constituencies. The town's young people will become increasingly active participants in the process. At each point in the discussion, there will be need for further reflection about the community's standards and expectations.

Youth charters evolve to meet the changing needs and composition of the community. Records may note general agreements and resolutions for action, but no youth charter can be written in stone. Standards and expectations are added, modified, improved, and more clearly understood as the discussions and the task force work move forward.

Youth charters generally reflect fundamental human virtues such as civility, decency, justice, truthfulness, the pursuit of excellence, courage, and compassion. In addition, a youth charter incorporates specific standards of behavior that are important for the particular community that establishes the charter. In this way, the charter is compatible with, but more comprehensive and more action oriented than, the well-known "pillars of virtue" approach reflected in the contemporary character education movement. (The "pillars" approach teaches children general concepts such as respect, responsibility, caring, and fairness—a valuable exercise, but one that needs to be linked to children's own behavior if it is to leave any deep or lasting effect.) A youth charter does more than name an abstract list of concepts that adults find desirable. It lays out direct expectations for youth behavior in the actual community contexts where youths spend their time. Moreover, a charter indicates realistic procedures for coordinating the expectations across the disparate contexts and for communicating them to young people.

Although any youth charter includes elements that are specific to the community that engenders it, there are some essential requirements for all youth charters:

1. It addresses core matters of character and competence— morality and achievement—that are required for becoming a responsible citizen.
2. It provides high expectations for young people's achievement and service.
3. It provides limits, prohibitions, and sanctions for behavior that violates the community's standards.

4. It is not limited to a collection of disconnected don'ts. Rather, it provides young people with a positive and coherent sense of purpose.

5. It focuses on areas of common agreement rather than on ideological distinctions, doctrinaire squabbles, or polarizing issues of hot controversy.

6. It includes mechanisms for identifying shared standards and negotiating among disparate parties with conflicting interests and opinions.

7. It includes mechanisms for communicating the agreed-upon standards and expectations to the younger generation.

When a teacher becomes disappointed in a child's performance or a police officer calls a parent into the station to discuss a misbehaving teenager, a youth charter can turn the emotional experience into a constructive developmental lesson. Because charters are powerful communication devices, they can help young people anticipate the reactions of others to their behavior. They provide conduits for regular feedback between parent and child and can create healthy links between young people and the entire adult community. Youth charters can provide the basis for rigorous academic standards at school, and they can be crucial in dealing with sudden crises, such as violence or school cheating scandals. They can be used to put in place the lines of communication that can constructively address the problem, thus avoiding the usual response of finger-pointing and mutual blaming.

A youth charter is a voluntary contract among members of a community. Ideally, a youth charter engages the whole community around the mission of fostering healthy development in all its young. It is not a political document that commands allegiance by virtue of legislated authority or a contract bound by force of law. In fact, it is not a formal document at all, although parts of it may be written down. Rather, a youth charter is a process, a strategy, a proposal, a goal, a working statement of intent, a set of procedures. It could be called a moral compact, whether written or verbal. But it has no compulsory force other than that of people's chosen senses of personal obligation.

A successful youth charter permeates every aspect of community life, from the home to the school, to the streets and the playing fields, the libraries and the workplaces, the churches, museums, boys' and girls' clubs, and the centers of entertainment. It transforms all the places it touches, vastly improving the effectiveness of the institutions that serve young people. Schools, for example, no longer find themselves alone in the struggle to motivate young people. The rest of the community accepts its obligation to support the school's academic goals actively. As a result, the school now has crucial allies in its most difficult and essential task: getting young people to want to learn. Others in the community are resources for the school rather than adversaries. Reciprocally, the school accepts its own obligation to support the wholesome out-of-school activities that outside agencies sponsor for students.

In times and places where there is a cohesive sense of community, a youth charter is simply assumed. It may be given voice by a civic leader or emphasized in school lessons and religious sermons, but even without such special efforts, the general standards and expectations are well known. In seventeenth-century New England, for example, it was taken for granted that children would be raised to respect their elders, perform household duties, study the Bible, obey the Ten Commandments, acquire proper manners, learn skills, work hard, and eventually find a calling in life and establish a family. Writings from that time reveal that these standards and expectations permeated every setting in a child's social world. There was little uncertainty about the importance of the standards for providing children with needed guidance. Other times and places have had youth charters founded on very different sorts of beliefs, but they have all worked to communicate clear directives and a positive sense of purpose across the generations.

Some places today have implicit youth charters and some do not. Those that do typically arrive at them spontaneously, through frequent interchanges among people who are in positions to influence the young. Naturally this happens most readily in small towns and other tightly knit communities. But it can happen elsewhere as well, including in large urban centers. Not surprisingly, young people growing up in communities with youth charters do better in almost every regard than young people who grow up in places without them.

The sociologist Francis Ianni, whose writings introduced me to the phrase youth charter, examined a broad range of American settings: inner cities, suburbs, towns, and rural areas. Ianni found that a set of coherent expectations among the people and institutions in a young person's life was the most striking ingredient in the young person's successful adaptation to life: "We soon discovered that the harmony and accord among the institutions and what their adolescent members heard from them *in concert* was what scored the adolescent experience."[1] Young people growing up amid a consensus of positive expectations tended to do well; those growing up in a climate of discord and mutual distrust often drifted into trouble. Ianni wrote that every youngster needs predictable structure—"a set of believable and attainable expectations and standards from the community to guide the movement from child to adult status." Ianni termed this implicit consensus of standards and expectations a youth charter. In his sweeping study of American communities, Ianni found places with strong and coherent youth charters and places where there was none in evidence.

Unfortunately, harmony and accord with respect to standards for youth behavior are more the exception than the rule in modern society. Schools, families, peer groups, local institutions, the media, and the job market send incoherent and even clashing messages to youth. The lack of coherence has created a fragmented and confusing context for youth development. Because the relationship between family, work, and school is so often characterized by discord in contemporary society, high standards and expectations are often hard for a young person to find.

In places where the sense of community has waned, young people may face conflicting demands and messages from each of these sources. Many communities have lost the traditional social networks that once guided youth into adulthood. Without these networks, role models are lacking, intergenerational guidance is rare, and isolation prevails. The institutions within the community blame one another for all the problems of its of youth. Such fragmentation is deleterious to youth development.

On the other hand, in places that operate like communities, there are many ways in which families, schools, sports teams, workplaces, youth agencies, and religious institutions connect with one another through their contact with youth. For example, schools can be responsive to the values and attitudes that students learn in their families. In turn, students' family lives can be positively affected by their quest for academic achievement, which fills their after-school time with productive homework and should be supported on the home front. A young person's identity formation, rooted initially in the family, is thus shaped by a sense of belonging in the community, through participation in sports teams, after-school clubs, religious institutions, and jobs. In such communities, there is concordance between the norms of the peer culture and those of adults.

Why a Youth Charter Is Not Just Another Youth Program

Imagine the case of a teenager who refuses to go to school. A special education expert may look for learning disabilities and emotional disorders. A guidance counselor may look for family and peer problems. A social worker may suspect abuse. A school reformer will find ways that the school could change its instructional strategy to appeal better to the child. A police officer will threaten the child and the family with a truancy warrant. A boys' or girls' club may offer the youngster a big brother or sister.

These approaches are all potentially effective and not necessarily incompatible—at least in theory. In practice, however, agencies that sponsor youth programs often end up at odds with one another. Each perceives the other as a threat rather than as a resource. Each thinks of itself as competing with the other agencies for scarce public resources. Each believes that it has the one best solution to the problem. Each thinks of the others' efforts as interference that must be fended off so as not to make matters worse. As a result, the young person's problems and prospects are not addressed in the comprehensive and coherent manner needed to make a positive difference. Instead, the youngster bounces from one agency to the next, bewildered, torn, and eventually inured against adult guidance in any form.

Risk-prevention programs suffer from the same fragmentation and sense of disconnect. A school sponsors a drug and alcohol abuse prevention program that teaches students about the biological hazards of addiction. As part of the program, students are counseled to seek advice if they feel signs of drug or alcohol dependence. Meanwhile, the police department has instituted a zero-tolerance policy, whereby the police immediately arrest and prosecute all minors caught in drug-

or alcohol-related offenses. Elsewhere in school, the school guidance counselor warns students in the college preparatory program that they can forget about admissions to elite institutions if they get police records. A young basketball player who has developed a craving for crack wants help but does not want to take a chance identifying himself or the friends who supply the stuff; a parent who knows that her child drinks at social events keeps the problem hidden because she is afraid that he will end up with a police record; a girl sees her closest friend getting hooked on pills but does not dare say anything about it. People who should be working together toward a common solution are forced into a paralyzed isolation by miscommunication and mistrust.

In a fragmented society, conflicts can arise around the most fundamental matters of youth behavior. A high school disrupted by a racial incident tries to respond by suspending the perpetrators. The local minister who heads up the town's civil rights commission wages a protest based on his belief that racism is deeply embedded in society and that individual students should not be held accountable. Instead of suspending the students, the high school decided to sponsor a day-long educational forum on diversity and tolerance. The forum is criticized as "politically correct" by one columnist in the town newspaper and "an empty charade" by a letter to the editor. On the day of the forum, someone leaves neo-Nazi brochures on tables in the school hallway. The students have a hard time taking the event seriously.

Even within professional fields, there are discord, mistrust, and fierce rivalry. Leaders of major school reform movements are called "gurus," and they vie for advantage over one another. Efforts at collaboration are sporadic and short-lived. Sex education is divided between those who would teach students safer sex practices and those who would insist on total abstinence prior to marriage. How can a young student make sense out of these opposing messages? The field of character education has become a competitive marketplace where hundreds of vendors promote proprietary wares. Some approaches stress loyalty and obedience, whereas others tell students to think autonomously and to question authority. Both approaches have a point, but it is rare to find attempts to integrate them into a comprehensive message. Meanwhile, proponents of the opposing approaches attack each other with a zeal that makes cutthroat corporations and law firms look tame by comparison.

The lack of coordination among youth programs has roots in the basic inclination to protect one's own turf. Every agency has a specialty, a catchment area, a raison d'etre. Every profession has its own area of expertise. Every brand of school reform has its own philosophy, its own principles and methods. Every youth program has its own twist. And the people who run agencies, reform efforts, and programs have jobs and egos to protect. Many of them believe that they have *the* answer to troubled youth. They are suspicious of, if not downright unfriendly to, others who may approach the problem from a different angle.

But children are not divided up into separate parts that correspond to the programs that adults invent for them. A child has one mind, one personality, one character. When a child learns something new, it must be woven into whatever the child already knows in this one mind, one personality, one character. Children are flexible, and they have great tolerance for novelty, but they learn best when there is a reasonable degree of consistency in the information and messages that they are getting. They do not learn well when they perceive only cacophony, discord, and disorder all around them.

Children learn skills and values through thousands of small experiences that are guided by key people in their lives: their mothers and fathers, their teachers, their friends, religious leaders, and other mentor. Each experience is different from all the rest, but the direction of guidance around core skills and values need not be. If everyone a child meets tells her to be honest, the child will take it seriously. If a teacher tells a child to be honest in school but the coach says it is okay to cheat a bit for the big game and mom says it is okay to lie about her age to get into the show free, the child will not consider honesty an important virtue. Repeat this scene over and over across a range of issues while the child is growing up, and the child will become confused and demoralized. In order to learn well, children need to find high standards that are presented consistently and coherently by all the people in a position to influence them.

This was not difficult to find in the days when communities were the norm rather than the exception of collective life. True communities have become hard to find. The waning of communities has impaired our capacity to raise the young; in their place, we have created youth programs and have tried to reform schools, but these efforts have not added up to community. The programs by themselves have not been able to deliver to young people the kinds of guidance that they most need, because they have not offered young people a consistent set of high standards and clear expectations. In the absence of a compelling community youth charter, the programs have failed to provide essential guidance to young people.

Most programs for youth remain uncoordinated with one another and distant from young people's personal lives. Because of this, children often cannot understand how their experience in one program connects with their experience in another—or, for that matter, to things that they really care about. For example, a child can spend hours reading and writing in an after-school program without seeing how to bring the skills she has learned to bear on her schoolwork. A child can learn social-problem-solving skills in one program, intergroup sensitivity in another, tolerance for diversity in a third, and still not see how any of it connects with his feelings toward children who look and act strangely to himself and his friends.

We will always need professionals for the expertise they bring, and we will always need good youth programs for the services they render. But neither professionals nor youth programs can provide a remedy for the unwholesome cultural climate that faces young people today. No expert working in isolation can provide young people with high standards and a sense of purpose. Only people who have close personal relations with the young—family, friends, teachers, direct mentors— can do that. All the programs in the world will not restore a sense of mutual trust and solidarity to our communities. Only people living in them can do that. We need to support useful professions and programs, but in order to make the best of them, we must surround them with a vigorous culture of high, positive expectations. In order to make a serious attempt at developing the full potential of every young person in society, we must create an encompassing sense of purpose for young people wherever they go. That is the role of the youth charter.

The youth charter is an approach, not a program, and it is an approach that must grow within a community. The need for it must be perceived from within. Discussions and activities must be organized by community members and supported by local institutions. Task forces to implement the recommendations must be composed of local citizens. Other than an occasional facilitator to help structure some of the early discussions, the process requires no experts.

A youth charter neither replaces nor supplants youth programs. Rather, it provides the missing ingredient: a sense of common purpose. It does so by uniting a community around a set of shared understandings about how to guide young people in healthy directions. When programs begin to direct their efforts *in concert* toward these shared community understandings, they will finally become able to accomplish their avowed missions for the benefit of youth.

Building the Conditions for a Successful Youth Charter

There are some fundamental conditions necessary for creating effective structures of youth guidance:

- Families, schools, and communities that provide a coherent sense of direction.
- Supportive relationships that embody and communicate high standards.
- Activities that will engage young people in pursuits that they find challenging and inspiring.
- Safe and reliable venues for young people for developing their skills to their fullest potential and for finding the purpose, meaning, hope, and aspiration that will bind their lives through good times and bad.

Many of the necessary conditions for youth development—solid community, guiding relationships, inspiration, clear standards, and high expectations—have been eroded. Young people today encounter a fractionated society broadcasting messages of low expectations, disbelief, cynicism, relative or nonexistent standards, isolation, and moral detachment. The guidance many young people need is missing from all the usual places. Their families' lives, their schools, their neighborhoods, and religious and other community organizations have been degraded by conflict or lack of support. The increasingly powerful mass media impart messages that are mixed at best and corrupting at worst, further confounding the youngster's developmental quest.

All of these conditions must be improved if we are to create a society where all children can reach their full potentials. Changing these conditions is a central part of the youth charter approach. It is the backdrop to, and the goal of, the youth charter meetings, discussions, and actions that I have discussed throughout this chapter. Improving the conditions feeds into, and draws from, the process of communication and coordination of effort that youth charter meetings initiate.

In one sense, improving the conditions is a *precursor* to a successful youth charter, and in another sense, improving the conditions is a *result* of the successful charter. Youth charters can work only when people and institutions in a community adopt practices and beliefs that enable them to work together constructively for positive ends. This requires improving many of the current conditions in families, schools, neighborhood, the media, and other key societal institutions. The meetings, discussions, task forces, and actions of a youth charter process can facilitate these changes.

The next six chapters describe the *conditions* necessary for youth guidance and recommend changes in policies and practices that could create the right conditions for a successful youth charter. Some of my recommendations are for parents, teachers, sports coaches, and other adult mentors who work directly with young people. My other recommendations are for citizens who influence or control large institutions, such as the mass media and governmental agencies (in our democratic society, of course, this includes the average citizen, at least with respect to government control). The purpose of all my recommendations is to show how we can ensure that the high standards and expectations that young people need for building their character and competence are reflected all throughout our society.

Chapters 4, 5, and 6 examine the face-to-face settings where children are raised. In these chapters I recommend a variety of specific practices for families, teachers, coaches, and others who work closely with young people. I discuss child-rearing practices for the homes, educational practices for the schools, coaching and mentoring practices for our neighborhoods, employment practices on the job, and responses to young people who have headed into trouble.

The chapters in Part III discuss the "macro" conditions, or broad societal forces, that influence families and children: the mass media, the popular culture, and the social and legal policies of modern government.

In the final chapter of the book, I describe procedures for initiating a youth charter process. These procedures can be used to trigger the discussions, meetings, committee work, and action plans needed to accomplish the changes that I recommend in this book. Of course communities may launch youth charter efforts to respond to their own particular problems or seize their own special opportunities as well.

Bit by bit, a youth charter effort can improve conditions for raising children. Town meetings that bring together parents, teachers, youth workers, coaches, employers, religious leaders, and police are certain to affect the ways in which all these people operate. Moreover, even at the heights of national politics, mass media, and popular culture, local citizens can make their voices heard. If enough citizens act with energy and determination, the direction of an entire society can be turned around. A youth charter process gives citizens a realistic means of joining forces for the sake of the young.

The conditions that I discuss in Chapters 4 through 9 are not going to be altered by youth charter meetings alone; they are too entrenched and too widespread for that. These meetings can initiate a process of examination and reflection that may trigger a change, but other types of committed effort will also be necessary. Efforts must be undertaken in homes, schools, neighborhoods, the mass media, and the arena of public policy, and they must reflect an essential change in mentality about children's developmental needs.

There is a "bootstrapping" relationship between this necessary change in mentality and a youth charter approach. The change in mentality, along with the improved policies and practices that it will bring, is important for a successful youth charter approach. At the same time, the wrong ideas, policies, and practices are not going to change by themselves. We must not remain passive in the face of conditions that sabotage our hopes for the next generation. This is why the youth charter process goes hand in hand with the standards and expectations that it represents.

Discussions, examinations, and constructions of community youth charters can be one step toward better ideas, policies, and practices. The youth charter process places citizens in an active role regarding the conditions that determine young people's competence and character. The process by itself will not entirely change the conditions or beliefs, but it can contribute to the necessary process of change. Many other changes in thought and action will also be required. A youth charter approach is one among many parts of the solution that we shall need. As with so many other relations in a complex society, the parts intertwine. The improvements will gain strength in concert. Like a campaign advancing along many fronts at once, we must move wherever an opportunity arises. The conditions will improve with each new victory.

PART TWO

SETTINGS FOR GUIDANCE AND GROWTH

4

GUIDANCE ON THE HOME FRONT

When speaking with parent groups, I hear similar kinds of distress everywhere I go. Parents say that major forces influencing their children's beliefs and behavior have spun out of control. They worry that their children are being led in the wrong direction by the mass media, by friends, even by teachers. Parents complain of feeling ignored, unsupported—in a sense, abandoned. Often they do not trust the child-rearing advice that they get from books and newspapers. Nor do they always trust the other adults in their communities to give their children the right kind of guidance. In short, many parents today feel alienated from their children's friends and teachers, distant from their relatives and neighbors, hostile to the mass media, and suspicious of child-rearing experts, police, sports coaches, business managers who employ the young, and in some cases even their civic and religious leaders.

As a result, many parents feel alone in a world of questionable values and people whom they cannot count on. They feel that their own sound intuitions about what is right for a child are constantly undermined by society. A parent tells a child to be in by ten at night, and the child complains that she will be an outcast, because none of her friends needs to be in before midnight. A parent abhors the sex and violence that media outlets expose her child to, yet the parent cannot spend every waking moment monitoring all the material that her child watches or hears. A parent wants his child to gain strong academic skills, but the child brings home banal schoolwork assignments that require little or no effort—and still the child cannot write a good paragraph, multiply with decimals, or find Brazil on a map.

Feeling isolated in a world seemingly spinning out of their control, many parents have drifted into a sense of powerlessness. But parents *do* have the power to shape the forces that influence their children's development—more power than they may know, both within and beyond the confines of their own homes. The key to unleashing this power is to resist the isolation that has divided and confused households throughout our society. Parents must open lines of communication to others who will join with them in a collective effort to impart high intellectual and moral standards to the entire younger generation. Parents will find many allies in this effort: neighbors, friends, relatives, schoolteachers, and some almost moribund community organizations (including some of our less active libraries, museums, and churches that will be brought to life by taking on the mission of promoting healthy youth development). A main purpose of a youth charter process is to help parents open these lines of communication and draw support from numerous sources.

Practically every community that I have visited has vexing concerns that have parents worried and baffled. One widespread concern is teenage drunk driving. The horrifying image of one's child smashed up in a drunken driving incident probably has passed before every parent's eyes at some time or other. Yet many parents tell me that they feel powerless to do anything effective about this. They know that stern admonitions are not enough. Their child has friends, the friends may have access to liquor, one of them may be at the wheel with their child as a passenger. What can any parent do to prevent such a thing? To complicate matters, no two families seem to agree on how to broach the matter of alcohol with their children. Some families abstain entirely, and their children never see an alcoholic drink in their house. In other families, adults drink with abandon, but the children are not allowed to touch a drop. Other families allow their youngsters to consume moderate amounts of wine or beer, especially on holiday and other ceremonial occasions. With all of the wide variation in drinking practices, parents often conclude that alcohol consumption is a private matter that must be left to individual families to work out. This leaves them with little to do but pray that their child does not end up in the wrong car at the wrong time with an inebriated friend at the wheel.

It *is* possible to reach a workable consensus on sensitive matters such as this. Through youth charter discussions, families can identify areas of agreement and joint courses of action on critical problems such as drunk driving, while agreeing to disagree on private matters such as whether to allow youngsters to drink wine on family occasions. For example, parents collectively can determine that liquor will no longer be available at *any* teenage parties that they will allow their children to attend. They can agree to communicate this standard to their children and to the parents of all their children's friends; and they can agree to enforce the standard whenever their own homes are used for parties. They also can agree that they will expect other households to honor the same rule. Moreover, they can publicly announce that they will expect that schools and other organizations will make special efforts to monitor all youth events that they sponsor to prevent alcohol consumption.

When adults thereby identify a concrete standard that they all see a need for—no drinking at teenage parties—they put their differences aside. The standard picks up strength and credibility as more people sign on. It becomes far easier to enforce a "no drinking at parties" rule when it is universally applied than when just one or two families try to do it on their own. Parents then feel an increased sense of control over a bothersome concern and a new sense of assurance that their children's social life has become a bit safer. The children listen to their parents' warnings with more respect, since all of their friends are hearing similar directives.

The Importance of Healthy Habits for Children's Character Development

A youth charter begins at home. The habits that children learn from their family can either support or undermine the standards of the community. In places where parents raise their children with consistent guidance and clear expectations, community-wide youth charters are more easily arrived at than in places where children have not benefited from such guidance.

In turn, widely shared community standards can support parents' efforts to impart healthy habits to their children. A parent who is confused about what to do when her child refuses to go to bed on time, or fails to do homework, needs to know how other parents in the community deal with the same issues. If all of the child's friends must go to bed by ten and if none are allowed to watch TV until their homework is done, the parent is in a far stronger position to uphold such rules than if the other children can do whatever they want. Some parents— against their own better instincts—let their children do whatever they want on the assumption that this is the way children are raised now. With better communication and with higher shared standards—in short, with a youth charter—parents can institute more effective child-rearing practices in their own homes. Moreover, the practices will have more credibility with the children because they know their friends are being held to similar standards.

This is *not* to say that communities should make it their business to intervene in private family life. A youth charter is a method of communication and mutual support, not an instrument of coercion. We have the great fortune to live in a free society, and no one should wish to see community members policing one another's child-rearing practices. The power of a youth charter lies in offering parents and other adults a clear understanding of the standards and expectations that they and other community members believe will provide a wholesome direction for their children's development, and it lies as well in establishing a network of support for implementing these standards and expectations in homes, schools, and other places where children spend time. On the home front, a youth charter can offer parents a sense that their efforts to impart beneficial habits to their children will be valued and supported by others in the community.

A child's character is founded on habits such as respectfulness, truthfulness, kindness, curiosity, loyalty, responsibility, and perseverance. Children begin to develop basic habits soon after they are born. The habits that a child acquires in the home have a powerful and enduring impact on the child's life, affecting everyone who comes in contact with the child. Healthy habits will dispose a child toward learning and self-improvement, cooperation with others, diligence and reliability, obedience to authority and social rules, self-control, and a sincere concern for others. There are unhealthy habits that do just the opposite, and these become increasingly difficult to correct as the child grows older.

By the end of childhood, a child's basic habits are well on their way to being formed. In this most crucial realm of personal growth, the home front is where the action is. A community youth charter can help parents understand this. It can provide useful insights about how to impart healthy habits to children, and it can provide a network of social support in the effort to do so. Contemporary means of communication can make a youth charter's shared insight and support readily available at any time. Parents can telephone one another when a problem arises or use e-mail to create an ongoing forum about parenting ideas and resources. Through on-line services, groups of parents can create an electronic bulletin board, or virtual e-mail network, devoted to discussing their community's youth charter. In this way, they can exchange suggestions, questions, and support with one another at any time.

Wonders of modern technology aside, we are nowadays starting at something of a disadvantage. Many adults today have lost sight of the importance of imparting healthy habits to children. In fact, many have come to believe that their children can actually be harmed by the kinds of parenting practices that encourage children to acquire strong habits. Such beliefs have been passed along by many popular baby books that emphasize autonomy and self-esteem as the primary goals of child-rearing[1] Many of these books suggest that parenting practices aimed at teaching children habits such as responsibility and obedience are deadly to self-esteem and creativity, because such strictures "overcontrol" children, preventing them from exercising their free choice.

The best research in the field of child development conveys a very different story. Talented youth—children and adolescents whose accomplishments in the arts and sciences outshine their peers—invariably have acquired a strong sense of discipline and habit. "Talent development," write the authors of the leading study in the area, "is easier for teens who have learned habits conducive to cultivating talent."[2] These youngsters are able to work hard and persistently at their crafts. Their creative self-expression does not wither as a result of their hard work; on the contrary, it blossoms.

Some of the popular child-rearing books also caution that children will become pressured and dispirited by parental enforcement of firm standards.[3] Parental inducement of shame, guilt, or other feelings of remorse for violating a family standard is portrayed as crippling to a child's self-image. This now commonly accepted "wisdom" is an off-shoot of the disabling cultural beliefs that I write about in Chapter 8.

As a result of these and other misconceptions, many children today are growing up without the capacity to follow rules, to learn well and work effectively, to be considerate toward others, to cope with frustration, to postpone gratification, or to conduct their affairs in a well-organized manner. The unhappy irony here is that growing up without consistent family rules actually decreases children's creative capacities and increases their sense of stress—precisely the opposite effects from those intended by those who advocate withholding the guidance that children need to build good habits. Wrong ideas can defeat the best of intentions.

In order to foster the kinds of habits that build character and competence in their children, parents have two obstacles to overcome; but they also will find two powerful allies to help them get past the obstacles.

The first obstacle is the self-centeredness that marks an immature mind. Children can be highly egocentric, especially in the early years of life. With very little social experience under their belts, they tend to see things mostly from their own perspectives. If they feel like getting up early on Saturday morning and making a lot of noise, why shouldn't they? One of a parent's most important jobs is to see that their child's early egocentrism is corrected by an appreciation of differing points of view. The child may feel great, but Grandma may be feeling sick; and this may require special acts of consideration or service on the part of the child. Children will not come to such realizations by themselves: they must be informed, and sometimes prodded, if they are to respect another's viewpoint. If a parent fails to direct a child in this manner, the child's early egocentrism can turn into enduring self-absorption and plain selfishness.

The second obstacle is that youth charters have become weak or nonexistent in many communities. It is a challenge to counter a child's egocentrism in the best of circumstances. In a time of uncertain standards, low expectations, and social isolation, it becomes an uphill struggle to impart a sense of purpose beyond a child's pursuit of easy thrills and immediate gratification.

Fortunately, parents have two allies in their quest to raise a child with strong character and competence. The first is the rich repertoire of natural moral dispositions that all children are born with. These dispositions, which include empathy and self-regulation, orient a child toward the rules, standards, and expectations of civilized life. Children enter the world prepared to get along with others, despite their early tendencies toward egocentrism. (In the language of child development theory, it is said that children are born sociocentric as well as egocentric.) This gives parents a lot to work with in a positive sense. In other words, a parent's job is not simply to resist a child's antisocial tendencies, as was once believed by Puritans who struggled to "break the will" of young children. Rather, parents can focus their efforts on nurturing and bringing to fruition their children's prosocial potential—for example, by showing children how to act reliably and effectively on their feelings of empathy for other people.

The second ally that parents have in their quest is the potential of community support. Even though we live in a fragmented society, the isolation is not complete, and many people crave a greater sense of community. A youth charter process can create this sense of community for parents who wish to raise their children with high standards and clear expectations. It can also help parents resist popular misconceptions about children's needs—the fashionable trends in child-rearing that make little sense to parents but that may seem compelling because they have been uncritically passed along by avowed experts. By participating in youth charter discussions, parents can gain a better understanding of how to guide their children at home, and they can form alliances with others in the community who can provide similar guidance to their children when they venture beyond the home. For example, in a youth charter meeting, parents can discuss standards for children's television viewing. How many hours per week should children spend in front of the TV set? What kinds of shows should they watch? Parents can share information and ideas with one another. One parent may recommend certain television shows with strong educational value for children. Another may describe her experience with setting weekly limits on television time in her family. In this manner, parents can share expectations and perhaps come up with standards that they can present with confidence to their children. Other youth charter discussions can focus on homework, bedtime, teen parties, or any other common matters of household contention.

Adult guidance is required to make the most of a child's natural moral dispositions, as well as to correct for a child's initial self-centeredness. A parental practice of presenting clear standards to a child will nurture in the child a habit of learning and living up to the standards. Children also need guidance in order to find out exactly how to do so. If parents and other adults offer guidance early enough, children will be ready (even eager) to hear it. When parents withhold such guidance, the child's natural moral inclinations will start to atrophy.

The foundation of a youth charter is the guidance that parents give children on the home front. A youth charter can enable parents to benefit from one another's wisdom about how to foster healthy habits in their children. It can also give young people the constructive message that their own family's rules and guidelines are in sync with those that regulate their friends' home lives. This kind of awareness motivates a child to internalize the rules and guidelines rather than simply go through motions and later complain to friends about how unfair one's parents are. In a community with a strong youth charter, there will still be such complaints (after all, children love a sympathetic ear as much as we do), but they will not be serious enough to reflect a true alienation from parental guidance.

In the remainder of this chapter, I discuss the kinds of parental guidance that a youth charter in our society could support in order to foster children's development of healthy habits, positive attitudes, and essential skills. Many of the principles may seem like common sense to parents who have already raised young children—at least I hope that this is the case. Part of my point is that it has become difficult for parents to follow commonsense principles in raising children. Beginning parents especially have trouble finding their bearings amid the cultural confusion and misconceptions in our fractious society. I do not deceive myself into believing that one more collection of written child-rearing advice will set this picture straight, but if the principles that I discuss— or others like them—are used as the home front component of a community youth charter, they could indeed help parents foster beneficial habits in their children. It is the principles in combination with a community youth charter that will make the difference.

The Habit-Forming Early Years

Newborn babies make their needs known loudly and clearly. They are born with a rich medley of ways to signal their parents whenever they feel hungry, cold, wet, sleepy, or simply wish stimulation. A baby's cries, smiles, and stares are all part of the adaptive equipment that ensures the baby's survival.

Parents are instinctively captivated by the many signals that young children send. Most parents are closely attuned to their children's basic needs. Parents naturally feed their children when they are hungry, comfort them when they are distressed, change their clothes when they are wet, put them to rest when they are tired, and play with them when they are eager to interact. These are the elements of caregiving—seeing that a young child's basic life functions, such as eating and sleeping, are well tended—that all responsible parents look after their children with love and devotion.

What parents may not realize is that each of these basic functions has additional layers of meaning for the child—layers of meaning that can shape the child's present and future orientation to the world. Feeding and comforting a child are essential not only in themselves but also in communicating behavioral standards to the child. The manner in which primary care is given plays a key role in teaching children how to act and regulate their own feelings.

There are two principles of child development that all parents should know: (1) children are amazingly proficient learners who pick up indirect messages from every nuance of every situation that they are in, and (2) common life functions such as eating, sleeping, eliminating bodily waste, and interacting with others carry multiple messages for children. These messages—and in particular, the way that these messages are conveyed by the child's home and culture—have implications for the child's behavior that go well beyond the satisfaction of the child's primary needs.

As I discuss in Chapter 8, we are living in a culture that chronically underestimates the intelligence and resourcefulness of the young. In the midst of such a culture, it takes a concerted effort to hold onto the following two principles: (1) children are quick and eager learners, and (2) they are acute observers. These two principles will be found in every part of the world. With these two principles in mind, let us consider the basic tasks of early childhood. I begin with eating and sleeping, perhaps the most basic of all, and then take up some other elements of a child's home life, such as the sharing of family rules and responsibilities.

All living people eat and sleep. This means, of course, that every living child accomplishes these elementary functions. What more is there to say than that? First, children learn many generalized habits of thought and behavior from the way in which they learn to eat and sleep. Second, many children have serious eating or sleeping disorders, which in some cases persist into adulthood. Depending on the nature of the habits that the child learns, the child's early experience can serve the child well or poorly throughout life.

Within our own culture, certain popular practices regarding eating and sleeping patterns clearly spell trouble for children who are subjected to them. These practices are easily avoided, to the benefit of child and parent. My comments and recommendations do *not* propose uniformity in cultural approaches to eating and sleeping arrangements. (Eating and sleeping patterns vary enormously throughout the world, and many have deep religious and cultural significance. It would be absurd to express preferences between different cultural practices of eating and sleeping. Children are constitutionally resilient and adapt well in a broad range of circumstances.) Rather, they focus on how we may avoid the unfortunate consequences of self-defeating practices that have become too common.

The underlying theme in my recommendations is that children need predictability in order to regulate their eating and sleeping behavior. This is one universal learning requirement that transcends the vast variability in cultural patterns. In all cultures, eating and sleeping are important opportunities for young children to learn essential habits of self-control—habits that are essential both within and beyond the spheres of food and rest.

It is hard for a child to learn self-control in eating when food is used as an emotional inducement almost as often as it is used as a source of nourishment. In our homes and schools, children are offered candy, cookies, chips, and other junk food through the day. To keep a child busy, a parent will sit the child down in front of the TV with a plate of brownies; to keep a child happy, a relative brings the child a candy bar every time she visits; to keep her students entertained, a teacher turns her classroom into a snack-filled party several days a month. Adding to the tempting mix, giant food corporations saturate shopping malls and schools with free candy as a means of cultivating even stronger junk food habits among the young. It is little wonder that the rate of obesity among children has risen constantly since World War II. Even more serious is the effect of all this on children's sense of order and self-discipline. The irregularity and overindulgence spawned by unwholesome eating patterns give young children a shaky start in their quest to develop stable ways of organizing their lives.

To compound the problem, at the same time as we are stuffing our children with heavy doses of high-calorie junk food, the popular culture excessively prizes low weight, especially in girls and young women. In fact, our culture *overvalues* the condition of being thin. Medical specialists have estimated that weight norms associated with aesthetic appeal in our society are 10 to 15 percent lower than those associated with good health.

These conflicting messages place young people in a bewildering bind. Early in life, they are plied with nonnutritional snacks meant to amuse, mollify, soothe, and occupy them. Many acquire irregular eating habits and dependency on food as an emotional comfort. Suddenly, around the time of puberty, the young person discovers that she is expected to be slender at all costs. The penalties for obesity include social ridicule and isolation, among the worst fears of any teenager. Is it any wonder that anorexia, bulimia, and other serious eating disorders flourish among our adolescent population? Children respond to a lack of predictability in their environments with extreme—and often self-destructive—attempts to regulate their own behavior. We would serve them better by giving them a more predictable environment and some guidance in acquiring early habits of self-control.

Children's sleeping patterns also benefit from predictability early in life. Children can acquire maladaptive sleeping habits if they do not have the chance to regulate their own sleeping rhythms when they are young. A parent who rushes to comfort an infant at every nighttime murmur does the child no favor—advice from some popular baby books to the contrary. Children need time to get themselves to sleep. In the absence of physical reasons for discomfort (which, of course, parents should check on), children spontaneously will find their own ways to unwind. For a child, learning to do so is one small step toward learned self-control. Again, as with eating behavior, the child who has never learned self-control inevitably will encounter real-world penalties before long. Our high schools are full of students who stay up half the night and sleep through their early morning classes.

Eating and sleeping patterns have personal, health, and social significance, and they presage many other behavioral challenges. The destructive binds that we often place our children in with respect to eating and sleeping have parallels in larger predicaments that children also confront in today's society. For example, we have created an educational system that is devoid of rigor in the early grades and filled with high-stakes testing in the later grades. The lazy thinking and sloppy work habits that children acquire during the primary school years prepare them poorly for the later requirement that they possess real skill and knowledge. From the child's point of view, schooling begins with frequent and unpredictable indulgence; then, without much warning, it turns into a cacophony of unsympathetic demands for performance accompanied by harsh penalties for failure. In this and many other ways, we place teenagers in a demanding drama with little rehearsal— while at the same time we rehearse young children for a play that never could (or should) be produced.

A community youth charter, because it is a comprehensive vision, can help us avoid these kinds of destructive binds. A youth charter places child-rearing and education practices in the perspective of our ultimate goals for our children. It forces us to ask ourselves, "If we encourage our children to acquire these kinds of habits, where will it lead them?" A youth charter makes it possible for parents to take a developmental perspective on their own child-rearing practices and offers them opportunities to exchange ideas and support with other adults who are also concerned with the future prospects of children.

In youth charter meetings, parents can discuss with one another all issues that concern them, including the most basic functions in children's lives—eating, sleeping, communicating, and playing. Parents can share ideas about how to foster good habits in children by establishing sensible household routines. Of course, the parents themselves will still hold the primary responsibility of deciding which routines best serve their own families' needs. It is the parents, not the community, who run the households and raise the families. But most parents need support and advice. Grandparents may be unavailable to dispense wise counsel. Pediatricians may not have the time to concern themselves with their patients' behavioral habits. Many parents feel too isolated from neighbors to broach intimate family matters, and many popular baby books are filled with guilt-inducing admonitions that lead parents to believe that their only duty is to rush to serve their child's every whim. In such a climate, parents need opportunities for open discussions with others who can share common sense and insights, large and small, about how to raise children with good habits.

Eating and sleeping are two occasions for learning the habits of self-regulation that can contribute to a child's prospects for attaining an orderly and purposeful life. Eating and sleeping are powerful occasions for learning because they begin at birth, they are necessary to survival, they are gratifying, and children engage in them frequently. Other early life functions also can offer similar opportunities for learning self-control; toilet training and social play are other obvious examples.

There are many constructive practices that parents may follow in teaching their children to regulate basic functions, and there also are a number of problematic ones that have come into widespread use. In all their broad variety, practices that are constructive have certain principles in common. The following guidelines reflect these principles:

1.   *Establish regular routines that create a sense of predictability and order in the basic functions of a child's life.* This guideline has two parts. First, the caregiver establishes rules, schedules, and consistent standards that guide the child's eating and sleeping behavior. Second, the caregiver makes sure that the child understands these routines, so that the child always knows what is expected and why. In this way, children learn to respect the rules of home. The habits that children acquire then become reinforced by their cognitive understanding of why such habits are important.

Although there is much legitimate cultural variation in the routines that parents establish for their children, certain routines are so advantageous for all children that parents everywhere would be wise to follow them. Breakfast for school-age children is critical to their academic performance. Children who leave for school without a nutritious breakfast are starting the day with serious physical and cognitive handicaps. Beyond that, they are failing to learn valuable habits of nutrition and personal organization. They are unprepared to enter the community of learners— another implication for the community youth charter.

Still, many parents accept without hesitation a child's protests that "I'm not hungry" or "I'm too tired to eat anything." Parents should realize that breakfast is an acquired habit with multiple benefits for school-age children. Sometimes a child needs to be urged to learn such habits. The same applies for all other eating and sleeping routines with long-term consequences. In youth charter meetings, teachers might remind parents how important a child's breakfast is for learning in school. This will give parents a way to explain the standard to their children, and it may increase a parent's resolve in helping her children acquire good breakfast habits while they are young.

The child's attendance at family mealtimes, such as dinner, affords the child irreplaceable opportunities for getting guidance and wisdom from parents. Regular bedtimes ensure that children get enough rest and teach children how to organize their affairs in a timely fashion.

As a bonus, such routines give parents an orderly household that they can count on for their own peace of mind. There is no need to hide this parental benefit from the children (as if it were a shameful sign of adult selfishness). Children need to hear on occasion that they are not always at the center of the universe. Consideration for other people is one perfectly good reason for children to learn to regulate their life functions. Moreover, when children discover that their own self-control can benefit others, this can be a highly motivating source of pride for them.

2.   *Strike a balance between children's desires and the home's basic routines.* Children's physiological needs must be met in a responsive manner. Children express desires for comfort and gratification that any loving parent will want to satisfy. At the same time, children need to learn that gratification often must be postponed and that nonessential desires sometimes must go unattended. As they grow older, children must learn to regulate and fulfill their own desires in the absence of their parents. Children cannot learn this if their parents constantly try to mollify their every whim.

Modern trends in child rearing have taken us in an increasingly child-centered direction. As a result, experts have been dispensing child-rearing advice that urges parents to give wide latitude to children's desires. For example, Penelope Leach's popular *Your Baby and Child from Birth to Age Five* suggests that sleeping and feeding patterns should follow the child's schedule, not the parent's. In addition, toilet training is a "choice" that, according to Leach, "is, and will remain, the child's." Urging a child to become toilet trained is a losing cause, she says, because children should be allowed to do as they wish: "Don't try to force the child to sit on the potty," Leach writes. "The clearer you make it that you really want him to sit there, the less likely he is to want to. Since toilet training can only succeed through his voluntary cooperation, battles will mean certain failure."[4] Such advice, although well-meaning, implies that it is futile for a parent to guide her child in the essential task of behavioral self-regulation. Children thrive on parental guidance of all kinds, including guidance about how to accommodate their behavior to routines of the household.

3. *Teach children to carry out basic functions in ways that augment their respect for their society's general norms.* Every society embeds basic life functions such as eating and sleeping in a rich web of cultural meaning. Manners, rituals, and customs regulate basic functions according to traditions and current requirements of a particular society. Each custom symbolizes a greater societal reality that transcends the individual's own needs.

Once children understand spoken language, adults can begin explaining this to them, to good effect. For example, parents can tell children *why* we in our society have three mealtimes, use forks and spoons, and wipe our mouths with napkins when we eat. Parents can read children descriptions of societies where people eat with their fingers, eat once a day, and share communal platters of food, describing the conditions that engender these particular practices and explaining the cultural meaning that they convey. (Libraries are full of sources of information about cultural practices around the world.) All of this will help children better appreciate the rationale behind the practices of their own society—practices that they are expected to follow. Parents can also explain to children what happens when one chooses not to conform to the customs of one's own culture (the social consequences, say, of eating spaghetti with one's fingers in the school cafeteria). Through such discussions, the child's habits become reinforced by understanding and conviction.

4. *Train early habits that help children cope with later demands.* Children do best when they experience continuity and coherence throughout their development. We must avoid putting children on a track that inculcates bad habits when they are young and then poses decisive tasks requiring exemplary habits later. (Misplaced priorities, such as overvaluing thinness or other superficial ideals, can add a further frenzied madness to this wrong direction.)

Parents should take a hard look at the tasks that their children must prepare for, identify the skills that their children will need to accomplish these tasks, and help their children acquire the habits that enable them to develop these skills. With this kind of developmental sequence in mind, parents can begin early, when it matters most, and in the areas that carry the most weight. For the young child, those areas are eating, sleeping, and the other basic life functions that provide fertile ground for learning enduring habits of self-regulation. A community youth charter can enable parents to help one another organize their child-rearing practices toward the shared goal of fostering these habits in the younger generation, to the benefit of the whole community.

Chores and Responsibilities

In most of the industrial world, the ancient custom of asking children to help out around the house has gone out of fashion. When asked why they no longer give children chores, modern parents offer three reasons. First, children have a lot to do anyway, with schoolwork, friends, and after-school activities. Second, children need and deserve free time in order to "cool out" from the pressures of their overprogrammed lives. Third, it is more trouble to get a child to make his bed or help empty the dishwasher than to simply do it yourself (or, in highly affluent families, to have the hired help do it). Many parents express pride over having enough family resources (household help, labor-saving appliances, their own time) to relieve children of the burden of doing chores. It is normal for parents to enjoy the feeling that their children do not have to perform the difficult and boring tasks that they had to put up with when they were young.

As the child's responsibilities around the house have declined, the child's rights and privileges have increased—part of the waxing of children's power. This can be seen clearly in the changing relationship between household chores and children's allowances. Two generations ago, it was common for families to expect children to perform household chores without remuneration. Many families were still feeling the Great Depression's effects; they needed their children to chip in if they were going to keep their homes afloat, and there was little money for extra spending. The subsequent generation had more money to work with, but children's help was still expected. Often the solution was to tie an allowance—some regular spending money—to the requirement of contributing help to the family. Now the spending money has remained but, in most families, the requirement of performing service has disappeared. (As a footnote to this small history, I note that some families today have changed the notion of allowance to mean money on demand rather than a constant weekly sum that the child must learn to budget.)

With each step of this progression, we have moved further away from providing children with the responsibility that they need to develop good habits and sound character. When parents tell me, as they often do, that their households work best when all chores are done by parents or paid help, I reply that families are not just about running households in the most efficient manner possible. Families also are about raising the future generation—and doing so in a manner that will serve society well. Home economics is not the bottom line of our families' ledgers: the character of our children is the bottom line, the ultimate criterion of a family's accountability to itself and society.

Personal responsibility is necessary for the development of sound character. So, too, is a sense of service—a sense that there are other people who deserve attention. Character growth means learning how to balance one's own needs with the needs of others. Children who are never asked to help, who are never given responsibilities for the well-being of others, from whom nothing is expected beyond the pursuit of their own desires, will fail to develop such a balance. A standard of service to the family home constrains the child's initial tendency toward self-centeredness and promotes an enduring orientation toward the common good.

As with all other good habits, a sense of responsibility and service are most readily acquired in the early years. The longer a parent waits to introduce such expectations, the more resistant the child will be. Children can help out in meaningful ways as soon as they can walk and talk—and, especially when they are very young, they almost always have fun doing so. For a young child, helping out is a rare and welcome chance to demonstrate competence and acquire important new skills.

In case there may be a reader who would overinterpret my recommendations on household chores, I am not referring to anything that looks remotely like child labor. The last thing I would like to see is a child trooping off to a day at the factory with a lunch bucket in hand or kneeling on a floor, Cinderella-like, mopping up for hours on end. The sorts of chores that I have in mind for young children are simple household tasks that should require no more than a few minutes each day: helping to straighten the house, feeding a family pet, watering the plants, and so on. As children grow older, they can do more: mow the lawn, wash the car, shovel the walk, take out trash, watch over a younger sibling or an aging grandparent who needs some company. The following are guidelines for children's household chores:

1.   *Children of all ages should be given assignments around the house that they will take responsibility for.* Even young children can do something helpful, be it no more complex than bringing a dish from the refrigerator to the table. Simple acts such as this, begun early, are the building blocks of cooperation and consideration for others. As for children of the wealthy, it is no favor to them to bar them from the kitchen, as I have seen in many well-to-do families. The operating belief in such families seems to be that shielding children from such chores instills in the children a special sense of elitism and pride. In reality, this misguided practice does little more than instill self-absorption and incompetence—two undesirable characteristics that will come back to haunt parent and child alike under even the most privileged economic conditions.

Some household assignments bring with them so many developmental benefits for a child that it is hard to see why any parent would refrain from giving them to a child. For example, any child who has a pet should feed, groom, and care for the pet. This is a motivating and engaging way of teaching children responsibility: the child can see the pet's lively gratitude every time the child fill's the pet's dinner bowl. Caring for a pet gives children an opportunity to find a useful expression for their empathic feelings. In this way, children expand and strengthen their natural capacities to empathize with others. Over time, the experience links the child's positive emotions to a sense of responsibility and effective action.

2.   *Children's household assignments should be modest, age graded, and regular.* Chores should not be so time-consuming as to interfere with schoolwork. Children also should have ample time to spend with peers, as well as by themselves, in pursuit of their own interests. Standards for household service should take into account a child's age and ability, without wildly underestimating or overestimating either. Children should be asked to do only chores that they are capable of doing or that they can learn to do in a reasonable period of time. If a child is having difficulty, the parent must be prepared to step in with assistance and support.

For the sake of the child's character growth, the most important requirement is that the child assume real responsibility. If the child's job is to water the indoor plants, he should feel that if he does not do it, the plants will dry up and eventually die—and this is not an acceptable outcome. If, for whatever reason, the child cannot fulfill this obligation, the child must make arrangements for someone else to do it, perhaps by asking his sister or a friend for a favor that later may need to be repaid. That is what it means to take responsibility for getting something done. A regular household chore can teach children the importance of taking responsibility, and it can help children acquire the resourcefulness that is sometimes needed to ensure that a responsibility is always fulfilled. Even the most modest chores can serve this character-building purpose, but they can do so only if parents refrain from stepping in and taking over the chore for the child. "The buck stops here" is a good attitude for anyone, young people included. It is better for a family to let its plants go thirsty than to let its children learn that skipping out on obligations is no big deal.

3. *Children should expect to do household assignments without money in return.* One of the many benefits of chores is that they give children the message that service to others is an essential part of life. In every community, everyone must contribute; for a child, a family should be a microcosm of the community. This is a fundamental principle of the youth charter.

A modest amount of regular chores should be seen as one way that a child can make a contribution. Linking monetary compensation to the chores undermines this message, because it indicates that the child's service is an extra, rather than a normal, contribution. It is as if parents were to keep track of the time they spent caring for the child and then later charge the child for it. If a child takes on a task above and beyond the normal call of duty, it is reasonable for a parent to offer the child special compensation for the extra effort. But it should be made clear to the child that this compensation does not apply to the child's regular household duties, which are assumed as part of the child's membership in the family.

This said, there is nothing wrong with giving children an allowance, which is a useful way of teaching children money management skills in budgeting, planning, and mastering self-control. As with all other responsibilities that parents give their children, an allowance should be consistent. Children should know what they are getting and when. Any change should be made ahead of time and only for good reason (such as the child's advancing in age).

Unlike allowances, money on demand does not teach children management skills and can breed loose spending habits; and it creates unpredictable inequities among groups of children that can weaken community solidarity. One useful role that a youth charter can play is to establish a shared norm for children's allowances. Parents can discuss with one another what amounts seem reasonable in their community, and they can gauge their own children's allowances accordingly. This understanding will immediately resolve one source of tension among children, and it will help all children in the community learn standards of financial responsibility and prudence.

Discipline and Family Rules

Many of the anxieties, frustrations, and confusions of modern parenting revolve around much-misunderstood concepts of discipline. In books written for parents, extreme positions abound. Some popular books have urged parents to refrain from "overcontrolling" their children through punishment of any sort. In reaction, others have urged parents to make a point of disciplining their children through spanking and other forms of corporal punishment.[5] This sort of stern advice has spurred a further reaction from experts who claim that any form of corporal punishment, including a mild smack on a child's bottom, permanently damages the child's psyche and thus constitutes a form of child abuse. In this climate of strident disagreement, it never surprises me that questions about discipline are among the most common that come up when I give talks to parents' groups.

What does surprise me—or at least it used to—is that many parents themselves swing back and forth across the entire gamut of permissiveness and control, from one extreme to the other, in their own homes. In fact, a parent may run through the entire gamut in a single episode of child misbehavior. This is the pattern of response that Thomas Phelan, in an excellent book about disciplinary practices, has called the "talk-persuade-yell-argue-hit syndrome."[6] The parent begins assuming that she can talk the child out of his mischievous impulses. Soon the parent discovers that her child is not yet wholly mature, perfectly reasonable, totally socialized, or impeccably intentioned. Getting nowhere fast, the parent gradually blows her top, escalating into a temper tantrum of her own.

There is a better way, for both the management of the home and the growth of the child: *authoritative parenting*, an approach that combines a firm enforcement of consistent rules with rational explanations for the purposes behind the rules.[7] The child always knows what she is supposed to do and why. The child is respected, and her opinions are heard, but at the same time, the child is expected to listen to the parent and follow the parent's lead. There is no assumption that a child's judgment is of equal value to that of the adult. In authoritative parenting, parents take a child's opinions into account and offer clear explanations for their decisions. But in the end it is they who set the household rules. The parents make sure that the child understands the rationale behind the rules and knows the parents' predictable response if the child breaks the rules.

At times, parents may need to resort to discipline in order to underscore the importance of rules. *Discipline* is a loaded word. Many understand it to mean nothing more than taking the child to the woodshed with a leather belt. When I write about parental discipline, I do *not* mean corporal punishment. I believe that there are always wiser, safer, and more effective means of discipline than corporal punishment—for example, withholding privileges. Parents can be strict without being threatening, firm without being harsh and violent. Children need to know that family rules will be enforced consistently and that breaches of family rules will be punished predictably and fairly. The earlier that children learn this, the less need there will be for parents to use punitive forms of discipline at all.

Many parents who feel compelled to deter their child's rebelliousness with angry threats and spanking have not managed to teach the child proper respect for rules and authority when the child was younger. The way to teach children such respect is through the consistent application of family rules and standards. In the long run, rules are best communicated to children by patience and persistence rather than by hot emotional outbursts.

Discipline is a means of communicating standards—a last resort. Controlling a child's errant behavior enables a parent to prevent any damage that the child might do to himself or to others. It also makes it possible to gain the child's attention so that the child will listen to the standards and the reasons for them.

Discipline is an essential means of implementing principles in a youth charter, because it demonstrates to children that adults take these principles seriously. In turn, a community youth charter creates a forum where parents can discuss disciplinary practices with one another. Such discussions will offer parents ideas, support, and information about what other parents are doing—information that can give parents and their children reassurance that their own practices are reasonable and in the children's long-term interests.

The following are guidelines for family rules and parental discipline in the home:

1. *Start communicating household rules to children early in their lives.* This is similar to the first recommendation that I made regarding children's eating and sleeping routines. The point in both cases is that young children do best when they grow in environments that are structured by predictable regularities and clear expectations for their behavior. Children who grow up in such environments acquire orderly habits that will make life's later challenges manageable.

Family rules that very young children can learn include politeness and kindness to peers, respectfulness to adults, good manners, picking up after themselves, truthfulness, consideration for others, and sharing. These, of course, are general categories of basic household rules. Each family can come up with its own specific versions (for example, "no loud music after 10:00 P.M.") that suits its own home.

2. *Consistency is all-important.* Family rules differ from household to household. Some families have a host of rules that they believe essential; others have very few. Within reason, the number and nature of family rules is far less important than the consistency with which they are upheld. A parent who enforces rules only when it suits the parent's whims (say, by punishing a child for playing loud music after 10:00 P.M. only when the parent is in a bad mood) causes the child to disrespect both the rule and the parent's authority. The most opportune moment for teaching a child respect comes at times when the parent has not personally been put out by the child's disobedience. The parent who bothers to sanction the child in such instances is acting in the child's interest rather than for the parent's own momentary satisfaction.

3. *As soon as they are able, children should be helped to understand the purpose of the rules that they are expected to follow.* Authoritative parenting combines firm standards with clear communication about the rationale behind the standards. Every rule has a purpose that a parent can articulate so the child can understand. The purpose might relate to the welfare of others (you'll keep us awake with loud music) or the child's own welfare (you need the sleep), or to both at once. The child's understanding of the purpose behind the rule is the best assurance that the child will continue to follow the rule in the parents' absence.

Explaining a rule to a child is not the same as using reasoning to persuade the child to follow the rule. The rule must be enforced, whether or not the child agrees that it is reasonable. This is essential to the consistency that makes authoritative parenting so effective. The parent's explanations must assume the child's obedience to the rule; they should not be seen as a means of getting the child to follow the rule. The value of the rational explanation is that it adds longevity to the rule by making it likely that the child eventually will adopt the rule as one of his own. Reasoning should not substitute for the rule itself; that is, it should not become an easy way for children to talk parents out of upholding the rule, except in unusual circumstances where the parents agree that the rule should not apply.

4.   *Sanctions for rule breaking should be calibrated to the child's age as well as to the frequency and severity of the violation.* One excellent disciplinary strategy for children of all ages is withholding privileges. For the strategy to work, the privileges to be withheld must be age appropriate. For a young child, a dinner without dessert may bring the message home; for an older child, it might take a night without TV; for a teenager, it might mean being grounded during an evening when friends are giving a party.

The punishment can match the frequency of the violation as well. Did the child repeat the same infraction? A day without dessert can turn into two days, three days, or a week if the child will not learn the lesson the first time. Administering gradually escalating sanctions in this way is a strategy that has made residential institutions such as the military into effective socializing environments for young people—even for young people who have become almost impossible to deal with after years of undisciplined and uncontrolled behavior. Such approaches can offer parents solutions for the most difficult and recalcitrant youngsters. Graduated sanctions may not turn the child's stubborn behavior around overnight, but if consistently applied, they eventually get through. Again, the solution works best if it is applied over a long term and with the help of a supportive network. A youth charter can provide this kind of stability and support by enabling parents to solicit help and advice from the whole community.

Sanctions also should match the severity of an offense. This principle seems obvious, but in practice it is often misapplied. The problem lies in how parents determine the severity of a child's offense. In a community where parents are isolated from one another, this can be a hard problem to solve. A parent may excuse a serious breach of standards because the parent assumes that everyone else does it. I recently heard a parent of a six-year-old caught stealing say, "That's pretty normal for this age," and leave it at that. But stealing is a violation of core standards in any society—standards such as honesty, trust, respect for other's property, and obedience to the law. A community youth charter would make it clear that parents do not need to consider stealing on the part of their children a normal and inevitable behavior. A youth charter enables parents to teach children to live up to a higher standard.

When Things Go Wrong: Family Conflict, Dissolution, and Loss

It seems that every social critic during the past decade has attributed the major problems of young people today to the breakup of the modern family. Endless treatises have been written on the epidemic of divorce, fatherless homes, and the general demise of the two-parent nuclear family. Among political leaders and policymakers of virtually every persuasion, there has been unanimity in the call to restore stability—and two parents—to every child's home. It is generally believed that not doing so will inevitably take us further along the path toward youth failure and social decay.

It is certainly true that a child raised with two parents in a stable home begins life at a tremendous advantage. Two parents usually can do more for a child than one, and stability in any part of a child's life—especially a part as central as the home—is to be treasured. Children raised in such advantageous conditions should be grateful for their good fortune. But what does this mean for children who have not been so fortunate? Are they doomed? Are they defective? Are they always headed for trouble—unless, that is, we can find a way to legislate the return of the stable two-parent family?

If this were to be the case, our society would indeed be facing a bleak future—but so would every other society in the history of the world, for families have always been subjected to the whims of fate, and some children have always had to cope with less-than-stable home conditions. Parents get sick and die. They lose their jobs and get depressed. Sometimes a parent must leave home to fight in a foreign war. Sometimes a parent leaves home to pursue a golden opportunity or to respond to the desperate call of someone in need. Sometimes parents run away;

sometimes they fight with one another; sometimes they collapse under life's burdens. Such events happen everywhere, and they always will as long as there are humans with families. So what point are our social critics making when they rail against the collapse of two-parent families? Are we going to legislate away personal catastrophes?

In fact, the problems of young people have little to do with the purported collapse of the two-parent family. As in every other period of history, there are plenty of single parents today who are raising their children splendidly (though admittedly under more difficult conditions than could be provided by an additional parent). Conversely, many children are raised poorly in families with two parents. The essential ingredient in child-rearing does not boil down to the number of parents that the child has access to. Rather, it boils down to the quality of guidance that a child receives at home and throughout the community. A single parent with high standards and persistent dedication can do a better job of providing guidance than do two parents who impart little in the way of standards to their children and expect even less. In communities with a strong youth charter, children can find more character-building sources of guidance, and single parents can find essential networks of support.

I do not make light of family breakup and loss. They are painful experiences for any child and potentially harmful as well, but their effects can be managed. Children are resilient. They can come through such experiences as strong as or stronger than they were prior to the difficulties. The tenor of our modern social critiques has led many people to stigmatize children who grow up in less-than-ideal family conditions. Stigmatizing a child, however, is a cruel way of giving up on the child, because it unnecessarily lowers expectations for the child, and no one should ever give up on a child. This is an unfair and socially destructive way of penalizing children for conditions in their lives that tell us very little about their real potential and can be managed in a way that prevents any loss of that potential.

Family adversities need not damage children's growth or impair their futures. In fact, adversity in the home, much like any other hardship, can facilitate the child's character development, particularly when the child is offered proper guidance and support. All experiences, pleasant or unpleasant, can be turned into learning opportunities if adults in the child's life have sufficient faith, wisdom, and dedication to do so.

A community youth charter can help adults coordinate their efforts to ensure that all children, and especially those enduring a family hardship, have access to the support and guidance of other community members. Following are guidelines for managing conflict, dissolution, and family loss in ways that can enhance rather than impair the child's character development:

1. *Tell children the truth, the whole truth, and nothing but the truth.* When adversity strikes a family, the question always arises: What should we tell the children? Understandably parents often hesitate to divulge anything to children that may upset them. It is common for adults to tell children half-truths (or even lies), to hide information, and to use euphemisms intended to soften the realities. I have heard adults tell young children that a deceased loved one has "gone away," is "at rest," or is "sleeping somewhere." In some divorces, long after both parents have determined to dissolve the marriage, children are led to believe that their parents eventually will reunite. Many children whose parents come down with a fatal illness do not discover that their parent is dying until the parent's last moments.

Children sooner or later must confront the hard facts. There can be no escaping them. What, then, is accomplished by not telling a child the truth? Three things are accomplished, none of them constructive: (1) the child becomes thoroughly confused by the vague euphemisms and other contorted explanations that are meant to disguise reality; (2) the child is thoroughly frightened by the whisperings, hushed secrets, and other veiled mysteries; and (3) the child begins to mistrust all communications on the matter. If the purpose of the deception is to reassure the child, that purpose is quickly defeated by the confusion, fear, and mistrust that the child experiences.

Adults chronically underestimate children's intelligence (a serious mistake that provides a continuing theme for this book). Children have acute observational powers. There is no way to keep emotionally charged family events from them for long. The most that adults can do is to unsettle and unnerve children through ineffectual cover-ups.

Deceiving children also squanders a unique opportunity for providing them with priceless guidance about how to handle adversity. There will be further conflict, disarray, and death in every child's future. A popular approach is to shield children while young from such painful realities, under the assumption that childhood should be a preserve of blissful ignorance. In the modern era, this approach has been taken to such an extreme that old fairy tales and poems—the Brothers Grimm, Hans Christian Andersen, even Mother Goose—have been bowdlerized beyond recognition in order to delete references to human cruelty, illness, and death and dying.

I do not believe that adults should gratuitously rub children's noses in life's miseries, but I am convinced that young children are strengthened rather than damaged by honest accounts of life's realities. Children are curious and ready to learn about the world. Naturally they will become sad when told of a loved one's afflictions, but feeling sadness is not in itself a harmful experience. Sadness is a normal and healthy response to tragic events. It is one of the basic emotional responses that children in their formative years can learn to cope with and to act on appropriately. We are always more helpful to children when we support their efforts to master developmental tasks than when we try to deter or postpone such efforts. It is not only futile but detrimental to shield children from the inevitable challenges of living in this world.

2.   *During any family adversity, maintain as much continuity as possible in all of the child's key interpersonal relationships and build a community of support and guidance for the child.* Isolation is the one condition that can turn a family adversity into a developmental tragedy for a child. Unfortunately, isolation during times of high family stress is difficult to prevent. The social conditions surrounding the child can quickly deteriorate to the point where the child has virtually no one to communicate with. The prominent adults in the child's life become frantically busy and wholly preoccupied by their own concerns. Suddenly, in the case of illness, death, or separation, a parent may be gone from the household entirely. The adults who remain may be loath to tell the child the whole truth about what is going on, out of misguided fears of upsetting the child further. Or—worse—if the absence of a parent arises from a family conflict, the one who remains may truly upset the child further by strenuously criticizing the one who has left.

To add to all this, children have a tendency to withdraw in the face of severe external pressure. Sometimes they blame themselves for conflicts and other mishaps that disturb their families. Sometimes they imagine catastrophic scenarios that go beyond the problems at hand. Unless a child has a close confidant to talk to during such stressful periods, the child's anxieties can fester in private until they immobilize the child's coping abilities. In such a state, the child's character development comes to a halt, because nothing can be learned.

Certainly children are hardy and resilient, but they are not made of steel. They have the inner strength and adaptability to survive most family adversities, and even to learn useful coping skills from their experience with them, but they cannot do so alone. They need the support and guidance of people who care about their welfare. If one such person is available, that will do; a surer route is a network of people who are ready and willing to provide the child with all the varieties of help and guidance that the child may need.

Families caught up in the midst of adversity should take as their first priority the creation of such networks for their children. They should draw on relatives, neighbors, teachers, youth workers, local agencies, the churches and synagogues, and all professionals or volunteers they have access to. In this way, a family in trouble can give their child the most valuable instrument for prevailing over adversity: a virtual extended family. In the process, the child not only gets crucial assistance but also learns how to deal with difficulties by finding social support.

While building networks of support for their children, parents also must be careful not to weaken or destroy key relationships that their children have built up over the years. This guideline is not always easy to follow during times of parental strife. It may seem more palatable for one parent to try to cut the other one out of the picture. But parents who violate this guideline pay a price later in the form of their children's emotional instability. Continuity for a child provides precious armor against the hazards of family instability.

In today's fractious social climate, it may seem impossible to overcome personal animosity, even for the sake of a child. After all, it takes more than one person to stop the animosity. Similarly, it may seem difficult for a parent to create a network of extrafamilial support for a distressed child. Again, the parent cannot do it alone; other people must be willing and able to cooperate.

This brings me back once again to the major overriding message of this book. In order to ensure success, we must strengthen the links among all the important people in a child's life. We must create communities where parents can turn to others for support when they need it and where children can find multiple sources of guidance. We must make the effort to establish a core understanding—a sense of common standards—among those whom we work with in the service of our children's future. Only in this way can we turn a fractious atmosphere full of conflict and division into a cooperative atmosphere full of shared purpose. A community of mutual support and a sense of high common standards are the two main purposes of the youth charter.

A youth charter starts in the home, with parent' efforts to build character in their children. As children grow, they move into other venues: the school, the neighborhood, the peer group, the community at large. The youth charter must move with the child, providing extended support, clear standards, and high expectations wherever the child goes.

5

SCHOOL SUCCESS

The educational lives of teenagers neither begin nor end in the schools themselves. . . . They are the result of how coordinated or divided the community is in proposing a learning environment for teenagers in which each is held accountable to a common set of educational goals.

FRANCIS IANNI, *The Search for Structure*

Like all other matters related to children, schools are attracting intense public scrutiny. In the mid-1980s, an influential report called the United States "a nation at risk" because of the dismal state of its schools. Leading government officials who had been mainly occupying themselves with weighty problems such as economics or foreign affairs began devoting their energies to fixing school systems. A high-profile council of state governors sponsored a series of education summits. Following their lead, Vice President George Bush campaigned for president in 1988 on a promise to become the nation's first "education president." The 1990s saw school reform become a standard item on every politician's list of promises—an end-of-the-century version of a chicken in every pot. By the 1996 presidential campaign, the improvement of schools had become a dominant theme in both parties' platforms, with both candidates naming education as "our number one priority."

The heightened public interest in schooling is part of a wave of concern for children that has swept through society during the latter part of this century. Yet the increased attention by itself will do nothing unless it is accompanied by sound insights about children's developmental needs and a realistic strategy for providing children with the guidance that their healthy development requires.

In the matter of schooling, the increased attention has generated much energy but no definitive blueprint for school improvement. Still, the experiments of the past decade have taught us some useful lessons. The first and foremost lesson that I take from our recent experience is that schools succeed only when they work in close concert with students' parents and other members of the community. Schools that hold themselves aloof inevitably fail to reach the majority of their students. Conversely, parents will not see their children properly educated unless they actively participate in their schooling. Education must be a collaborative venture between parent, teacher, student, and other community members who can add to the students' repertoire of skills. A community youth charter can make this kind of collaboration possible by opening lines of communication and joining all the parties around a common set of learning goals. In addition, a youth charter can prevent conflicts and misunderstandings that can derail a school's educational mission.

A great many parents these days feel distant—almost barred—from their children's school. Except for one or two routine conferences and parent nights each year, and an occasional report card, most parents have little way of knowing what their children are doing at school. There are few opportunities for parents to provide input about the school's learning goals for their children, let alone to develop a solid working relationship with their children's teachers. As a result, parents are often suspicious of the feedback that they get from teachers, and teachers are almost always lacking the intimate knowledge of a student's strengths and needs that a parent could provide. Students, meanwhile, fall between the cracks, deprived of the continuity of guidance that they would receive if parents and teachers were working together. Students' motivation also suffers: it is demoralizing for students to perceive—and they do—that their parents and teachers disrespect one another.

There is a story that I have heard, in one version or another, dozens and dozens of times. The most recent version was told to me by a friend with a daughter who was refusing to read in school. The parent was teaching the child to read at home and knew perfectly well that the child had the capacity to learn. When the parent went in to speak with the teacher, she was abruptly told that the child must have a "neurological problem." This lay diagnosis was made by a young teacher with no medical training whatsoever. The parent tried to tell the teacher what *she,* the parent, believed was the reason that the child might be hesitant to read in school. The parent also had some suggestions about reading methods that the child might respond to. The teacher showed no interest in the parent's information or ideas and responded with her own theory (or perhaps one that she picked up in graduate school) about the cultural peculiarities of the English language. The teacher then ended the meeting by referring the child to a school psychologist. The parent is hoping to meet with the school psychologist before he begins examining her child, but given her experience with the school, she worries that she may not be permitted to do so. The child faces the prospect of being bounced from one specialist to another, each with his or her own professional approach to the problem, and none of whom is prepared to join forces with the person closest to the child.

In a community with a strong youth charter, it is the child's developmental needs that are front and center, not the specialized expertise of those who work with children. The school is embedded within the community, not walled off from it. A school's standards and expectations for its students—its learning goals—are in the public domain, not the sole and secret province of an elite school staff. The youth charter process brings parents, teachers, and other community members together to discuss learning goals for students. One result is that parents come to understand and wholeheartedly support the school's learning goals, and this support is important for bolstering student motivation. A second result is that teachers and parents begin a conversation that can lead to a trusting, mutually respectful relationship. In a community with a strong youth charter, my friend's teacher would have been eager to hear what my friend had to say about her daughter's reading, and the teacher would have been better prepared to articulate the school's reading standards in a way that made sense to a parent of a child who was refusing to read. There would have been no question that the parent would have had immediate access to the school psychologist or to any other professional who was called in to assist with the child.

There is a vast array of destabilizing school conflicts that a community youth charter can help to allay. One source of such conflicts is the competition between progressive and traditional approaches to school reform. A youth charter, because it focuses on the child's needs rather than on the expertise of the specialist, can help keep such conflicts in perspective.

Competition between school reform approaches has been triggered by a recent wave of interest in improving our schools. In the United States, this wave of interest began with some influential reports showing that U.S. students performed poorly on achievement tests in comparison with children from the rest of the industrial world. Educational critics argued about the causes. Some cited poorly funded schools, others the lack of a good national curriculum, others the inadequate classroom practices of teachers. No two critics quite agreed on precisely how schools should change, but all agreed that change was in order. As a result, educators and politicians alike dedicated themselves to "school reform." A movement to break the mold was enthusiastically supported by a broad coalition of government, corporations, and philanthropists. Dozens of new approaches were put forward, and fierce debate has swirled around the question of whose approach achieves the best results.

The single greatest philosophical divide in this debate has been between progressive and traditional approaches. In general, progressive approaches emphasize thinking skills, understanding, and creativity, whereas traditional ones emphasize facts, cultural literacy, and the mastery of conventional academic disciplines. This is a modern version of an ancient philosophical divide between progressives and traditionalists.

A large number of educational questions have become polarized along progressive and traditional lines. Should reading be taught through whole language or phonics? Should history be taught as a store of facts or a method of interpretation? Should math be taught as formulas or as logic? Should moral instruction emphasize autonomous reasoning or absolute standards of right or wrong? Should immigrant children receive bilingual education during a transitional period after they arrive, or should they be immersed in English-only instruction from the start?

I see no sign that any of these questions is about to be settled. To the contrary, divisions appear to be deepening, to such an extent that they have emerged as contentious political issues in many localities. State legislatures now vote whether public schools should use methods such as whole language instruction or bilingual education—matters once thought to be squarely in the realm of curriculum design. As these educational issues become increasingly politicized, the two sides draw further apart. The divide between progressives and traditionalists persists and deepens without any signs of resolution. Perhaps this will always be the case. The perennial split may be inevitable, since these are two complementary perspectives on the human condition: both change and stability are essential in human development, as they are in life. The hard questions remain: When do we need change and when stability; and how do we get the right balance between the two?

In education, though, many of the issues that divide traditionalists and progressives are false oppositions. Good teachers of reading use both whole language and phonics instruction when appropriate. Each method has its uses, and there are students who benefit more from one than the other. Mastery of math requires both knowledge of the formulas and the capacity to reason logically. In history, children should learn that interpretations of events can vary, but they also must learn the vital facts. Moral education should help students think autonomously about difficult moral choices, but it also should impart to students a deep respect for their society's common values.

A successful school resists polarizing and oversimplifying these complex issues. It aims instead to give its students all the tools that they will need to master the challenges that they will encounter in their lives. I have known good schools that lean toward traditional precepts, good schools that lean toward progressive precepts, and good schools that combine the two in an eclectic manner. Moreover, I have seen dreadful schools of all types. I also know many progressive-minded parents who happily send their children to traditional schools, and I know traditional-minded parents who choose to send their children to progressive schools. Since this is a telling litmus test, it stands as confirmation that educational philosophy does not define the quality of a school. The contentious split between the two approaches is unnecessary and potentially damaging; it can rend the fabric of an educational community. On the other hand, a community that achieves core consensus about its standards and expectations through a youth charter will be able to focus on student learning goals rather than divisive nuances of educational ideology. Such a community can be flexible and agnostic with respect to the competing approaches while remaining firm in its determination to achieve learning goals for all its students. In order to accomplish these goals, the community will need to support many kinds of educational experiences for its young, including instruction in places other than school—for example, in community resources such as museums, libraries, workplaces, and religious and recreational settings.

Another contentious issue roiling the public conversation is the debate about whether parents in a public school district should be allowed to choose between schools in the district, or even another district—to select for their children, for example, a school with a reputation superior to that of neighboring schools or a school whose approach matches their own beliefs about education. Those in favor of school choice believe that parents should be allowed to send their children to any school they wish and that public funds from tax revenue should support such choices. Those in opposition, such as some teacher unions and other specialists, have fought against school choice on two grounds. First, they say, parents will not know enough to make good choices. Second, school choice places schools in competition with one another, depriving the "losers" of needed resources and thus penalizing the students who still will be left attending them.

In contrast to the progressive-traditionalist split, the school choice debate is moving toward a resolution. Societies everywhere are gradually adopting principles of school choice, giving parents of public school children more and more freedom to select from available public schools. In the United States this is happening quickly, whereas in other countries it is proceeding at a slower pace. This movement is perhaps inevitable. Once people envision freedom in any area of their lives, it is hard to turn them back.

There remains some doubt about certain important matters, such as whether parents will be allowed to use tax-funded vouchers to help pay for private and parochial schools, and whether there will be enough good choices for parents to select from. Whatever the resolution of these matters, the clear direction of public policy in our time is to give parents more autonomy to choose their children's schools. As a result, new options for schoolchildren are cropping up like grass growing through old pavement.

The combination of school reform and school choice opens a world of possibilities for parents, educators, and students. It also creates a number of dilemmas. How can parents choose wisely from among all the new options? What is the best strategy for teachers to follow in their classrooms? How can educators use the reform movement to create the best possible schools? And—reflecting the mission of the youth charter—how can citizens throughout a community make the best use of the schools that they choose, support, and participate in? In this chapter, I address these questions from a youth charter perspective.

Parents in a World of Choice

We are fast entering into an emancipated era of education in which parents will gain more control over their children's educational destinies. In most part, this is a salutary turn of events. Parental choice increases the likelihood of parental support: parents who have freely chosen their child's school will be likely to participate in the school's educational mission by attending meetings, volunteering time, monitoring homework, and backing the teacher in matters of discipline and evaluation. This kind of parental support will significantly advance the child's chances of educational success beyond anything else the school may do. Reconciling parents and teachers in our age of divisiveness is a primary element of the youth charter approach, and school choice can provide the conditions for such a reconciliation.

Yet in schooling, as in everything else, new choices provide only a start, a promise of things to come. What counts is whether the promise will be fulfilled. Will the emerging options be better than the old ones? How can we make sure that they are? How can we make the best use of the ones that do emerge? Just about every parent today is asking, How can we choose the right selection from the rich menu of new choices now before us? For parents facing the often puzzling prospects of school choice, I present some criteria for identifying a good school. Schools with the characteristics noted operate in a manner consistent with a community youth charter:

1. *Leadership.* Does the school have a principal who commands the respect of teachers and staff; who has a clear sense of priorities; who can articulate in a convincing way the goals and standards of the school; who communicates openly and frequently to parents; and who knows and cares about students as individuals? A youth charter meeting can often give a principal the chance to communicate with parents so that parents can assess the quality of the school's leadership.

2.   *Commitment.* Do the teachers act as if their occupation is just a job, or do they show a sense of commitment to their craft and their students? There are several positive signs that parents may look for: teachers who readily stay after class when needed, who give and read extra assignments, who encourage students to engage in educational activities outside school, and who find ingenious ways to trigger students' interest in classroom materials.

3.   *Mission.* Does the school emanate a sense of purpose throughout the day? The best schools are alive with the spirit of learning everywhere a student goes. Nothing is wasted. There is no sense of drift or disorder. Instead, there is a palpable feeling of productivity in every classroom. People are busy, and they know what they are busy about. Everyone from the principal to the teacher's aide is aware of the mission and acts on it.

4.   *Community.* Does the school project a sense of inclusiveness that makes students and parents feel central rather than peripheral, a sense of identity that gives students and parents pride in the school, a sense of collegiality that helps students and teacher collaborate with one another, and a sense of compassion that imparts a mutual obligation of respect and concern for one another?

5.   *Standards.* Does the school uphold high academic and moral standards? Does the school communicate these standards clearly, and with great certainty, to all students? Are the standards applied firmly and consistently by the teachers and staff?

Parents can find out about a school's academic standards by asking to see the school's grade-by-grade curriculum goals. (If the school has never prepared goals, that is one sure sign of lax academic standards.) Parents can inquire about the school's classroom and homework assignments, and they can inspect sample tests from past years. It does not take an expert eye to gauge whether the curriculum goals are credible, the assignments challenging, and the tests rigorous.

One sure test of a school's standards—in this case, both academic and moral standards combined—is the school's response to cheating. Cheating has become common in both public schools and elite private academies, yet many schools have ill-defined policies about cheating. To the extent that they have explicit cheating codes at all, their teaching staffs often disagree about the codes and refrain from enforcing them. I have spoken with many teachers who believe that cheating is an inevitable and minor offense. The teachers say things like: "Kids today feel very loyal to their peers; you can't punish them for cooperative behavior that we happen to call cheating." Or: "The tests have no meaning for these students, so why wouldn't they cheat?" Or—the most common one of all—"Everyone else in our society cheats. What's the big deal?" Although such responses intend to be sympathetic to young-sters, they undermine the integrity of the school as well as its students' intellectual and moral development. In a school that functions as it should, values of academic integrity will be shared and defended by all who work there. A fundamental part of a school's job is to teach posi-tive academic and moral values to its students. These values are as important as anything that students learn from their lessons. Parents can discuss such matters with teachers to ascertain their willingness and ability to impart such values to their students.

Teachers in a World of Choice

All of these guidelines for parents place a spotlight on the conduct and skills of teachers. Indeed, the very notion of school choice creates such a spotlight, because it enables parents to compare teachers across schools. In order to make such comparisons, parents will be spending more time in the schools, will be examining teachers more closely, and will be making evaluating judgments about what they see. Teachers, in turn, will rise to the occasion with new vigor. Proponents of choice believe that increased parental involvement and a spirit of competition are just what schools need. When parents can freely choose schools, teachers will think twice before cutting them off in the high-handed and insensitive manner that my friend with the nonreading daughter experienced. This, in fact, is why many parents, at great financial sacri-fice, send their children to private schools. Public school choice will bring the same advantages to parents who cannot afford independent schools.

Opponents of school choice worry that the increased competition will bring unproductive pressures to bear on already overburdened teachers. My own view is that school choice opens a possibility for teachers to *reduce* the pressures and frustrations of their jobs.

Many teachers today confront a set of demoralizing conditions. For the most part, teachers enter the profession with high hopes of educating the young. They usually begin their careers dedicated to learning, optimistic about their capacity to reach students, and idealistic about their goals. But soon they are confronted with a number of harsh realities. A large proportion of their students fail to respond to their best teaching efforts. Some students drift through class with little effort; others disrupt the classroom agenda. Many parents refuse to support the assignments that the teacher sends home or the grades they give. Some accuse the teacher of pushing their child too hard, some worry that the teacher is impairing their child's creativity, some complain that the teacher is not recognizing their child's true gifts, and others charge that the teacher is not working with their child's special needs.

In the end, the teacher's performance is usually assessed by one uncompromising, hard-and-fast measure: how well the students do on the standardized achievement tests given to her students at the end of the year. Standardized tests do offer one useful index of a student's knowledge, and every school should give them in a rigorous and objective manner. But no standardized test can reveal the full depths of a student's skills, understanding, or motivation. For example, a standardized test will tell us whether Sally can multiply fractions together to solve a word problem—an important thing for us to know about Sally as a student—but it will not tell us whether she could use that same knowledge to fix a bike wheel, or whether she would be resourceful enough to go to a library to get the right formula from a book in order to fix the wheel. In the long run, Sally's resourcefulness may be more important than her specific skills. It too can be taught and assessed, but not through multiple-choice achievement tests. Sally's standardized test performance is just a small slice of the know-how that she will need to succeed in life. When educating Sally, we must keep her test scores in perspective. If Sally is lucky, her teachers will gear her instruction toward the entire range of competencies—including but not limited to test-taking skills—that will help Sally approach the world intelligently.

Aware that they will be judged mostly by their students' standardized test scores, many teachers attempt to teach to the test, using their classrooms to drill into students the limited kinds of facts and problem-solving skills that show up on the multiple-choice exams. This teaching may help students gain some points on the tests, and it does convey certain useful knowledge and skills, but it also can divert a teacher's efforts away from other kinds of in-depth presentations that students need to acquire a full range of understanding.

Moreover, too great an emphasis on test taking can exact a toll on student motivation, perhaps the most crucial factor in long-term student achievement. Motivation in a student is cultivated by showing the student why it is important to strive and learn. This can happen only by forging connections to the student's interests or future prospects. A student's attention almost always focuses on activities that the student has already found stimulating or on activities that the student sees as potentially rewarding, such as those connected with producing something important in the world of work. A student who cannot find such connections in the classroom will have little reason to become motivated. The kind of practice and drill required for standardized tests may help a student acquire good learning habits—a worthwhile effect—but it contributes little toward the critical job of building such connections. When practice for test taking consumes too much class time, more motivating kinds of activities such as instructional projects get squeezed out.

The combination of all these conditions places teachers in a frustrating bind. They are expected to prepare students for success on the job and in life, yet they (and their students) are judged by measures that do not capture some of the most valuable lessons that they teach. They are expected to induce skills, good citizenship, and a love of learning in students who are often uninterested in academic pursuits, yet they cannot count on the crucial support of parents in this formidable task. They are criticized for both failing to correct deep-seated student problems and intruding into the private lives of students and their families.

School choice, together with a community youth charter, can release teachers from such binds. For reasons that I noted above, school choice increases parental support. In schools that parents have chosen, teachers are likely to receive cooperation from parents rather than indifference, skepticism, or hostility. This partnership transforms the school into a working community rather than an isolated and besieged bastion of educational expertise. The climate change is conducive—perhaps necessary—for learning.

In a school that has strong parental and community support, teachers have a ready-made network of resources for expanding and deepening the learning opportunities that they can offer students. Youth charter meetings can make teachers aware of the community resources available to them. For example, local businesses and professional organizations can offer youth internships that will give students a chance to apply their academic skills to real-world problems. Museums and libraries can coordinate their exhibits and other activities with school curricula. Community members can express their availability for assisting students with special projects, such as an oral history study of lives of successive generations within the community. In this way, the education of students moves beyond the classroom and into the dynamic life of society. Students gain a firsthand sense of why it is important for them to build their academic skills and knowledge. This sort of motivating experience is the surest way to guarantee results in the long run. In order to spur motivation, teachers must draw out the special talents and interests of each student, building vital connections among classroom, community, and the workplace.

All of this requires a community with a strong youth charter—that is, a place where parents and other citizens have thoughtfully discussed and determined the learning goals that best serve students from that community. In such a community, test scores can be placed in the broader perspective of what children need to know in order to succeed in life. The whole range of academic and vocational skills can be placed on the learning table, and all of the community's resources can be tapped in order to foster these skills. Teachers who are trying to bring out the fullest potential in every student will receive fuller and more understanding support from parents and the rest of the community, even in the face of mixed test scores. Through a solid youth charter, teachers can explain with credibility that students who do not test well still have bright futures, as long as they are offered meaningful educational opportunities. Teachers can then concentrate on doing just that rather than futilely trying to raise class norms on tests that bear an uncertain relationship to children's future prospects. The point is to view these prospects broadly, from the perspective of all the standards and expectations of the youth charter. When the school's learning goals match the youth charter's standards and expectations, teachers will be able to teach to the future rather than to the test.

The following principles will enable teachers to accomplish this primary youth charter goal:

1.   *The teacher's first priority should be fostering the motivation to learn.* Motivation is the single strongest predictor of a child's success in school and beyond. It far outweighs the child's socioeconomic background, IQ, gender, ethnicity, birth order, or any of the dozens of factors that educators and parents often worry about. It is far more important than the three R's, cultural literacy, foreign languages, or computer skills, however valuable these other assets may be.

Teachers must recognize the importance of student motivation and make direct efforts to foster it. Such efforts may contribute little to students' performances on standardized tests, but teachers should make them nonetheless. Teachers must realize that motivation is more important than test scores. Moreover, motivation will not be revealed by test scores: a child's performance on a standardized test cannot tell whether the child has a burning desire to learn or whether the child is content to just get by with the minimal possible effort.

Psychologist and author Daniel Goleman has written a groundbreaking book about the value of "emotional intelligence" in work, personal transactions, and one's relations with the society at large.[1] He defines emotional intelligence as the judgment of the "heart and gut" rather than the head—a practical street smarts that people rely on in real life when the chips are down. Motivation, he writes, is a central component of emotional intelligence. Goleman makes the convincing case that a child's emotional intelligence far outweighs the kinds of skills that determine a child's IQ and standardized test scores. This is what employers look for, often in vain, when they hire young workers; and it is what enables a young person to advance in whatever career he or she has chosen.

Other related components of emotional intelligence are overlooked by standardized tests yet play a key role in learning and life. These include self-control, optimism, and cooperation. A good teacher will work to foster all of these characteristics in students, although none will show up in the test scores that most schools have traditionally used to gauge teaching effectiveness. In the long run, motivation and other features of emotional intelligence show up in improved student ability, achievement, and conduct. These are the educational outcomes that parents and other citizens value. In a community with a youth charter, they will be the accepted mark of a good teacher.

2. *To spur student motivation, teachers must draw connections between the classroom and the rest of the student's present and future life.* Children are motivated by goals that they acquire in every part of their lives. For most children, classroom activities are not especially motivating unless something happens to make them so. That something is a realization that classroom work can be linked to broader life goals. This realization can occur in the form of instrumental awareness, as when children figure out that they will need the skills—or the credentials—that their school offers if they are to get where they want to go. Or the realization can take the form of an insight based on more intellectual or expressive grounds—for example, when children discover that the poems they read in class articulate their feelings in aesthetically pleasurable ways.

There always will be a few talented students who take readily to school as if it were made expressly for them. Nothing can hold such students back. Give them access to books, computers, and teachers, and they will receive an excellent education under virtually any conditions. These students are the fortunate minority in the student population at large. For most students, school has meaning only when someone makes a special effort to show them why classroom efforts are interesting and important. The best way for teachers to do this is by connecting classroom instruction with the student's life experience and goals. For this, teachers need the help of the entire community. In a youth charter meeting, teachers can explain their learning goals for students to a broad array of community members. When a teacher discusses literacy goals, the publisher of the town newspaper may decide to invite student contributions, or a local cable station may sponsor an essay contest with the prize winner reading the essay on the air. When a teacher discusses numeracy goals, a Little League coach may decide to ask players to compute their own batting and fielding averages. When a teacher discusses goals for improving children's technological skills, museums and libraries may devise interactive computer exhibits geared to the educational needs of the young. Parents who understand a school's learning goals not only can support the goals while their children are doing homework but also can help connect their children to community activities that will enhance the goals. All of this bridge building requires the extensive open lines of communication made possible by a community youth charter.

There also are a variety of methods for applying academic skills to real-life problems during classroom instruction. In my own writings for teachers, I have advocated the use of long-term instructional projects that require students to learn basic academic skills if they want to accomplish a captivating mission.[2] My research staff has designed projects around familiar formats such as writing and performing a play, designing a playground, building objects that fly, creating a nutritional snack program, and producing a newsletter. For many children, working on such projects provides unique opportunities for learning literacy and numerous skills. They find authentic uses for academic skills, such as writing and calculating, that previously may have seemed arbitrary and unimportant to them. Instructional projects are good vehicles for fostering motivation as well as other aspects of emotional intelligence. For example, they encourage cooperative group work between peers and collaborative relations between teacher and student; require students to acquire self-control and discipline in order to master challenging tasks; evoke performances that give students a feeling of success and optimism about their abilities; and provide engaging tasks that stimulate the application of thinking skills.

3.   *Teachers should create networks of support with parents and other members of the community.* Students become motivated to excel when parents, relatives, neighbors, and friends support teachers in their educational mission. Without the guidance of these other people, most students will neither acquire nor sustain the proper motivation. Unless we find ways to create active networks of support around our schools, most students will continue to find the classroom an alien and barren place. A fundamental task of a youth charter process is building such networks of support around teachers. This is the part of the youth charter process where teachers can play their most valuable role.

One obvious way a teacher can create a network of support around her classroom is to bring students' families into school whenever possible. In most schools, meetings between teachers and parents are limited to perfunctory occasions such as evaluation conferences or yearly back-to-school nights, unless a student is in trouble—and by then it is too late to cultivate the trust necessary for a truly supportive relationship. Teachers need to do more to enlist parents' full energies behind the classroom agenda. Parents should be routinely invited to informational sessions, special events, exhibitions of student work, and discussions about all the programs that the school offers.

At the same time, teachers should find out about the interests of the parents and the educational resources that students may find in their own homes. Teachers can then draw out student motivation by playing off these familiar interests and resources. A child whose parents play musical instruments or sing in a choir may be captivated by a music lesson. Teachers who know the strengths and limitations of each student's home will be in an excellent position to individualize instruction so as to sustain the motivation of each student.

Teachers also can bring into their classroom people from the community who are leaders in the arts and the professions. Not only will students find these leaders inspirational, they will also learn from them the efforts that it takes to succeed in these endeavors. Textbooks and classroom lectures can tell only part of that story. It is important, for example, for a student to learn to read and write well if the student is interested in a career as a journalist. But it is also important to know how to formulate a story, do the investigatory research, and get published. This kind of practical knowledge will motivate students to dig deeper into their homework assignments in order to gain the basic reading and writing skills that they will need. Only a living-and-breathing worker in fields such as journalism can supply this kind of engaging background information to students. Local professionals are usually delighted to volunteer an afternoon or two of their time to visit a classroom at the behest of a teacher, so it is well worth the teacher's time to cultivate such opportunities. Far from distracting students from the real business of the classroom, such visits encourage students to take the acquisition of academic knowledge seriously.

Teachers can initiate links between classroom, home, and community, but they cannot build all the necessary connections by themselves. The community itself must be responsive to such initiatives; this is one role of the youth charter. In addition, the school must support the teacher's efforts. Often schools do not support such efforts; they have been content to exist apart from their communities, protective of their own privileges and power. Ideally, building community connections should be high on the agenda of any school reform movement to change this orientation.

4.   *Teachers should uphold high academic and moral standards for all students, without exception.* The surest way to lose students academically is to fail to challenge them. The surest way to lead students into trouble is to project low expectations for their behavior. Nothing so bores a child as a lesson that seems too easy. Nothing so disheartens a child as a message from adults that they believe the child to be incapable of assuming responsibility.

In many classrooms students encounter precisely these disheartening conditions. Curricula have been watered down to the point of utter vacuousness. Instruction proceeds at the pace of the slowest students. In fact, since teachers usually underestimate the abilities of the "slow" students, instruction often proceeds at a pace that is boring even for them. Many of them have been considered "slow" only because they have never been challenged. High behavioral standards, too, are conspicuously absent from many classrooms. Even in matters central to the school community, such as cheating and stealing, teachers hesitate to voice a clear message.

The dearth of high standards most affects children who are easily stereotyped. Girls are told in multiple ways during their school careers that they are unlikely to do well in math or science courses. I once sat in on a meeting where a math teacher "reassured" a female student that she would not be held to the same standards as the boys; this was done with the benign intention of trying to bolster the girl's confidence, but in the long run it always has the opposite effect. Minority students face this kind of condescending stereotyping all through their academic careers. Again, it is done with the best of intentions but the worst of judgment. The assumption is that these students are genetically inferior and therefore require a lower set of standards than other students, for their own good. This wrong and foolish assumption permeates our educational system, from colleges down to elementary school. A couple of years ago the president of Rutgers University made headlines with an argument along these lines. An insightful study of primary schools concluded: "Teachers are aware of these [institutional] constraints and lower their expectations for black achievement and effort accordingly. . . . Oppression can arise out of warmth, friendliness, and concern. Paternalism and a lack of challenging standards are creating a distorted system of evaluation in the schools."[3] The lower standards start a self-fulfilling cycle: minority students are told that they are expected to do less, they are given less to do, they succeed less frequently, and thus the wrongful stereotype is confirmed, sealing the students' downward fate. It all amounts to an unnecessary and tragic waste of potential, for the student as well as the community.

All students, despite their gender, ethnicity, or background, can perform at the highest academic and moral levels. They are all born bright and energetic, full of curiosity and ready to learn. Teachers should approach every child with this belief in mind. Every child can be taught and inspired to achieve. Every child wants to learn. The job of the teacher is to make the classroom into a place where the child's natural thirst for knowledge can be satisfied. The way to do this is to provide instruction that connects with children's interests and challenges them to reach beyond what they already know. Motivation and high standards are the keys to school success.

Not only must teachers encourage their students to perform at high standards, they also must give their students honest feedback about how they are doing. An honest assessment method is one that is not inflated—for example, one that does *not* tell all children that they are doing above-average work. But the assessment should be centered on the work and not on the student. The student needs to be told two things: (1) you did not get it right the first time, but (2) you *can* do it if you keep trying; there is nothing wrong with your learning abilities that a little more effort cannot cure. Teachers who withhold honest assessment out of the fear that it will somehow lend a harmful, competitive atmosphere to the classroom misunderstand the nature of learning and motivation. Children do not crumple when they are given honest feedback about their work, nor do they succumb to invidious comparisons between themselves and their classmates. Teachers serve students best when they urge students to reach for standards that they have not yet attained. Failure, with constructive feedback, is a beneficial opportunity to learn something new.

Teachers cannot do this alone. Parents must support teachers in their efforts to give students accurate, constructive feedback. When teachers send home less-than-ideal grades, parents must resist the urge to call the teacher and lobby for a better grade. Parents should not be acting as their children's agents or lawyers. When a child receives tough feedback from a teacher, the parent should tell the child that the teacher's standards are valid, that the child's job is to live up to them, that the child *can* do it by trying harder, and that the parent is there to help the child reach the goal. A community youth charter can ensure this kind of supportive relation between parent and teacher.

During one meeting that I attended, teachers and parents discussed their expectations for students' math learning. The meeting took place in a nonaffluent community of recent immigrants to the United States. A math teacher began his presentation by telling parents that he was committed to the success of their children. The teacher said that it was important for children to learn basic math skills so that they could get good jobs that required quantitative skills. I believe that the teacher identified bus driving, clerking, and auto repair as three of the occupations that he had in mind. The teacher said that he believed that most children from this community could qualify for such jobs if they could learn the simple math lessons that he was offering them in his classroom.

After the teacher's presentation, a parent stood up and, in a heavy Spanish accent, said something to the following effect: "Excuse me, sir, but my son, who is in your class, is a brilliant and hard-working student who wishes to attend the California Institute of Technology. He will become a great scientist one day. What are you doing to get him ready for that?" Some other parents made similar statements. *Startled* is perhaps too strong a word for the math teacher's facial expression during all this; but the presentations certainly got his attention and that of the other teachers in the room as well. In one afternoon meeting, math standards at that school were dramatically raised—to the great benefit, I am convinced, of all the students. This could never have happened in the absence of a face-to-face discussion between teachers and parents. The encounter that I observed was supportive but also probing and challenging. This is the nature of youth charter meetings at their best.

Teachers also must have the support of their own schools. Too many excellent teachers have been eliminated or worn down by cynical school environments with low standards. A good teacher will not last long in a school satisfied with mediocrity. This is where school reform comes in. The school reform movement is a golden opportunity to create environments where good teachers can flourish. This opportunity will be realized only when the right kinds of schools are built. We have not yet gone very far in this direction. Countervailing trends (the lowering of standards) in our culture generally, and in education specifically, have been too strong to resist. We must fight these trends. This too is a job for a community youth charter.

Schools and School Reform

We must avoid the mistakes of the past. It may be helpful to look backward for a moment, in order to understand how our school system has fallen short and why we have come to replace it. Knowing history may not always prevent us from repeating it, but at least it gives us a fair chance.

During the past half-century or so, our great public school tradition has lost its sense of mission. Since their inception, public schools have been dedicated to promoting intellectual skills and knowledge in young people from all walks of life. This mission began with Horace

Mann and has continued through the waves of immigration at the turn of the twentieth century, during both world wars and the economic depression spanned by the wars. The public school was there through all this, during good times and bad, ready to equip children with skills and values that could enable them to reach heights undreamed of by preceding generations.

Now, at the end of the twentieth century, this noble mission has had to take its place among many other priorities—to the extent that the mission is still honored at all in the minds of public school administrators. In our complex modern society, there have been other things to worry about—a host of seemingly more pressing concerns that have forced academic instruction to take a backseat, even in the classroom.

Public schools have been given nonacademic mandates from every level of government, national as well as local. American public schools in the 1990s are required to sponsor extensive special education programs for students with a loosely defined array of characteristics known as learning disabilities. Most public schools also must host gender-role discrimination programs (including, in many cases, separate math and science classes) for building girls' self-esteem; AIDS awareness days; "drug-free schools" courses; safe-driving courses; conflict resolution training; recycling programs; save-the-environment "green" days; global peace days; voluntary and compulsory community service programs; and a burgeoning cascade of other programs that have captured the imaginations of local or federal school officials.

All of these peripheral activities represent worthwhile priorities for the society as a whole—indeed, they deserve to be pursued in other venues—but they have distracted the public school from its original educational mission. When taken together, these peripheral activities have so crammed the time and attention of public school staff that they have squeezed out the original core items on the school's agenda: the three R's, as they once were called. In the process, the public school's magnificent capacity to raise children from the most humble beginnings to lives of unlimited aspiration has been weakened, fatally in some cases.

Along with the weakening in their capacity to impart basic skills to their students, schools have ceased conveying a love of learning. Again, the problem has been one of priorities. Texts, especially in social studies and the humanities, are read more for implicit social messages that they may contain than for their value as works of art or scholarship.

Teachers are more likely to assign *The Adventures of Huckleberry Finn* as an illustration of poor race relations in the nineteenth century than as a grand aesthetic experience in storytelling and satire. The poems of T. S. Eliot, the paintings of Winslow Homer, the writings of Jane Austen, and the memoirs of Winston Churchill are used to discuss social class and gender influences rather than to cultivate an appreciation for literary insight or artistic merit. The authors' and artists' skills, intentions, and accomplishments are often ignored, as are any claims to beauty or truth that the works may have.

This cynical tone has been set by higher education, which itself has been busy deconstructing classic works in the humanities, social sciences, history, and even the hard sciences. By now, this cold-blooded insensitivity to the beauties of creative work has filtered down to schools at all levels. It is depriving students of a sense of why artistic, historical, or scientific texts are created in the first place, of what their original purpose was, and of what they add to human life when they are truly understood for what they are. The dent that such nihilistic instruction places in students' appreciation of creative work is as great a disservice as failing to impart basic academic skills.

To add further distraction, public schools have become economic institutions first and foremost in many people's minds. The public school system is the primary workplace for vast numbers of people. In some nonaffluent school districts, it is by far the largest employer. As a result, teaching has developed its own economic priorities, some of which have little to do with the educational mission. From a career perspective, teaching can be a job like any other, with fixed conditions that define the role and its obligations. Thus it may not seem surprising that teachers' unions in some school districts have made it a formal violation of work rules for teachers to remain after school with a pupil. A teacher can get in trouble with a union boss for volunteering extra instruction to students who need it. The union treats this as an act of professional sabotage akin to rate busting on a factory assembly line. Such practices are antithetical to the age-old notion that teaching is a calling, dedicated to the noble mission of illuminating the young. There is nothing wrong with a union job regulated by the time clock, but teaching cannot be reduced to that. Students do not roll off assembly lines. They cannot be educated by mandated procedures and shop rules with preset time limits.

A six-year-old may have a reading block that a few minutes of personal encouragement at the right time could break, before it rigidifies into a clinical learning phobia. A ten-year-old may be on the verge of finally grasping fractions; she needs just a few more demonstrations to make the idea of numerical ratios click. A twelve-year-old keeps acting up in class and needs to be spoken to away from the peers who provide him with an audience for showing off.

These are the intense, personal, guiding practices that are needed for children's learning and character development, unlike many of the inconsequential exercises that pass for school curricula these days. Everyone knows this intuitively. But such practices are not often taught in our schools of education, described in teacher magazines, or conveyed in materials about teaching put out by today's professional associations. They are unmentioned and unmentionable—in part because they conflict with union work rules and in part because they are considered to be the "art" rather than the "science" of teaching. Current educational theory is silent on such practices—not so much because it is unfriendly to them but because such practices do not fall easily into the overspecialized categories of educational research.

With teachers acting like union workers rather than dedicated mentors, modern public schools take on the character of factories. Teacher-workers put in their time on predefined tasks, earning their living by showing up and performing a set routine. Their performance is evaluated by how well they conform to work rules and how well their students do on tests that may bear little relation to what they would like to accomplish in the classroom. To the extent that teachers still pursue their original instructional ideals, they must do this on their own, as a kind of off-time activity.

All this makes for an odd institution: a factory that does not manufacture what it was built to produce. The "products" that the factory was supposed to deliver—learning, motivation, the development of sound skills and work habits—cannot be produced through the factory's preset routines. So the factory becomes more like a holding pen than a manufacturing plant. When they are not idle, the student occupants of the holding pen are kept vaguely busy on scattered and random activities for their prescribed six-hour days. I will not extend this metaphor to its logical conclusion of what happens to occupants of holding pens—that is, the livestock kind—once their time is up.

The modern ethic of public schooling has demoted learning to a secondary priority, behind personal and social agendas such as self-esteem boosting, fostering interpersonal skills, and recreation. The results are plain to see. Students leave school without the motivation or knowledge required for advanced training or meaningful employment. Plentiful jobs for workers with a mastery of high school algebra are going begging because not enough students have acquired this knowledge in school. Colleges cannot keep up with the demand for remedial courses. Literacy of every kind (linguistic, scientific, numerical, cultural) diminishes further with each generation of youth. The love of learning is fast becoming a bygone relic.

Many of these shortcomings have been documented in a spate of school critiques with titles such as *The Shopping-Mall High School; Horace's Compromise; Ed School Follies; Dumbing-Down Our Kids; We Must Take Charge;* and, noteworthy for its raw lack of restraint, *Inside American Education: The Decline, the Deception, and the Dogmas.* In addition, several excellent books have suggested steps that schools may take to remedy some of these shortcomings: *Reclaiming our Schools* by Edward Wynne and Kevin Ryan, James Comer's *School Power*, David Perkins's *Smart Schools*, and Howard Gardner's *The Unschooled Mind* are the best among these.[4] These books are full of practical ideas and methods. Here are a few recommendations that I consider to be at the heart of the matter, because they are closely connected to the learning agenda of the youth charter:

1.   *Schools must reinstate student learning as their first priority, and they must be careful not to crowd out student learning by taking on conflicting social priorities.* Every hour of the school day is precious and should be jealously guarded. An hour here and a day there add up. Before long, there is not enough instructional time in the school day for serious work. This also imparts an unfortunate message to students: book learning is expendable. There may be places where such a message is appropriate, but school is not one of them. Schools must defend their own mission on their own territory. They are charged with fostering young people's intellectual skills. Schools must fulfill this charge, because they are the only societal institution constituted to do so. Other social agendas, no matter how worthy, must not be allowed to interfere with this essential duty. Communities, in youth charter fashion, should coordinate their resources so that other

venues beyond the school are found to pursue worthy causes outside the academic mission.

For example, many schools today sponsor programs for educating students about the dangers of alcoholism, casual sex, drugs, and guns. The schools have taken on this responsibility because nobody else in the community seems to be doing it effectively. Similarly, many schools sponsor safe driving programs because so many of their students are ending up as casualties of traffic accidents. In addition to their risk-prevention programs, many schools spend considerable classroom time teaching about citizenship issues, such as world poverty, racial and ethnic equality, and environmental preservation.

All of these are worthwhile causes, yet all of them take time away from the core academic curriculum that the school is attempting to deliver. (In some cases, it may be possible to teach about, say, an environmental problem in a rigorous way that promotes literacy, numeracy, and knowledge of basic science, but this requires a sustained effort by the teacher as well as a special project-based plan of instruction.) As long as a school feels obliged to educate students about a constantly expanding array of social issues and personal risks, its capacity to foster students' mastery of core academic disciplines will be pinched.

One solution to this contemporary squeeze on schools is a youth charter meeting where resources beyond the school can be identified for the purpose of educating children in nonacademic areas of life. A coalition of citizens, including parents, police, local media, sports coaches, and religious leaders, can devise risk-prevention educational programs that can be delivered in every child's home through videos, printed materials, and parental instruction. Programs on social issues can be sponsored by the town's libraries, museums, and churches and synagogues, and they too can be discussed and supported in children's homes. If there is a special concern about teen driving in the community, a youth charter meeting can alert the local drivers' schools and motor vehicle departments to the need for better training and more stringent examinations. When the entire community shares the responsibility for youth development in this way, schools can focus on the work that they do best: the academic instruction that imparts key skills, disciplinary knowledge, and the ability to learn.

2.   *Schools must treat teachers as colleagues rather than as laborers, and teachers must focus on the needs of their students rather than on work rules and employ-*

ment conditions. The teacher is the most important resource of any school. Teachers can never be replaced—not by books, not by new buildings, not by computers, "distance learning," or any other advances in technology. If young people are to learn, they need to have sustained relationships with people who care about their intellectual growth. Any school reform effort worth its salt will ensure that these kinds of caring relationships are available to all students.

This will be possible only when teachers are given the autonomy and the community mandate to cultivate intellectual skill, motivation, and the love of learning in their students. For this to happen, teachers cannot be bound by work rules that constrain the time that they spend with students, nor should they be evaluated by limited indicators such as standardized test scores alone. In return for greater autonomy, teachers must orient to their work as if it were a calling rather than a time clock–punching job. A necessary step toward school improvement is building a teaching staff with a collegial attitude and a dedication to student learning.

3. *Schools should teach the art and science of great works prior to teaching the critical interpretations of the texts.* Curricula should be designed, first and foremost, to impart scientific, literary, artistic, historical, and other scholarly understandings. Students should acquire an appreciation of great works in all the basic disciplines. Students should discover the works through the eyes of the creators. The school should inspire a sense of awe and wonder at the grandeur of great creative achievements. Only then, after the student has gained a sympathetic understanding of the works and the intentions behind them, should social critiques from a present-day perspective be introduced. The critiques should be kept in perspective: no critique can match the contribution of a groundbreaking scientific discovery or a captivating artistic expression. Schools should always seek ways to thrill students with the power of art and knowledge. Encounters with great works of discovery and expression can accomplish this if students are encouraged to share the visions of the creators. It is in this way that a school cultivates the love of learning.

4. *Schools should base their standards for students and teachers on a broader range of indicators than standardized test scores.* Scores on standardized tests are important, but they do not constitute rigorous academic standards in and of themselves. Scores indicate test-taking ability, and they can predict

success in strictly academic settings. This is useful information, but it must not exclude other measures of student and teacher success. It is also important to assess the progress that a student makes from day to day in learning new material; the student's performance on authentic tasks; the student's effort and motivation; the student's willingness to collaborate with teacher and peers; and the student's conduct in and out of the classroom. These indicators require ongoing assessments by teachers with clear instructional goals and personal knowledge of all students. In such an atmosphere, teachers treat students as individuals, working with each student's particular profile of skills.

This is the kind of educational environment required for cultivating the entire range of potential in our student population. High standards play an essential role in cultivating potential. This is why it is important for a school to implement standards in a genuine rather than a superficial way. I have heard school officials confuse standards with everything from high IQ scores to admissions to prestigious colleges. These are not the kinds of standards that give direction to a youngster's intellectual and character development.

Academic standards must be derived from specific learning goals, grade by grade, across all the key academic disciplines; history, math, English, science, and so on. Moral standards for character development must be derived from core moral values that are widely shared in the community. A youth charter can help a school define academic and moral standards for its students and communicate the standards so that the students will take them seriously. Naturally this is done most effectively in discussions among parents and others in the community. Such discussions are at the heart of the youth charter process.

5. *School reform must derive from the needs and values of the community.* Good schools, like good teachers, maintain close links to their communities. They are part of their communities rather than standing apart from them. Unfortunately, too many school reform efforts have taken the opposite tack, attempting to build elite schools virtually walled off from community input. The aim has been to create enclaves of expertise (or "enlightened practice") rather than networks of community support. The result is schools that are unaccountable to and disconnected from the parents of the children they serve. Inevitably, this has been the route to failure. The school ends up feeling isolated and besieged, the parents

unheard. It is one reason that home schooling, little noted by professional educators, has become the fastest-growing "school reform" movement in the United States.

In the long run, besieged enclaves of expertise are unsustainable. They also constitute barren learning environments for students. Young people do not live in classrooms alone. They travel back to their homes and neighborhoods too, and they pick up attitudes everywhere they go. Unless other key people in students' lives are deeply supportive of what goes on in the school, classroom learning does not have a chance to capture the students' allegiance. Students will drift through the school day and reserve their real energies for activities out of school.

Learning is not a matter for intellect alone. It involves the whole child—mind and morals, attitudes and motivation, character and competence, all working together. To engage the whole child requires a whole network of people working together. Teachers in classrooms cannot do it alone. Schools that open their doors to parents, take advantage of local resources, and make determined efforts to embed themselves in their communities will be able to create such networks for their students. They will develop standards that students will recognize and respect, and they will find welcome allies in their efforts to educate the young.

6

BEYOND HOME AND SCHOOL: SPORTS, FRIENDS, MENTORS, JOBS

It does not take long for the child's universe to expand beyond the home and the school. Well before the school years, many young children spend hours each day with peers and adult caregivers in day care settings. A child's playmates, relatives, and neighbors can influence the child's development. Eventually many others typically enter the picture: coaches, camp counselors, art and music instructors, clergy, close friends (including, by adolescence, romantic ones), and employers. Every one of these relationships shapes a child's character and competence, in small ways or large.

In today's dangerous world, some parents try to protect children from outside influences. But outside influences are inevitable and children must learn to make the most of them rather than hide from them. The goal of parents should be to help children choose outside influences that are constructive rather than destructive.

The home and the school are primary settings for child development, but they are not the only ones, and they are limited. Much of what children need to learn cannot be found in homes and schools. Howard Gardner has written that to develop fully, every child should have three "apprenticeships": one in academics, one in the arts, and one in athletics.[1] This is a splendid idea that I return to later in the chapter. For now, I simply note that none of these three can be reliably provided by most homes. Schools, too, are usually insufficient, at least for the arts and athletics: most public schools do very little for their students in art and music instruction, and they focus their athletic coaching only on the top athletes who make the teams—a small minority of the student population.

If children are to explore, in a serious way, all facets of their intellectual, moral, aesthetic, and athletic potential, they must gain access to community resources beyond the home and the school. Parents and teachers should facilitate children's explorations, guiding them in productive directions, and the community must provide the resources. In keeping with the principles of the youth charter, community members must make sure that these resources reflect the same high common standards that children should find in their homes and schools.

Sports

Sports are a valuable resource that can teach children both physical skills and enduring character lessons. Regrettably, participatory sports has become a dwindling resource for young people. It also has become a misunderstood and underappreciated resource, largely because of highly publicized abuses. In this section, I discuss why sports are important for youth development and examine how we can avoid the misuses that have discredited youth sports and diminished their support in many communities. The standards and expectations that children confront on the playing field can be a key component of the youth charter. In turn, a youth charter can play a crucial role in making sports widely available to young people and ensuring that youth sports in the community reflects the highest standards.

The first benefit of sports is increased physical fitness. This may seem obvious to all the adults who are huffing and puffing their way through middle age on bikes, exercise machines, jogging paths, and tennis courts in search of health, vitality, and trim figures. But what may not be so obvious to middle-aged adults is that, as a whole, today's younger generation shows no sign of following in the older generation's sweating footsteps. Among the population at large, youth participation in active (nonspectator) sports has declined dramatically since World War II.[2] Not accidentally, childhood obesity has risen in lockstep year by year. As for youth health indicators such as stamina and endurance, I quote from a research report published in 1996, describing the results of an elementary school program designed to introduce urban schoolchildren to common exercise routines:

> Teachers had seen the initial responses of their students to vigorous physical activity and were concerned with the physical development of their students. These initial responses showed that the children could not sustain vigorous activity for more than 1 to 2 minutes without becoming distressed or ill. Many of the students panted or started coughing and gagging after just 15 seconds of activity, were physically ill, sweated profusely, and had to disengage from the activity.[3]

There is little question that children increase their physical fitness when they play sports, an advantage with long-lasting consequences. Bone and muscle configurations formed early in life tend to endure, as do the habits that built them. A child with an active lifestyle has a better chance of maintaining health during maturity than a child with a sedentary one.

Apart from physical health—a worthy goal in itself—participation in sports offers a child key social and psychological benefits as well. The old saw that sports builds character is still valid. When children and coaches conduct sports in the right way, children learn self-discipline, persistence, and cooperation. They also learn good sportsmanship: that is, fair play, how to win and lose gracefully, how to manage competition, how to take initiative while staying within a common set of rules, and how to balance the desire to win with the need to maintain a good working relationship with opponents who also want to win.

These lessons in good sportsmanship have enduring significance for a child's later relationships and engagements.

Unfortunately, sports are not always played in a way that imparts these beneficial lessons. A "win at any cost" mentality infuses modern sports, filtering down from professional sports to the Little League and toss-up basketball. Despite Vince Lombardi's other contributions to the world of sports, he did our society no favor when he famously proclaimed, "Winning is not the main thing, it's the *only* thing." In fact, winning should *not* be the only thing, especially for youngsters. An older maxim remains sounder: "It's not whether you win or lose but how you play the game."

For young people in their formative years, the benefits that sports can bring have nothing to do with winning. There is no difference between winners and losers in the amount of exercise available in a sports game, nor is there a difference in the opportunity to learn and demonstrate good sportsmanship. For a young person, these are the enduring benefits from participating in sports, far more rewarding than the immediate thrill of coming out on top.

Now there is nothing wrong with playing to win; it can be a healthy effort for young people, but only when it is kept in perspective. When conducted fairly, vigorous competition can add to the spirit of any sport. But it is another thing entirely to break the rules and violate common codes of human decency in order to win. When this occurs, sports are corrupted, and their potential to promote character growth among the young is diminished. Winning is a fine goal, but the benefits of sports are threatened when all that matters is winning.

The corruption of sports is not a new phenomenon, nor is the cynicism of young people when a sports hero reveals a less-than-noble side. The young Chicago White Sox fan who called out, "Say it ain't so, Joe!" to Shoeless Joe Jackson after the player was caught throwing the 1919 World Series spoke (perhaps apocryphally) for disillusioned youngsters of all eras. Nothing as dramatic as a thrown World Series has plagued sports in recent years, yet the spotlight of the mass media has shone brightly on many instances of unsportsmanlike behavior by leading sports figures. Young people have watched sports heroes caught throwing spitballs, insulting umpires, taking steroids, and encouraging a hit man to rough up an opponent. Children have seen players, coaches, and team owners blatantly deny responsibility for these and other incidents, even when the incidents were observed by millions. Parents have observed such behavior, and they naturally have wondered whether sports is indeed a good influence on the young.

On the local level, sports coaches of youth teams often forget that their first priority should be to provide moral mentorship for youngsters rather than merely to win games. Unruly sports coaches provide youngsters with some of the worst examples of adult conduct that they will ever see firsthand. In 1996 alone, according to the Texas University Interscholastic League in Austin, ninety high school basketball coaches were ejected from games for "unsporting behavior." This is hardly the way to teach adolescents lessons in character.

When conducted in a sportsmanlike fashion, sports can help young people learn how to win graciously and lose with dignity. Sports can promote the virtues of civil behavior, honesty, decency, and courage. It is the responsibility of adults who run youth sports programs to ensure that training is conducted—and games are played—with this educational purpose as a top priority.

One of the benefits of youth charter meetings is that they provide opportunities for parents, teachers, coaches, and other citizens to discuss the educational purpose of youth sports. This discussion can help people agree on their priorities for youth participation in sports. Coaches may start by assuming (sometimes correctly!) that parents lust for victory as much as they do. In the reflective atmosphere of a youth charter meeting, citizens can examine such assumptions, placing their understandable desires to win in the context of the more important moral mission of fostering positive youth values. During the youth charter meeting, parents, teachers, and coaches can identify their shared expectations for youth conduct in the home, in school, and on the playing field. They come out of the meeting with a common mandate to focus on the character of the young people in their charges, and they now have a network of support in pursuing this goal.

Another reason for skepticism about youth sports is that many adults have come to believe that the ethic of competition is in and of itself harmful to children, a notion that has affected academic education as well, leading some schools to dispense with grades and other forms of comparative assessment. But competition can be motivating if it is managed right. Children do not crumple when they lose a contest or see peers accomplish something that they cannot yet do. Instead, they are more likely to feel a desire to accomplish more themselves. Shielding a child from competition can dissuade the child from the pursuit of excellence. It also removes crucial opportunities for the child to build skills. Nevertheless, many parents today distrust competition and place a low priority on activities such as sports that are associated with it.

All of these reasons—abusive behavior, poor sportsmanship, distrust of competition—have combined to demote the status of youth sports in many communities. No longer do sports receive the widespread, unequivocal support they once enjoyed. Communities, especially in financially strapped urban areas, have withdrawn funding. As a result, facilities of all kinds—playing fields, equipment, uniforms, leagues, and teams—have become increasingly scarce. In places where youth sports once flourished, they have been squeezed out by other pursuits: lessons, television, hanging out at the mall or on the streets.

Carl Taylor, a social scientist who grew up in a working-class Detroit neighborhood, recalls that "My childhood always involved some sort of sports. The community, both within my block and the city at large, was supportive of recreational programs." After examining present-day community support for youth sports in the United States, he concluded: "In the 1990s, America, and, in particular, industrial centers, began to see the results of cutting programs for sports and recreation. Such reductions, although often seen as financially necessary, have left a void that handicaps many communities and neighborhoods in their attempts to provide experiences to their youth that promote positive development."[4]

Yet the news is not all bad. There has been one countervailing trend that has improved the athletic prospects of over half our youth population: girls are now welcome in many team sports that, less than twenty years ago, were virtually closed to them. As a result, large numbers of girls are taking up soccer, baseball, softball, basketball, and ice hockey. And the games have become more interesting. In girls' basketball, for example, players no longer need to stop at half court and look on helplessly while someone else takes the ball down to shoot. We have at last figured out that girls can run up and down the whole court, just like boys. Gender equality has brought sports to a new population of girls— although a separate shift in our social priorities has decreased the athletic opportunities available to some populations of boys.

Sports can play an indispensable role in a community youth charter. Sports can be used to support the standards of home and school, but they also can provide a unique training ground for habits that are essential for both physical and character development. In order for sports to fulfill this role, opportunities for active participation must be made widely available to young people throughout the community. Most important, youth sports must be conducted with the highest possible standards. The following guidelines are directed toward these ends:

1. *We must make youth sports a priority for public funding and other forms of community support (space, facilities, volunteer coaches).* Calling for more resources always sounds like an easy and rather banal recommendation. I have refrained from doing so in most of this book, even for resource-needy areas such as schooling, because I believe that a focus on standards and community is more urgently needed in public discussions about youth. But I take the situation of youth sports today to be something of an exception. For one thing, youth sports have been defunded in many communities that need them most. For another thing, attempts to restore funding or create new programs have met with uninformed derision. As a consequence, it has become necessary to make an explicit case for supporting youth sports as a high community priority.

In the United States recently, politicians successfully attacked a proposed anticrime bill because it had provisions for youth sports programs. In their attacks, they singled out a program called "midnight basketball." Its name clearly made it sound like an easy target. That program and others like it were called "pork" because they supposedly added "fat" to the crime-fighting bill. In the end, the punitive parts of the bill were passed, but provisions for youth sports and other preventive measures were eliminated or drastically reduced.

Of course, this is the way the democratic process is supposed to function: opposing sides examine bills and budgets carefully in order to minimize waste. The problem is that youth sports leagues are not wasteful in any sense. They do indeed prevent crime, especially in communities where young people encounter many temptations and few constructive alternatives. Unlike many of the politicians who railed against midnight basketball, I have seen these programs in action. They provide havens for young people in beleaguered neighborhoods, healthy outlets for adolescent energy, positive team experiences, and a needed structure of rules, discipline, and adult guidance that is all too rare in their young lives.

Community leaders at every level of government must resist the temptation to score easy political points at the expense of valuable youth programs. Politicians who want to sound tough and thrifty should pick targets that they know more about. Almost everyone who works with young offenders knows two facts: (1) the best way to get youngsters off the criminal track is to get them interested in positive engagements such as sports, school, or work; and (2) the surest way to lead youngsters to a life of serious crime is to incarcerate them for long periods of time with hardened criminals. Yet politicians continue to make political hay from simplistic attacks on youth sports programs and from passing bills that provide long sentences in adult prisons for youthful offenders. The public should stop buying such worthless hay and invest instead in community resources that promote healthy futures for all young people. Youth charter meetings can help citizens become informed about their community's youth sports needs. The youth charter meetings also can give citizens a chance to communicate these needs to their political representatives, some of whom can be induced to attend the meetings.

2. *Parents and coaches should emphasize standards of conduct as a primary goal of youth sports.* Sports must be conducted in a way that places competition within a framework of fairness, respect for rules, cooperation, and courtesy. Parents and coaches should commit themselves to the idea that how you play the game is more important than winning, and they must communicate this ethic to young players through words and deeds. This includes paying close attention to the incentives that influence youthful behavior in sports.

Children should be strongly praised for trying hard, contributing to the team, and playing well, even when they lose. They should be reproached when they break the rules, treat opponents unfairly, and act inconsiderately or egotistically—even when they win by doing so. Prizes and awards for youth sports should take sportsmanship into account. Coaches also can make special efforts to inform players that standards of conduct are a high priority with them. They can clearly state their expectations concerning sportsmanship and team behavior.

One example of this is a recent practice that I have observed in several youth sports teams. In prominent areas of team locker rooms, coaches have posted lists of the virtues promoted in Michael Josephson's "Character Counts" materials. Among the virtues are honesty, fairness, respect, and compassion—all central to sportsmanlike team conduct. This is a useful way of imparting the message that virtuous behavior really does matter to the coach.

Emphasizing standards of conduct does not require doing away with the desire to win. Young people can understand complexity. Winning is a proper goal of sports. It brings zest and vigor to the game. My point is not that winning should be devalued, but rather that it should not be put forth as the first and only goal. Young people should learn that winning has value only when the game is played honorably; otherwise it is worthless. Participation in sports should teach children that even the most vigorous competition can be conducted with high standards of conduct. Such an approach will prepare them well for the world of work, where success always will be important, though not at any cost.

3. *Young people should be provided opportunities to participate in individual as well as team sports.* Youth sports does not always need to revolve around team competitions. There are developmental benefits to single-person sports such as running and swimming, where children can test themselves against their own previous performances. Such sports offer young people a refuge from the anxious cheers of overeager parents and coaches who are looking for surrogate victories. Single-person sports can provide a moratorium from social pressure, enabling children to acquire physical skills at their own pace. Of course, single-person sports cannot usually provide a child with opportunities to learn cooperation and teamwork. A comprehensive sports program for a young person will balance team experiences with individual ones.

4. *Youth sports programs should encourage broad participation by ordinary players as well as stars.* Too many youth sports programs are organized around a quest for glory for the team sponsor rather than the physical needs of the youth population that is supposedly being served. In single-minded pursuit of championships or other victories, these programs bathe their star players with attention and ignore the rest. In many cases, only the very top athletes get to play at all. The star athletes are provided with highly intensive training, often at great expense, while the majority of youngsters are not offered even the most minimal opportunities to participate. This is another manifestation of the win-at-all-costs mentality that has diminished the value of modern sports for most youngsters. We must reorder our priorities and spread the resources around, so that all youngsters have ample access to both team and individual sports in their communities.

5. *Sports programs for youth must be carefully coordinated with other community events and activities for young people.* Aside from the ethic of win-at-any-cost, the greatest source of antagonism against youth sports arises from scheduling conflicts. Religious leaders complain that league games are held during church or synagogue services; parents complain that they interfere with the parents' work responsibilities; teachers complain that

they cut into school events or homework time. In busy lives, there always will be unavoidable scheduling conflicts, but today there is a widespread public perception that youth sports leagues make no effort to resolve such conflicts. This perception has eroded the already shaky public support for youth sports. Before the season schedule is arranged, coaches should speak with community leaders to ensure that all unnecessary conflicts are avoided. In addition, they should use this effort as an opportunity to build a network of support that can help them reach as many young people in the community as possible. The resulting network of support can be an important leg of the community's youth charter.

Peers and Close Friends

Long ago the Swiss psychologist Jean Piaget wrote that children live simultaneously in two social worlds: a world of adults and a world of peers. Both are crucial for the child's social development, but in different ways. From adults, children receive guidance, a sense of direction, and respect for rules, authority, and the social order, as well as a host of habits, skills, and goals that prepare them for their lives as responsible citizens. From peers, children learn cooperation and mutual respect, the rules of friendship, and the importance of fair play. The psychiatrist Harry Stack Sullivan later added that children's peer relations provide them with a crucial forum for intimate communication. In their close friendships, children share secrets and private messages. They talk about their self-doubts and insecurities. They confide thoughts that they will keep hidden from everyone else, including their parents. Sullivan wrote that the capacity to open up to another in this way is the cornerstone of mental health; in the long run it enables a person to be honest with self and others. The peer world is the main forum for the acquisition of this essential life skill.

As every parent and teacher knows, the peer world is also fraught with dangers. Most of the destructive behavior that young people engage in comes about as a result of contact with peers. Young people usually carry out antisocial behavior in groups; in many cases, they direct it at one another. Even self-destructive behavior, such as dangerous driving, substance abuse, unsafe sex, eating disorders, and suicide, frequently comes in response to peer influences of one kind or another.

All of this—the essential developmental benefits along with the life-threatening hazards—makes the peer world a high-risk arena for young people. As a consequence, most parents no doubt wish at times they could simply choose their children's friends. This may seem like a temptingly direct solution to parents' classic fears that their children will fall in with friends who will lead them into trouble. But young people are never going to let parents determine their friendships for them. It is even a fantasy for parents to believe that they can have any impact at all on which peers their child will take a liking to.

The peer world has its own dynamics, and parents, after all, are parents, and not peers. In fact, when parents *do* try to act like peers, out of a modern-day egalitarian impulse, they may relinquish the legitimate authority that they must have to provide the child with guidance in other key areas of life. For better or for worse, these key areas of parental influence do not extend to the child's peer affections. The two social worlds of the child always will remain separate to some degree. There is nothing wrong with this; in fact, it is probably necessary if each sphere is to retain its own integrity and its own power to nurture a young person's growth.

Separation between the two need not mean conflict, nor must it imply lack of contact. There are many things that parents, teachers, and other adults in a community can do to create the conditions for wholesome peer relations among young people. This too is a primary role for a community youth charter.

Adults can promote activities and events that give children opportunities to develop constructive friendships. A youth sports program is one example, but there are many others. At the same time, parents need not sit by passively if they see their children engage in self-destructive or antisocial peer behavior. They can work to remove conditions that corrupt and degrade relationships among young people. In many indirect but powerful ways, adults can create a community climate that enables their children to receive positive rather than negative developmental influences from their friendships.

How can parents help young people maximize the benefits of their friendships while minimizing the risks? First, it is necessary to identify both the benefits and risks. The benefits are easy to recognize, because they are timeless and universal: peer loyalty, mutual trust, cooperation, and intimate communication. The risks, on the other hand, vary from place to place. In some places gang violence stalks the peer world. In other places, the wrong friendships can lead to serious, irreversible problems with the law. (I know a judge who warns juvenile offenders, "It's your friends, not your enemies, who will get you in the most trouble in life.") In other places, the main dangers of friendship are drunk driving, or drug dependency, or HIV infection, or premature pregnancy, or compulsive gambling, or school failure.

Without good networks of communication, such as those provided by a youth charter process, it is not possible for adults to stay current on these matters. Most adults are unaware of the particular risks that confront youth peer groups in their community until a crisis arises. With better information, the crisis might have been avoided.

In a youth charter meeting, citizens can help one another identify local trouble spots where youngsters may be getting into trouble. In one meeting that I attended, people informed one another (and the police) about a spot under a neighborhood bridge where drug dealers from outside the community were making contact with local youth. In another town, people exchanged information about a pizza parlor that had become home to a teenage gambling ring. According to a later report, citizens launched a successful boycott of the pizza parlor until the owner put a halt to his youthful customers' gambling activities. In another town that I observed, the tables were turned: it was the store owner who insisted that he would close his doughnut shop early in the evening unless parents told their youngsters to respect his property (and make some minimal purchases) while they hung out there. The parents saw the shop as a safe, substance-free place where their teenagers could congregate, and so it was in everyone's interest to ensure that young people behaved properly there. Because a youth charter meeting affords citizens the opportunity to exchange information about how young people are acting in the settings where they spend time, it can help citizens avert many of the risks that youngsters often encounter in these settings.

Of all the risks surrounding the peer relations of young people today, the drug trade affects the largest number. It is also our society's most cancerous problem, spreading rapidly wherever it takes root and decimating the lives of those that it affects. Teenage drug use stabilized at a high rate during the early 1990s. Since then, drug use and trafficking have reaccelerated among young people in all sectors of society, from the inner-city streets to the leafy green suburbs.

Eliminating illegal drugs from our neighborhoods would immediately improve the climate of peer relations for a large number of today's young. Drugs have poisoned far more than the physical health of many young people. As many youngsters have been drawn into drug trafficking, the key social relationships in these youngsters' lives have been corrupted. Simple friendships quickly become underground trafficking associations, and these merge into gangs in an explosive mix. In neighborhoods with heavy drug trade, children's peer relationships often are based on nothing more than exploitation and instrumental gain. These "friendships" hover on the brink of betrayal at all times, and they can turn lethal at a moment's notice. Drug trafficking has turned once-safe neighborhoods into menacing places splattered with gang-related graffiti, unwelcoming to any people or institutions who could provide children with positive friendships and mentoring.

Because the drug trade holds out the allure of quick and substantial profits, it has afflicted many disadvantaged communities where money is a scarce commodity. A deal can make a youngster more money than he could otherwise earn in a year—perhaps more money than he has ever seen. The allure can be hard to resist, especially when those who could dissuade the youngster from such a course have been scared away. As a consequence of the illegal drug trade, many proud communities have become barren wastelands by day and fearful battle zones by night. Affluent areas have been able to protect themselves better against the drug blight than disadvantaged ones, but beneath the surface there are less obvious signs of blight even in places that were once considered invulnerable to social problems.

Among affluent youngsters, another frequent problem in substance abuse is binge drinking, usually at teen parties. Alcohol abuse among teenagers has risen steadily over the past two decades, with all the attendant problems of automobile calamities, antisocial behavior, and sexual misadventures. Many parents are desperately seeking ways to curb binge drinking among their teenagers, but they have concluded that alcohol abuse is uncontrollable in youth society today.

The other risk-laden peer activity that many adults have come to see as uncontrollable is teenage sex. For many young people, sex has become a kind of Russian roulette—a sport for thrills that flirts with disastrous consequences such as AIDS or other life-changing ones such as early pregnancy. The 1995 movie *Kids* provides a glimpse into the growing culture of high-risk teenage sexuality. The movie's main characters, two adolescent Lotharios, compete for sexual trophies and practice unsafe sex with abandon—all with unremitting encouragement from girlfriends and boyfriends alike. At the time the film appeared, reviewers objected that the film was nothing more than sensationalized fiction. Two 1994 studies published by the Henry J. Kaiser Family Foundation suggest that these film critics, like many other adults, need a clearer view of today's adolescent peer society. I quote from each of the two studies in the Kaiser report:

> There is a high rate of sexual activity among urban white youth. Knowledge about contraception and fertility is incomplete or erroneous; birth control is used inconsistently and often ineffectively. . . . Pregnancy seems to be a taken-for-granted or even desirable outcome of sexual relations.[5]
>
> In the glaring absence of a strong family unit, a close-knit group of 'street girls' often fills a social, moral, and family void in the young girl's life. . . . The street kids become increasingly committed to their peer groups, surviving by their wits, being "cool," and having fun. Some girls may begin to have babies by age 15 or 16, and soon others follow. In the minds of many, at least in the short run, this behavior is rewarded. . . . As the girl becomes more deeply involved, the group helps shape her dreams, social agenda, values, and aspirations. . . . As the babies arrive, the peer group takes on an even more provocative feature: The early play and social groups develop into "baby clubs." The girls. . . . use their babies to compete, on the premise that the baby is an extension of the mother and reflects directly on her. The young mother often feels the need to dress her baby in the latest and most expensive clothes "that fit" (rather than a size larger that the baby can grow into): a $50 sweater for a 3-month-old or $40 sneakers for a 6-month-old.[6]

Teenage pregnancy brings into the world a new generation of children who are placed at risk by the conditions of their birth. Many unwed teenage mothers are illiterate. Many, in the words of the Kaiser report, quickly become "surprised by how much time and involvement being a mother takes." As in the case of the "baby club" members, teenage mothers often adore their babies as extensions of themselves.

They lavish the babies with goods and affection, but they are unprepared to raise them with guidance, discipline, or instruction. Unless an older generation of grandparents comes to the rescue (which, happily, does indeed happen in some cases), the baby becomes one further casualty of the mother's risk taking.

Because communicating about peer relations is difficult across generations, parents often have little influence over the risks that accompany young people's friendships. Once again, it is helpful to look beyond the home for other people and institutions who can support the parents' efforts to guide youth friendships in a wholesome direction. The first need of all adults is good information about how young people are spending their free time. Every parent should ask: In our community, what are youngsters doing when they are with their friends? In particular, what are the peer group risks that we should know about? With sound information, parents, teachers, and other adults can take effective steps to avert the risks, while at the same time supporting the child's friendships. A youth charter process can play a key role for both information gathering and helping community members formulate balanced responses to the benefits and risks of children's peer relations. The following guidelines are dedicated toward this end:

1. *A parent's first priority with respect to a child's friendships is to encourage and guide the child's initiatives rather than to block or obstruct them.* Every child needs to explore the social world, and every child needs close friendships where intimate peer communication can be exchanged. In the hazardous climate of modern society, some parents try to wall their children off from all adverse social influences. They restrict their children's social life to the extent that it is impossible for the children to build a network of peer relations. One insightful sociological study called this a "bounding" strategy of child-rearing.[7] The strategy is understandable but misguided. Parents do better by helping children explore the outside world in a safe way than by shutting them off from it. Peer friendships are a critical developmental need. For young people, the greatest risk associated with peer relations is isolation.

2. *Parents cannot create or select their children's friendships, but they can connect with the child's peer world in constructive ways.* Children do not look to adults for opinions about which peers to like or not like. Affection among peers grows spontaneously, and attempts to control it from above always

lead to defiance and resistance. In extreme cases, parents may be able to keep a child away from a relationship that is clearly headed for trouble, but in the long run no parent can successfully micromanage a child's friendships. Peer relations have their own dynamics that operate on their own terms.

But the peer and adult worlds can come together on many fruitful occasions. Respecting the integrity of a child's peer relationships does not require staying apart at all times. From a historical perspective—and from a cross-cultural one as well—our society is age segregated in the extreme. Adults tend to stick with adults and kids with kids, without much mixing. In fact, there is not even much mixing across closely adjacent age ranges (such as older adults with younger ones, or teenagers with children). Such rigid age segregation limits the possibilities of positive influence across generations. It is even unnecessary on recreational grounds. Adults can create occasions—parties, trips, charitable projects, entrepreneurial ventures—that bring the generations together around a common purpose.

In the course of such joint activities, adults get to know their children's friends. Moreover, the activities can provide natural and nonthreatening ways for adults to impart high standards of behavior to young people and their peer groups. This is a more effective means of communicating standards than lectures and admonitions presented out of context.

In our divided society, it may take special efforts to think up authentic occasions that mix generations in the pursuit of engaging goals. These are precisely the kinds of efforts that a youth charter meeting can help launch. Community members can brainstorm ideas about joint projects that engage the interests and talents of both adults and youngsters: charitable activities, conservation work, improvements to local facilities, new building projects, commercial and noncommercial ventures, travel and exploration, arts and science exhibits, media shows, special entertainment events, and so on. Such efforts have multiple payoffs, not the least of which are the new avenues that they open between the worlds of adults and young people. These avenues are two-way streets as far as learning is concerned. They open the way for adults to offer young people the benefits of their experience and for young people to offer adults their own experience of the world that their generation is creating.

3. *Adults should keep themselves informed about risks associated with youth peer groups in their particular communities.* As in all other areas of human life, information is power. This sounds self-evident, but I am always shocked by how little parents know about the youth peer life in their communities.

The best source of information is the children themselves, and parents should go to this source whenever possible. A parent-child relationship that has been open, trusting, and honest from the start will pave the way for the frank disclosures, and, in some cases, these conversations can provide parents with an accurate view of the current peer scene.

But even the best of parent-child conversations will sometimes come up short in this regard. Young people do not always know about everything that is happening around them, and they are often blind to the risks that face them, out of denial or naiveté. They frequently dismiss a danger that has befallen a peer as something that "could never happen to me." Both in their own minds and in talking with adults, they will tend to minimize risks that arise in the course of their friendships. For a complete perspective, parents need information that goes beyond their own children's perceptions.

A youth charter process can serve this purpose. In small-group discussions, parents can trade stories and information with other parents, teachers, police officers, social workers, and community leaders. The discussions end up identifying common problems, including the risks that adults have observed in young people's peer activities. This kind of community forum can open a window onto the social world of children, offering parents a far clearer view than that provided by media accounts, which are often guarded, random, incomplete, or distorted—or ignored or hushed up in the first place.

I have witnessed occasions where parents say that shades have been lifted from their eyes by community-wide conversations about young people. In one town that I visited, several sets of parents had come home after nights out to find their houses trashed in the course of drunken parties thrown by their teenage children. (Sometimes the parents knew about the parties in advance, but none expected the drunken bashes.) What I found most startling was that most of the parents were unaware of the other incidents, since they had all been kept off the pages of the local paper. Only the town youth officer knew the full extent of the problem. When parents had a forum to discuss this new teenage trend with other parents and the youth officer, they realized the need to supervise their children's parties more closely. Once the information became available, the solution became obvious.

4.   *Community members should build coalitions among themselves and local institutions for the purpose of eliminating the hazardous conditions surrounding young people's peer friendships.* In places where the drug trade dominates peer engagements, citizens must join together to eradicate it. Drug traf-

ficking thrives on fear and apathy. A united stand is the only way to make the drug trade unattractive to those who find the prospects of easy illegal profits tempting. Similarly, coordinated efforts among parents and other citizens can help avert the other risks of youth peer relations.

When parents support one another—and when they enjoy the support of established institutions such as schools, churches, and synagogues—their warnings and directives gain credibility. It then becomes plausible for them to tell their children that alcohol abuse can harm themselves and others, that unsafe sex can be deadly, that an early pregnancy can wreck their futures, that it is irresponsible to bring children into the world before they are prepared to raise them properly, and that none of these behaviors is acceptable. In the absence of community support, parents often feel pressured to back down from such assertions. This can compromise the principles behind the parents' assertions, sapping the effectiveness of the guidance that they are trying to offer. Such compromises can turn out to be fatal for the young people who need the guidance. Community solidarity enables parents to give their children the unequivocal messages about risks that the children deserve.

The key to community solidarity on hot issues such as drug use or sexuality is to work out a common ground among all the controversies surrounding the issues. It is clear that there will always be disagreements among adults about how to respond to the risks of children's social lives. Some adults are determined to "just say no," others will tolerate some experimentation as long as the risks are controlled. No youth charter will be able to resolve such differences for all time, but it can identify the points of agreement and formulate action plans based on those points.

With respect to most matters of youth development, it is possible to find a common ground for effective action amid fundamental differences of opinion. In one meeting that I observed, some parents said that they had never taken illegal drugs themselves; they felt it immoral to do so and have told their children to stay clear of all controlled substances—including alcohol until they have reached age twenty-one. Other parents said that they had experimented with softer drugs such as marijuana during their own youth; they drew a distinction between these and the harder addictive drugs, talked straight with their children about their own past actions and present views on the matter, and as far as alcohol was concerned, believed in the European approach of offering young people an occasional glass of wine or beer so that the youngster learns to handle it. The group could have spent the entire meeting arguing about which approach made more sense. Instead, they resolved that every parent was opposed to trafficking in illegal drugs and driving under the influence of any intoxicating substance. The consensus opened up a discussion of specific measures that could prevent these behaviors, including an energetic, townwide educational campaign, carefully targeted police patrols, and a task force made up of local citizens to monitor progress.

In Search of Callings: Mentors and Jobs

Early in the chapter, I noted the importance of apprenticeships beyond the classroom, such as in sports and the arts. These are but two of the many nonacademic areas in which children can learn life-enhancing skills. In fact, most of what young people need to know must be gained through pursuits outside of school, through some sort of extracurricular mentoring. On the playing fields, in libraries and museums, on part-time jobs, in music and drama groups, and in neighborhood clubs, community mentors teach young people practical knowledge that extends far beyond their schoolwork. The fortunate young people who have access to this kind of community mentoring will draw upon this practical knowledge throughout their entire careers.

What do I mean by a community mentor? A note in the March 11, 1997, *Wall Street Journal* provides a good example: "Joyce Garrett, director of the acclaimed 90-member Eastern High School choir in Washington's inner city, enjoys seeing more of her students going to college. Using the slogan 'Excellence Without Excuses,' she sees the choir as a vehicle to teach values, like loyalty, perseverance, and teamwork. Mrs. Garrett . . . has coached 2000 EHS choir members over 25 years."

Community mentors also can impart to young people something even more valuable than practical skill: a sense of mission regarding their occupational interests. In traditional times, a young person was said to seek a calling. The notion of a calling implies a belief in the larger purpose of one's accomplishments. The most rewarding work-related gift that we could bestow on young people would be to bring back this notion, which unites personal ambition with the goal of serving humanity. The notion is central to the youth charter because it places every young person's quest for achievement in the context of the community's needs. For the young person, it provides a sustaining sense of dual aspiration (for the advancement of self and others) and can provide an enduring motivational structure to underpin the young person's vocational efforts.

Education has become an urgent national priority. As the evidence of our children's lackluster school performances mounts up, heroic efforts have been made to improve schools. The classroom has become the focus of intense scrutiny and the recipient of widespread attention and public largesse. But education is a broader concept than schooling, and we sometimes forget this. The school is only one part of the community. Young people must find mentoring and learning experiences in other parts of the community as well. The kinds of achievement that schools teach and measure provide only a small part of what most young people will need to know for their careers.

Some may believe that schoolwork is the real business of youth, and the school the place where students acquire serious job skills—and that all else is aimless play. If so, this belief exaggerates the usefulness of school knowledge and underestimates the value of skills picked up elsewhere. No school can teach the exact knowledge that young people will need in the future, for the simple reason that much of it still waits to be created. What school could have taught Jonas Salk to develop a polio vaccine or Steve Jobs to build a personal computer? These inventors, and others like them, forged the way for whole new industries that could not have been imagined by the teachers of those who ended up creating them. School learning certainly played a part in the inventions, but many other kinds of learning were needed as well, including practical and creative thinking skills that are alien to the culture of almost every school.

Not only are schools necessarily unaware of future career developments; they can also be oblivious to present trends. School systems across the United States have dropped instruction in the arts from their curricula, on the assumption that the arts are frivolous pursuits in comparison to the kinds of technical training that can offer students solid employment opportunities. All the while, U.S. technical jobs have been dispersed to the four corners of the earth, mostly to countries with pay scales too low for U.S. workers to compete with. As for the arts, it turns out that there *is* an industry there after all, with a secure economic base and attractive employment prospects: the media and entertainment fields, which have grown like wildfire, consistently producing America's largest balance-of-trade surplus. These fields rely heavily on young people with training in art, music, dance, film, and video. If this lively industry is to find the new talent to fuel their future growth, they will need young people who have been taught by mentors working outside the classroom, in community settings where the arts are performed and media are produced.

In virtually every field, young people can find apprenticeships through internships or part-time jobs. Some developmental psychologists worry that part-time jobs may interfere with young people's schoolwork. There are always extreme cases that can be cited; it is true that some teenagers skip classes, neglect their homework, and deprive themselves of sleep in order to earn as much spending money as possible. These are abuses that parents should discourage.

But part-time work can be an instructive experience for young people if held in balance and responsibly supervised. For many young people, a part-time job offers a unique opportunity to learn skills, self-discipline, and productive attitudes. Even the much-derided fast food stint can be edifying when the manager acts like a mentor to young apprentices. During a community youth charter meeting that I once participated in, I heard a restaurant manager describe how he counsels his teenage employees who start the job with poor attitudes toward the customers (something he frequently encounters, he said). This manager tells his teenage employees, "Every day you should select the crabbiest customer you can find and see if you can put a smile on the customer's face." This is a difficult challenge, he tells them. But if they can master it, they will have a future in any business where human relations is important (just about every business, of course). I am sure that the young people who worked at this manager's restaurant quickly became high-morale employees eager to learn more secrets of the trade.

The principles of good mentoring are very much like the principles of good athletic coaching. Excellence in performance is the mentor's first priority, but it is not the only one. The mentor also holds out high standards of conduct—the ethical infrastructure of the trade. In the finest examples, the mentor projects a larger vision of the enterprise's role in the life of the community. What broader purpose does this work serve? How does it contribute to others? How does it express the talents and aspirations of the person who produces it? How can the work fulfill the dual goals of personal ambition and service to humanity? When a respected mentor urges a young person to begin asking questions like this, the mentor sows the seeds of a calling in the young person's mind.

If we are to prepare every young person for a productive future, we must move in two directions beyond schools: *horizontally,* by creating mentoring opportunities for youth all throughout our communities, and *vertically,* by linking every young person's talents with mentoring experiences that will lead to a future vocation, or calling, for the young person. The bidirectional movement—horizontal across all the settings in a young person's life, vertically toward the young person's future— defines the community and developmental agendas of a youth charter. Only in this kind of comprehensive manner can we ensure that all young people are truly educated in the broad sense of the term and that none falls between the cracks. The following guidelines are directed toward this end:

1.   *Community institutions of all kinds should create apprenticeships for teenagers, and parents and teachers should encourage students to seek them out.* Some students find part-time work, internships, or instruction in the athletics or the arts, but many do not because the opportunities are too scarce. Every community has many potential mentoring resources that remain untapped—public agencies, newspapers, libraries, law firms, clinics and hospitals, arts leagues, media outlets, small and large businesses— all of which could host an internship program for students. It is worth the effort not only for the inexpensive extra help that it brings but also for its contribution to the future of the community. If those who manage for-profit and nonprofit organizations realized the importance of youth apprenticeships for the complete education of the entire youth population, every organization would sponsor an apprenticeship program. We need to move beyond the occasional opportunities that now exist, toward a systematic set of options that all young people can select from. Such options would help fulfill the now-neglected potential of the many young people who will never have much interest or success in school. A youth charter meeting can provide an occasion to solicit or announce apprenticeship opportunities for local youth.

2.   *Parents and teachers should open lines of communication to those who provide outside mentoring for young people.* Clear lines of communication ensure that young people encounter the same expectations and high standards of conduct wherever they go. The core principle of the youth charter is that young people learn standards most readily when all the important people in their lives share those standards. Parents, teachers, and other youth mentors can hold one another accountable for upholding the community's common values in their transactions with young people. For example, during a youth charter meeting, a parent can explain to the manager

of a fast food restaurant that parents expect the manager to insist that teenage employees not smoke on their breaks. Teachers may ask the manager to monitor the number of hours that each student is working, so that the work does not interfere with the student's homework. The manager might ask parents to support him in his efforts to get his teenage employees to show up on time. This kind of communication and cooperation, facilitated by youth charter discussions, can have a powerful effect in promoting good habits among young people. This works for everyone's benefit. Parents certainly want the values that they teach their child reinforced when the child is away from home. Those who provide jobs or internships to young people want the youngsters to conform to basic codes of decency, show up on time and dress neatly, act politely, be dependable, be honest and trustworthy, and strive for excellence. It is in the enlightened self-interest of adults, and in the developmental interests of the young, to see that all parties are on the same page with respect to the standards that they impart to young people.

3.   *Those who employ and instruct the young should seize the opportunity to provide them with mentoring.* First and foremost, good mentoring means imparting high standards of conduct and upholding the community's common values. It also means getting to know the youngster well enough to understand the youngster's goals, talents, and interests.

Such knowledge enables the mentor to connect the young person's worldview with the work experience in a meaningful way. The mentor then can point out what the young person needs to do in order to acquire missing skills and accomplish the desired goals. Moreover, the mentor can show the young person how it is done in day-to-day activities. This kind of continual coaching is both highly motivating and highly instructional for a young person. It is what school should be in the best of circumstances but all too rarely is. Because of structural and substantive limitations of academic schooling, most young people must look to other institutions for this kind of invaluable mentoring.

4.   *Every young person should be offered multiple opportunities to receive mentoring.* No matter how problematic a youngster's prior history, there is an excellent chance that the right mentoring can turn the youngster around. The world is full of young people whom everyone had given up on until they were taken under the wing of a caring mentor. Through guidance and coaching, these young people found activities that nurtured their interests

and skills, instilled pride and a sense of responsibility, and ultimately led the way to a bright future. It is in every community's interest to provide such opportunities, especially for their most troubled youngsters. When a young person discovers the thrill of doing something well—especially something that matters to someone else—many supposedly "deep-seated" behavioral problems start to disappear. Absorbing work is the surest antidote to self-absorption, and service that is valued by others is a good remedy for demoralization. It may seem expensive or overly time-consuming to create apprenticeships for troubled youngsters, but in the long run it is the most economical—and the most humane—solution that we could find.

There is another antidote to self-absorption and demoralization, one that may require mentoring of a different sort. The antidote is spiritual faith. The data are especially clear on this one: young people who hold serious religious or spiritual beliefs are those least likely to drift into trouble during the adolescent years.[8] I have often thought that we should add another type of apprenticeship to the list of those that enhance children's education (again, in the broad sense of the term): a spiritual apprenticeship that can lead a child to a belief in something that transcends the self. (One town's solution to this challenge is described in a report in the Appendix of this book.) All children need something to believe in, a devotion to a larger purpose. A spiritual sense is a sure antidote to self-absorption and demoralization.

In our pluralistic society, there is an enormous variety of routes to this end. Children can acquire a sense of spirituality from any of the world's religions, as well as from service to others, art and music, travels in nature, and reflections on the mysteries of life and death. In all of these areas, we can provide opportunities for young people to receive mentoring from those who have thought deeply about these matters, and we can create occasions for children to express their own sentiments, interests, and curiosities. We must fight against division and conflict. We must coordinate our efforts so that all young people have access to spiritual wisdom and guidance. In youth charter fashion, this will help us harness our community resources toward the goal of fostering the full potential of every young person.

PART THREE

The View from the Top

7

THE MASS MEDIA

Every day the mass media affect us intimately, infusing our thoughts and shaping our experience. The media's influence is everywhere, around us and within us, from the time we are first able to watch and hear. At the same time, the mass media somehow feel beyond our reach, outside our control. Who can do anything about the overpowering images and ideas that envelop us like the very air we breathe?

This chapter is about how we *can* do something about it, especially with respect to the mass media's effects on the young. In fact, we not only can but *must* do something about it, for the influence is too powerful to be ignored. If not turned to the good, the mass media can overwhelm other efforts to guide young people in a positive direction. When used to impart high standards and useful information to the young, the media can become an important part of a community youth charter. No community should ignore the mass media's potential to help young people develop the skills and understanding they will need for lives in the twenty-first century.

There is no way to overstate the influence of the mass media on young people. On the average, young people today spend more time watching and listening to media presentations than on any other activity. Children learn about the world through television, movies, radio, videos, music recordings, books, magazines, newspapers, computer games, on-line services, and the Internet. Each media outlet presents a view of reality that shapes children's knowledge, values, hopes, fears, and dreams.

I have heard many parents worry that the mass media harm young people by filling their minds with violent images, tempting them to experiment with sex, stereotyping people in derogatory manners, luring children away from more meaningful pursuits, promoting alcohol and tobacco, and distorting or watering down the truth. All of these concerns are valid.

But it is also important to note the many benefits that media can bestow on young people. Many of these benefits have not yet been fully exploited, yet they are there for the asking once we learn to use media in the right way. The main purpose of this chapter is to show how mass media can be used to make positive contributions to the education and socialization of young people.

Parents should join forces with other parents, teachers, and community members to exert influence on those who produce, broadcast, and sponsor media shows for children. There is a great need for community-level action. A June 1997 report on the state of children's television concluded that "local broadcasters believe that communities *do not care* about their children's educational programming efforts." This is an unacceptable state of affairs, because it means that local broadcasters feel no incentive to improve their efforts on behalf of children. It is also an unnecessary state of affairs, reflecting a misperception on the part of the broadcasters. The report went on to say that parents *do* care—it is just that they are "confused . . . about how to provide feedback."[1]

I can vouch for this myself. Whenever I speak before parent groups, I am always struck by how many parents feel anxious and frustrated about the media shows that their children are exposed to. These parents sense that there is no way to control the media programming that producers and broadcasters are filling children's minds with. This lack of control, parents correctly believe, is diminishing their capacities to provide their children with constructive guidance.

There are a number of ways that a youth charter meeting can help parents regain some control over media influences on their children. In a youth charter meeting, parents can exchange information and advice about the social and educational value of shows that are available to children in the local media market. Parents will then have a sounder basis for helping children make selections that will promote rather than retard intellectual and social development. Also parents can discuss supervision strategies such as setting limits for children's television viewing. In a community where four hours per week, for example, becomes a commonly accepted norm, children can be more easily dissuaded from excessive consumption.

Perhaps most important, a youth charter meeting can give parents and other citizens a chance to make collective statements to the people who control local and national media sources. Such statements, especially when repeated in multiple settings, can have a powerful impact on the choices that producers, sponsors, and media outlets make.

Currently, ratings are the primary means by which television producers and sponsors receive feedback about public sentiment regarding particular shows. As a result, television programming is largely driven by the ratings. The problem is that ratings for children's shows are notoriously vague and unreliable. In order to speak up for quality shows that contribute positively to children's development, parents must find other means of providing feedback that bypasses the ratings system. Alone and isolated, parents feel powerless. Acting together, parents can contact broadcast stations, producers, and companies that sponsor children's shows, and they can have reasonable confidence that their collective voice will be heard.

In the rest of this chapter, I offer principles that parents can use in their own families and in conjunction with other parents in order to help their children derive the most benefits and the least harm from the mass media. Some of these principles may be enhanced by collective effort through youth charter forums—as when parents join forces to create a market for wholesome programming. Of course, when children watch television and videos, the main venue is the home. Since this is where most of the action is, the main parts of my recommendations center on how parents can work with their own children to select worthwhile programming and get the most out of it.

The spirit of the youth charter is that adults in a community can and should use the media actively, as instruments in children's education.

In order to do so, we must learn to work with the mass media rather than around them. Parents can do this by helping their children select wholesome and edifying programming, providing their children with feedback about what they see and hear, showing their children how to get the most out of media presentations, and being vigilant consumers. In today's rich media marketplace, there is an abundance of shows that parents can, with a clear conscience, encourage children to watch. But this requires guiding children toward programming that they will both enjoy and benefit from. As Plato said long ago, "The first task of every parent is to teach children to find pleasure in the right things."

How do we know which programs are beneficial and which are harmful to children? Some of the signs are obvious: a show that teaches a science in an engaging way (for example, *Bill Nye the Science Guy*) is useful for children; a show that glamorizes violence (say, *Natural Born Killers*) sends a message that could lead young children down destructive paths, unless someone is there to help them interpret the movie from an anti-violence perspective. Other signs may be less obvious. For example, the way that a show uses characters and dramatic climaxes, integrates multiple modalities (for example, art and music), and encourages social participation between children and adults can make a difference in how a child watches the show and what the child learns from it. The more obvious features pertain to the content of a media presentation, the less obvious ones to the way in which children cognitively process the presentation.

Savory and Unsavory Media Content: The Effects on Children

Media programming that contains heavy doses of violence is clearly detrimental to children. We know from reams of studies that violent programming leads to increased levels of hostile activity in many children.[2] The effects are not large, but they are significant, and they have been found consistently enough to be troublesome. In addition to increasing levels of aggression in some children, violent programming has a numbing effect on young viewers, desensitizing them to the horrors of bloodshed. This is an especially pernicious effect, because it wears away the natural barrier of empathy that normally makes the thought of harming another person repulsive.

Incredibly, children's television programming contains more violence than adult TV. The cartoons, westerns, and crime shows that children watch are filled with human slaughter. One study found that 66 percent of children's shows contain acts of violence, in contrast with a rate of 57 percent (already high!) for all types of programming combined.[3] And this finding pertains only to violence that is rather strictly defined as physical attacks. If we were to count taunts, sneers, snide comments, and expressions of just plain unfriendliness toward others, no doubt the figure would rise well above 66 percent. The world that children are viewing through their TV sets is a very nonharmonious place.

Most of the violent acts in children's cartoons, westerns, and crime shows are justified by a "you shot first!" ethic that Hollywood popularized long ago. ("Go ahead, make my day" was perhaps the most charming statement of this ethic: it took a Clint Eastwood to be charming behind a .44 magnum that was about to blow the other guy's brains out.) There is nothing wrong with the principle of self-defense, but the aggressive posturing of many heroes is more like someone looking for an excuse to shoot. For the show's sponsor, this is a good thing. Imagine the audience's disappointment if the hero got the villains to put away their weapons and apologize.

Not only is violence made to appear justified, but it is also made to appear pretty. The villain is shot with a glamorous flash that leaves no ugly traces of gore. Violence that is both beautiful and "fair" has a magnetic appeal for young viewers seeking simple solutions to social problems.

Like violent shows, overly sexualized programming also can have an effect on young people. Studies have shown increases in sexually permissive attitudes among adolescents who have been repeatedly exposed to popular TV shows.[4] The messages that TV broadcasts about sex are almost invariably salacious. One study found that two out of every three statements about sexual intercourse referred to couples who had little or no emotional commitment to one another, whereas only 14 percent referred to married couples.[5] Aletha Huston and John Wright, reviewing studies that have examined sexual content in TV shows that young people watch, summed up their conclusions in the following way: "Sex is shown as recreational; themes of competition and emphasis on physical attractiveness and sexuality as a defining attribute of masculinity or femininity are frequent. The partners involved are usually not married, at least to each other, nor are they in a committed relationship."[6]

Beyond the hot emotional issues of sex and violence, children's attitudes toward matters such as intellectual effort and achievement also can be adversely affected by what they see on TV. It is typical for comedies to portray any character who is studious or ambitious as a "dork," a "dweeb," or a "nerd"—someone who is "uncool" and "clueless." Unflattering stereotypes such as these are readily picked up and passed along by child viewers. This may have an especially invidious effect on children who are struggling against other stereotypical beliefs that reinforce the same anti-intellectual notions. For example, girls with an interest in math already must resist a cultural belief that math and science are unfeminine pursuits. When this belief is compounded by stereotypes portraying all intellectuals as nerds, a girl's motivation to pursue math and science may be sapped.

Just as the wrong kinds of media content can lead children toward negative attitudes and behavior, the right kinds can foster positive attitudes, values, and achievement. For example, *Mr. Rogers' Neighborhood* often consciously promotes the theme of persistence in the face of difficulty: "If you don't succeed, try, try again." One study found that children who watched *Mr. Rogers* demonstrated more sustained attention spans during preschool play than children who watched other shows.[7] *Mr. Rogers* has also received high scores on prosocial content. Studies have found that children who watch the show are more likely than comparison groups to share, resolve conflicts peacefully, and express respect for others.

In general, prosocial television shows can have a strong positive influence on children's social values and behavior. Studies have found that children who watch shows exemplifying positive social behavior tend to think and act that way themselves.[8] They are more likely to control their own selfish and antisocial impulses and less likely to stereotype others in a negative way than children who have not watched such shows. Most strikingly, children who watch shows portraying acts of generosity, nobility, and courage have a marked tendency to perform acts of altruism on their own.

The strongest positive effects occur when children talk about a highly prosocial show with a parent or friend. The combination of observation and discussion is a developmentally powerful one. A combination that does *not* work is violence mixed with positive messages—as, for example, when a bloody conflict is followed by a moralistic statement about the virtues of nonviolence. Children remember only the violent part, perhaps because that is so much more dramatic than the moralizing part. What children remember, they are more likely to copy. Research has found that combining moralisms with violence in media presentations leads to increased rather than diminished childhood aggression.[9]

The implication of the studies is clear: it matters what children watch. The content of the presentation is the most important determinate of whether the influence will be in a positive or a negative direction. What can parents, teachers, and citizens do to see that the content of mass media presentations serves children for the good rather than for the ill? I propose the following guidelines:

1. *Exercise control at the family level.* This is the most direct solution, yet one that many parents feel powerless to follow. I have had many conversations with parents about their distress over the salacious and violent material in the shows that their children see. When I ask why they do not simply turn the shows off, some common replies are: "Bobby would never let me. He'd have a fit." Or: "How can I ask Karen to miss the shows that all her friends are talking about all the time?" Or: "The kids would find a way to see these things anyway." Conversely, when I ask why the parents do not find beneficial programming for their children to watch, often I hear responses like: "Tim finds those shows boring." Or: "I can't find enough of those shows that are on at the right time." Or: "I just don't have a chance to do all that monitoring every minute."

These are all realistic responses. I certainly do not mean to criticize the parents who have said them to me. In their own way, these protestations demonstrate the need for comprehensive approaches of the youth charter variety. If parents start to communicate constructively with other parents about their children's media exposure, it will become possible to develop collective viewing standards that all children in the community are expected to abide by. The short-term effect will be that children no longer will be able to tell their parents that their friends get to see shows that they are not allowed to see. The long-term effect of this kind of collective youth charter action, if repeated many times over in many communities, will be an improvement in mass media programming: stations and networks will see ratings for their junk shows decline and ratings for their worthwhile programming rise.

But even parents operating in isolation, without the benefit of a community youth charter, can start to exercise some effective control. First, they can set limits on the amount of noneducational programming that their children are allowed to watch. The limits can distinguish between entertainment and educational shows. For example, a family could allow their children two hours' total TV time per day, half entertainment and half chosen from educationally oriented listings. Family rules can also contain total prohibitions against material that is clearly harmful or inappropriate for children before certain ages. Such rules are not difficult to enforce in a household, especially if parents are consistent and begin early. Children accustomed to parental guidance from the time they are young are likely to accept it gracefully as they grow older.

There is one nonobvious message in this seemingly obvious guideline. I added the phrase *at the family level* intentionally, in order to exclude the idea of control at the governmental level. Control by the government amounts to censorship. Apart from important constitutional issues, which I shall not discuss here, there are at least two things wrong with public censorship.

First, governments that try to restrict access to media materials do so in erratic, muddled, arbitrary, and relativistic manners. Whoever happens to have power at any particular time sets the standards, and these standards will shift whenever the government changes. Even during a single administration, standards will be bent by political pressures. They will be compromised and watered down. Ultimately, what begins as a benign attempt to protect the public turns into a cynical attempt to advance the interests of those in power. Young people are smart enough to see through this. They are quick to become demoralized by the cynicism and the inconsistencies. The guidance that they need requires a steady commitment to core values. This guidance is beyond the capacity of any government agency to provide.

Second, censorship is futile in the long run. People always find ways around it—children no less than their elders, because children are among the most clever and curious people on earth. Unlike control from a respected parent, censorship from a distant government source only adds to a child's attraction for forbidden material. Moreover, modern media have made the task of the censors virtually impossible. Restricting materials is no longer as simple as pulling *Ulysses* or *Lady Chatterley's Lover* off the stacks of the local library. (My references date me. Now it is *The Adventures of Huckleberry Finn*, for an entirely different—and equally misguided—set of reasons.) Television, movies, and the Internet contain material that is at least as shocking and far less socially redeeming than any of these banned books. No governmental restriction could clean it all up. The Internet in particular is too large and free-form to be comprehensively regulated.

The place for media control is in the home, not the legislature. Parents can restrict access to materials that they consider unwholesome for children. They can turn off the TV set and install V-chips, approve or disapprove of movies that their children see on video or on screen, and purchase software that safeguards their children's Internet wanderings. Here it is important for parents not only to protect children from what they may see but also to protect them from people who will prey on children whom they have "met" through the Internet.

The media too should be exercising their own sense of social responsibility in producing decent programming for children. More control at the home level, especially if it becomes widespread and uniform, can help in this regard; it might give media executives' senses of responsibility a nudge in the right direction. The nudge is called for. We know the kinds of media content that helps children, and we know the kinds that harm them. It remains for the media to replace the harmful content with beneficial content. Parents and other citizens can provide the executives with incentives to do so.

2. *Provide children with guidance by opening up dialogues with them about the shows they have seen.* Suppose a child comes home from a friend's house and mentions he has just watched a video of *Natural Born Killers,* a film in which the heroes run rampant through the countryside in an orgiastic celebration of splashy violence and hostile sex. What is more, the child mentions that he thought that the movie was neat and that the heroes were cool. What can the parent do?

The parent, of course, could blow her stack and tell the child that he should not be watching movies like that (and, as I have noted above, it would be reasonable—and wise—for the parent to exercise such control when she is able to, in particular within her own home). But in this case, the child has already seen the film. Proclaiming a prohibition is like closing the barn door after the horse has already left. Nor is this an unusual case. In an open society, there is no way to keep children shielded from violent or salacious media content forever.

But the parent can use such occasions to provide invaluable guidance about the meaning of gratuitous violence and sex, topics that might be difficult to broach in a different context. The parent could begin by asking the child to explain, in a serious way, why he admired the movie and its heroes. What about the victims of the violence? How did they feel? Do you think, in real life, that the gunshot wounds would look as "neat" as they did in the Hollywood movie? Did the movie's sex scenes show the kind of romantic relationships that you would find fulfilling? Very likely these kinds of questions would provoke the child into evaluating the movie from a more critical and humane perspective. The questions, though, are just a beginning—a way to open up a learning dialogue in which the child actively participates. As the child responds, the parent can—and should—express her own point of view. The parent can tell the child why she finds glossed-over portrayals of violence abhorrent, and she can describe to the child the damaging toll that such activities always take.

The most unsavory media meal can be made into nourishing food for thought by providing the child with constructive guidance about the experience. A violence-filled media presentation can be used as an occasion for a discussion about its real human consequences and about ways that the violence could have been prevented. A scene ridden with sexual innuendo can give parents an opportunity to explain the risks of casual sex to a child. The child may even find it easier to ask delicate questions in the context of a media show, as long as the family is receptive to the child's curiosity. Parents should create a family atmosphere that encourages productive discussion of this kind. When they do, it is one of the surest ways to offer children direction about highly emotional matters.

In previous writings, I have described such an atmosphere as one of "respectful engagement."[10] Through respectful engagement, adults can: (1) create a dialogue around a common experience that the adult and child have shared; (2) use the dialogue to introduce the adult's perspective to the child; (3) encourage the child to participate actively in the dialogue and solicit the child's free expression of beliefs (however mistaken these beliefs may seem to the adult); and (4) express, in ways that the child can comprehend, the adult's own reactions to the media content and the child's perspective on it. Together these four elements of respectful engagement create dialogues that can have a lasting, constructive influence on the child's perspective.

Respectful engagement establishes, through open communication, a climate of tolerance for the child's opinions. Tolerance need not imply, as some have wrongly deduced, that adults should refrain from expressing a position of their own. In fact, when adults refrain from expressing their own values, it can actually discourage a child from exploring the issue more deeply—the opposite effect of that intended. Adults who fail to confront children with the real beliefs that they themselves genuinely hold will engender in children an attitude of passive indifference—even cynicism—toward the enterprise of moral choice. Why should a child bother working through a moral problem or risk taking a stand when the child's adult mentor refrains from doing so?

In their reactions to media presentations, adults should confront children with basic moral principles that are clearly stated and sincerely held. Principles such as compassion, fairness, honesty, and responsibility need not be compromised. When adults unambivalently express their convictions about such principles, they act as models of conviction. Children respect this. In fact, this kind of guidance increases children's respect for authority in general. At the same time, the open discussion encourages children to orient toward their own natural moral feelings and to use these as the foundations of strong moral values. Respectful engagement dispenses with the common assumption that children's respect for authority and their autonomous judgment stand in opposition—that one must be traded off for the other. Respectful engagement connects the two moral stances, prompting them to develop in synchrony.

3.   *Look for ways to add complexity and depth to overly bland media presentations.* We live in an age of extremes. At the same time as some media shows are exposing children to every scurrilous horror known on earth, other shows are removing anything that could be the least bit controversial from the stories that they tell. Classics of literature have been expurgated beyond recognition in order to produce "acceptable" children's versions. In this climate, even Brothers Grimm tales never make it onto children's TV with all their vivid details intact.

Children can handle the vivid details of great works of art. They do not scare easily, and they are fascinated by the rich texture of life as portrayed through art. A small dose of reality's dark side in an artistic work can inoculate a child from fears of the outside world, especially if the child has a chance to discuss the artistic work with a supportive adult. Moreover, children can handle complexity. The process of wrestling with challenging material spurs their intellectual growth. Again, guidance rather than protection is the route that leads most directly to the development of character and competence.

It is important for us to combat gratuitous violence and sex in children's media shows, but we must not allow every disturbing wrinkle to be taken out of the shows. Blandness is *not* a satisfactory solution. Children cannot thrive on watered-down diets of oversimplifications and euphemisms. They thrive on challenges, truth, and the excitement of deep probings into life.

Hollywood will continue to turn profound works like *The Hunchback of Notre Dame* into children's cartoons with cute characters like "Quasi," "Victor," and "Hugo." If we leave it there, this kind of show takes something out of our culture. We can respond by asking our children to read the book or by reading it to them. Only in this manner will they discover that Victor Hugo was not the name of two gargoyles, that along with Quasimodo's hunchback came misery, rage, and nobility rather than a lovable personality, and that there is more of a message to Hugo's tale than a simple cheerful tolerance for those who are different from us.

Can a child appreciate all this? I know that I stumbled across Hugo's novel when I was in sixth grade. I was neither a prodigy nor an egghead (far from it, I was a sports devotee). Our school had a program that allowed us to buy one cheap paperback a month. From its title, I guessed that *The Hunchback of Notre Dame* was a football story about a college lineman, but I read the novel anyway, not wanting to waste the fifty cents. It was a stunning experience, and I remember it to this day. I would be amazed if my thirteen-year-old daughter, who has just seen the Disney film, will remember her experience in a similar way forty years hence.

4.   *Create media content that is uplifting and educational while still amusing, authentic, informative, challenging, and fun to watch.* High-quality media programming requires individual initiative and personal vision. Neither the strongest community pressure nor the most nagging sense of responsibility can produce a show that children will watch with pleasure. Producing shows that are entertaining as well as educational is a creative effort that cannot be legislated.

The challenge for society today is not to preserve a creative spirit that is alive and well throughout the mass media. Artistic integrity in media programming already is endangered by the cynical view, widely accepted among media executives, that only junk sells (or, to put it another way, that intelligent shows will never gain enough market share to be worth caring about—another pessimistic assumption). Such entrenched beliefs have decimated the quality of films, music, and television shows, especially with respect to programming for teenagers. This is a problem that a community, acting in concert, can do something about—*not* by placing censoring pressures on producers but by making its concerns felt as a market force.

A youth charter meeting can get this process started by offering the community opportunities to identify shared expectations for youth media programming. In a youth charter meeting, a community can find its common voice and make that voice heard by the media industry. This sort of communication need not be confrontational. In fact, it can provide media producers with valuable information about the needs and wishes of their market. If, as I believe, those who make up the market are becoming increasingly uneasy with the "dumbing down" of media shows for young people, it is in producers' best interests to hear this kind of sentiment before it has adverse effects on their business. It is in everyone's interests to serve the legitimate needs of a market.

I conclude this section with a note to media producers and all those in positions to influence them, including consumers, advertisers, fellow citizens, and members of the community. It is time to exercise a new kind of creativity in producing material for young people—a creativity that does not accept as inevitable a conflict between market appeal and programming that is truly informative and uplifting. Rather, the kind of humane creativity that I have in mind seeks ways to join the two. This has been done many times before, in art and in the media, but never often enough, and it is rarer today than it once was. Shakespeare proved it in his time: the profound can be popular. In our time, *Sesame Street* has shown that the most basic educational messages can be made entertaining, for even the very young. If more of our media producers dedicated their creative talents to this challenge, we would not need to create an elaborate system of controls for children's viewing. As a public, we must exercise the kind of responsible consumership that provides compelling, market-driven incentives for creative and humane effort.

The Nature of Modern Media: The Effects on Children's Cognitive Processing Abilities

The content of a media presentation is not the only dimension that parents should be concerned about. The nature of the medium—that is, the special way that the medium conveys information, apart from the information itself—also can affect thoughts and attitudes. This was the point made by eminent communications scholar Marshall McLuhan, who put forth the now-famous maxim that "the medium is the message." In fact, McLuhan argued, the nature of the medium eventually determines its content. When a new medium is invented, he wrote, it starts out showing content developed for a prior medium. Before long, it develops content that suits its own formal properties. So, for example, radio in the 1920s began by simply broadcasting the vaudeville troupers who were then appearing on stage throughout the country. Soon radio invented its own disk jockey format, with programs of prerecorded music, news bulletins, and live sportscasting. Television began by broadcasting the content of radio shows, then moved on to its own programming. Now, the Internet fulfills McLuhan's prophecy by starting out printing newspapers and magazines verbatim; later, Internet users will invent who-knows-what content to exploit the potential of the Internet's new formal properties.

Following from this insight, McLuhan and his followers made a dramatic claim—one that is either frightening or cheerful, depending on how you look at it: that the nature of a popular medium alters the consciousness of those who use it. After a new medium such as TV becomes dominant, people come to process all information in the way that they have learned to watch a TV show. Thus the formal features of popular media in any epoch determine the nature of human intelligence during that period of time. This strong claim led McLuhan's fans at the time to conclude that we had entered an "age of television" in which thinking would emulate properties of TV—such as its rapidity, superficiality, nonlinearity (that is, freedom from logical sequence and literal meaning), and flashiness. Young people who were just forming their intellectual abilities would be the ones most radically affected.

Many social critics viewed this outlook for the future of human intelligence as bleak. McLuhan, born in 1897, wrote mostly about film, radio, and pop music, but the social critics who followed his reasoning focused mostly on the newer medium of television. Television was spreading like wildfire into homes worldwide, reaching far more young people than any other medium in human history. With the "channel-surfing" mentality that it brought, TV seemed to exemplify McLuhan's principles of rapidity and nonlinearity more closely than any previous medium. Distinguished and influential critics such as Jerome and

Dorothy Singer lamented what they considered to be TV's inevitably deleterious effects on the young.[11]

But the age of computers and the Internet has turned this critique on its ear. Champions of computers and the Internet believe that we have entered into a new world of communications that will irrevocably transform human intelligence *for the better*. This is McLuhanism taken to its rhapsodic conclusion. The claims of these boosters are intriguing. Computers, they say, take thinking even further along the road to non-linearity than does television. "Surfing the net" makes watching television, even with channel surfing, seem slow and constrained by comparison. When people skip from Web site to Web site, they follow their own idiosyncratic interests. Viewers do not end up at a TV "station" that tells them a story with a narrative sequence for a half-hour time slot. Nor is there a uniform logical sequence in one's selections of Web pages. This is nonlinearity beyond anything that television or any other previous medium has ever promoted. In this manner, it is argued, computers and the Internet will create a new popular culture with more mobile, creative, and productive rules of discourse.

Moreover, the argument goes, young people are the masters, and beneficiaries, of this new culture. They take to it more readily than those of us whose thinking has been rigidified by older traditions. Young people understand computers almost instinctively. Their own intellectual abilities are shaped and stimulated by their participation in computer and Internet activities. As a consequence, computers and the Internet will enable the younger generation to leapfrog past the intellectual constraints of the past.

As provocative and visionary as these claims are, I cannot accept them, at least in their most extreme versions. The claims do not accord with what that research has told us about the nature of human cognition, child development, and the media's influence on both. For one thing, the claims overestimate the power of a medium's formal information-processing features. For another thing, the claims underestimate the role of traditional bodies of knowledge and belief in the development of a young person's character and competence. A young person needs the guidance of those who went before in order to build basic skill and values. No single medium of communication, however bold and new, can provide that by itself.

McLuhan's maxim was charming, but it turns out that it was only partially correct; what is more, McLuhan overstated its implications. The nature of a medium is important, but it by no means overrides the content of a media presentation. Decades of research have shown that the content that McLuhan's maxim so cavalierly dismissed is in and of itself a force for parents to reckon with. In fact, studies since McLuhan's time have shown that content has a far greater effect on young people's social behavior (though not necessarily on their cognitive processing) than the nature of the medium through which it is presented.[12] This means that the violent episodes that dominate movies and TV (including children's cartoons!), the "gangsta rap" images of sex and violence that permeate pop music, the desultory talk that abounds in TV sitcoms and soap operas, and the inane programming piped into homes from every airwave in and of itself can have a harmful effect on young people unless parents and other community members guide children through it in the manner that I suggest. Conversely, prosocial and educational content, regardless of how it is presented, is beneficial to children and should be encouraged.

Still, McLuhan's maxim contains at least a grain of truth. His insight helps us appreciate a subtle yet indisputable fact: the particular ways in which the media present information can leave a mark on young people, especially during their formative years. Television, movies, and pop music all have their own particular ways of presenting information, and each form can influence attitudes, thoughts, and values.

In order to appreciate fully the magnitude of this subtle-sounding influence, we must keep in mind that children consume an enormous amount of mass media programming. Children in the United States watch an average of almost four hours of television per day, in addition to what they see and hear on videos, films, compact disks, tapes, radios, magazines, and computers. Processing so much information through these presentational forms inevitably affects the way in which a young mind develops. This can be for the ill or for the good. As with all else, there are risks that need to be avoided and benefits that can be seized. I begin with the risks, some of which were first identified by McLuhan and his followers in the 1960s and 1970s.

Developmental Risks of Modern Media Forms

Passivity. Some presentations are so distant from the child that they place a child in a passive role regarding the information that is being presented. This contrasts with a more direct presentation that enables the child to manipulate the world, ask questions, make mistakes, receive correction, make progress, receive praise, and figure things out through trial and error. If the passive mode becomes habitual, it can turn into a disposition toward inertia that limits a child's capacity to explore the world.

McLuhan pointed to film as one medium that places viewers in a passive role. It did not take McLuhan's followers long to make television the prime culprit of this critique, no doubt because of television's rapid spread into virtually all homes since the time of McLuhan's initial writings on the matter. The image of the passive "boob-tuber" quickly caught on, and certainly with some justification. But it is important to recognize that traditional media such as books also can be passively consumed, and a boring lecture at school can be every bit as passive an experience as a stupefying television show. Conversely, movies and TV can be transformed into active experiences for a child.

Fleeting Attention Span. Commercial TV often is structured around quick transitions and abbreviated chunks of information rather than a step-by-step development of ideas. This is most noticeable on the actual commercials that pay for commercial television. Usually the quick transitions follow one another in rapid succession, without any apparent connection. This unpredictable patterning is dissimilar to the logic of traditional narrative sequences: before and after, cause and effect, if-then, and so on. It is also dissimilar to the thematic structure of educational shows such as *Arthur* and *Mr. Rogers.*

The quick transitions add velocity to media that are already fast paced, and the newer the media, the faster the pace. Films move quickly when compared with books, because a film must pack its story into less than two hours. TV shows and music recordings make films seem relatively slow-paced. Market forces exacerbate this trend toward speed. Televised airtime is at a premium because of expensive per-minute advertising costs, especially during prime time. People who watch television become accustomed to short takes, sound bites, abrupt changes, and the reduction of complex stories to headlines and highlights.

For a child, processing information in this way stands in stark contrast to the hard effort of sustaining attention and acquiring habits of patience and perseverance. It can train a taste for the flashy, the erratic, and the mercurial. It also can lead to a disinterest in continuous, in-depth story treatments that are more carefully descriptive of people and places.

The extensive research studies conducted on child viewers of *Sesame Street* have shown few if any such effects, but this tells us nothing about all the children who watch commercial TV programming for several hours per day.[13] It is likely that *Sesame Street* is more logical and more organized than other children's TV shows. It also may be that all children's attentional abilities are robust enough to withstand some TV viewing. In either case, common sense tells us that a sustained attention span is an essential capacity for children to develop and that this capacity is not advanced by quick blasts of disconnected information.

Expectations of Instant Power. Action shows portray fabulous feats by characters with phenomenal powers. This is especially noticeable in cartoon shows, but it is also true of many shows with live actors as well. Heroes vanquish fearsome foes through supernatural strength or magical weapons, usually without enduring so much as a scratch themselves.

Traditional literature always had its larger-than-life heroes, but the older print traditions usually made an effort to show heroes acquiring skills through determination and preparation, often when they were young. Such a treatment can set a useful example for a young audience. Moreover, heroes were portrayed as susceptible to risks, such as wounding or death. They could make mistakes, and they could be hurt. Now, a hero's powers are instantly granted and applied with impunity. Valor comes cheap because there is never a price to pay. Foolhardy acts of bravado are rewarded with inevitable success. Children take readily to this appealing notion. Anyone who has observed children after they have watched an action show will see them zapping and buzzing their way through opponents, tasks, problems, and imagined challenges of all kinds. A moderate degree of this is in the scope of healthy childhood fantasy. When carried too far, an expectation of instantaneous power can substitute for the serious effort required to attain real skills.

Scanning for Climaxes. In contemporary movies and television, there has been a drift toward packing climactic action into practically every scene. The appeal is obvious. It is like junk food prepared with recipes that are calculated to deliver quick sensations in every bite. Children who become acclimated to this kind of high-energy dramatic experience learn to scan everything for climaxes—literature included. They will ignore context and meaning in search of action. They become bored with literature that does not translate readily into vivid images, and have little tolerance for stories that are not resolved definitively in a clash of right versus wrong.

Each of these risks can lead children to acquire habits of superficial and lethargic thinking rather than the critical, tough-minded approach they need to make their way through the complexities of life. But none of the risks is inevitable; all can be averted by good programming and intelligent usage by parents and children. What is more, the risks are not the whole story. Modern media also contain features that can powerfully enhance the thinking and learning habits of young people. The media critics of McLuhan's day were unaware of these positive features, because they were not privy to all that we now know about how thinking develops. More recent writings in cognitive science and psychology have given us the basis for a more balanced and more hopeful picture.[14] These writings have underscored two points that can help us extract from the mass media the maximum benefits for young learners:

1. Learning takes place in a diversity of ways, resulting in a multiplicity of intellectual abilities, habits, and character dispositions.
2. Elements of modern media have the potential to mesh better with some of these ways of learning than do older media forms, such as print.

A modern media presentation can be an active, participatory, and profound experience for a young person. This is not to say that this is the norm, or even that it occurs with any significant frequency at all, but the potential is there—and not because modern media contain the same features that have made traditional literary experiences active, participatory, and profound for audiences. Rather, it is there because modern media have their own features that create new opportunities for audience engagement. Because these features have not been deployed as often as they should be—and because detrimental features have been deployed with great frequency—we tend to think of mass media influences as inevitably negative, as ones that we must guard our children against, rather than as valuable instruments that could help us attain educational goals for our children.

Potential Benefits of Modern Media Forms

Integration of Diverse Modes of Understanding. Television and movies offer children presentations that combine visual, musical, and narrative forms of meaning. Prior to modern mass media, only the very privileged had access to presentations of this kind and even for those children, the experience was rare. Shows that combine art, music, and drama offer children frequent opportunities to develop and integrate the diverse facets of their intelligence: logical, visual, musical, sensory-physical, social, narrative, and personal. This is a thoroughly modern opportunity that brings with it the potential for expanding the power of every child's intelligence.

Interaction with Cybernetic Symbol Systems. With the advent and spread of Internet access, mass media are becoming more and more interactional in nature. Children can tap into their home computers, bring up education databases, surf the net, write and receive e-mail, and participate in group chats and their own on-line entertainment. This type of activity is far from a passive experience.

Future innovations no doubt will bring the interactivity of the Internet to television as well, drastically changing the nature of the medium. Children will become able to respond immediately to shows they see, communicate with fellow viewers, and even have some input on the programming itself. When this happens, TV watching will become a far more active process than it is now. It will give children real control over instantaneous electronic modes of thought and communication. In addition to this impending change, there are other things that television programmers and parents may do to ensure that TV watching is an active, stimulating experience for children. I note these in the guidelines below.

Social Participation. Modern media afford children unique opportunities to share their thoughts and feelings with other people. Television, radio, musical recordings, and films all lend themselves to joint viewing or listening. Children usually watch TV, listen to music, and go to movies in the company of other people. This opens a door to valuable shared experience and communication.

While watching a show with parents or friends, a child receives guidance, information, feedback, opinions, and new ideas. After the show, children often talk about the meaning of the events that they have just seen. This also may happen when two or more children have seen the same show separately from one another. Children commonly share pop music that they have heard through allusions, "musical quotations," dancing, and other symbolic gestures. Only the mass media could cre-

ate points of reference that are so readily understood by large populations of youth. These widely shared points of reference create an almost
universal language among young people. Such a language, when used
inventively, can advance young people's friendships and improve their
social skills.

Our task as educators, parents, and citizens is to come to grips with the
special nature of mass media, guard against the intrinsic risks of each,
and exploit the strengths and advantages of each. In the light of the
risks and opportunities that I have identified, I propose the following
guidelines for the use and production of mass media. They pertain to
the formal properties of media—the McLuhanesque dimensions—such
as the ways that the media present information, engage audiences, and
shape the nature of audience participation.

1. *Make it an active experience for the child.* Any media presentation can
be transformed from a passive to an active experience. There are many
ways that adults can encourage children to process the information actively
in a media presentation. Prior to the presentation, the adult can prime the
child to participate by posing questions that link the presentation to the
child's own experience and interests. For example, a child who is about to
watch a family sitcom can be asked to notice ways in which the TV family is
similar or different, funnier or sadder, more or less organized, closer or
more distant, than the child's own family. These questions are likely to get
the attention of the child's other family members too, and the ensuing discussion is sure to enhance the child's social understanding. Or a child who
is about to go to a movie about baseball can be asked to notice whether the
movie captures any of the joys or frustrations that have accompanied the
child's own attempts at sports. And so on.

The point of such queries is to get children to increase their powers
of observation, inference, critical examination, and generalization—all
fundamental cognitive skills that will serve the child well in all areas of life.
The kinds of queries that prompt children to use these powers are not hard
to think up, and the particular query is not as important as the fact that it
has been asked. Children, in fact, may forget or ignore the exact request,
yet they will remain primed to watch the presentation with an observant
eye. After sufficient exposure to such queries, children begin spontaneously asking similar questions of themselves. In this way, they internalize

the questioning process; in effect, they prime themselves. When this occurs, the child acquires an enduring learning disposition that enables the child to process information powerfully wherever the child encounters it.

After the show, parents and teachers can ask children further questions about the presentation, solicit children's own questions about it, and point out things that the child may have missed.

2. *Make it a limited experience for the child.* No matter how well we prime children to extract valuable lessons from a media presentation, the experience still cannot substitute for real-life individual or social activity. Children learn best by doing and participating in social relationships. Actively processing a media presentation can build a child's arsenal of skills and understanding by adding ideas, facts, language, and insight. But the foundations of the arsenal always come from real life, where children tackle actual challenges, communicate with other people, exchange positive and negative emotions, learn from successes and failures, receive direct feedback on their own actions, and receive real rewards or sanctions based on their own conduct.

No secondhand media presentation—whether in the form of books, films, TV shows, music recordings, or computer software—can deliver the forceful lessons of real-life experiences. The lesson for parents is simple: do not let children spend too large a proportion of their waking time consuming mass media presentations. Limit the child's exposure to television to no more than two hours per day, part of which (perhaps half) should be educational in nature. This is the amount of TV that research has shown most conducive to children's intellectual growth.[15] (In fact, children who watch up to two hours per day of TV tend to read at least as much as children who watch less TV—and, of course, they read more than children who watch more.) Make sure that there is plenty of time in the child's schedule for family life, schoolwork, sports, friendships, the arts, hobbies, helping out, and other extracurricular activities. When the child has reached the limit that you set, turn the TV off. This may sound far-fetched in today's world, but it is not science fiction. It can be done.

3. *Make it an integrative experience for the child.* Modern media combine dramatic story lines with music, dance, and spectacular visuals. In fact, the capacity to produce and broadcast captivating combinations of sounds and images is at the heart of modern media's market appeal. This is one of

modern media's strongest assets: a breakthrough in presenting information to audiences in ways that they find instantly compelling.

The commercial value of such combinations is clear. Glitzy ads that tell their stories through compelling sounds and images have sold millions of cars, candy bars, and tubes of toothpaste. Now it is time to exploit the educational potential of modern media's capacity to combine narrative, song, dance, and artful images.

Again, there are many things that parents and teachers can do in order to wrest maximum educational benefits from this natural capacity of modern media. The time for doing these things is during the early childhood years, when children are first exploring their many intelligences and forming lasting attitudes about what they are good at and interested in. Encouraging a young child to pursue as many avenues of endeavor as possible will broaden the child's intellectual horizons. Showing children how they may integrate diverse modes of intelligence—song and dance, logic and image, narrative and social understanding—will expand the power and flexibility of the child's overall intellectual approach.

Each mode of intelligence is important in itself, and it is in the child's best interests to develop as many modes as fully as possible. Beyond this, learning to combine the modes creatively will enable the child to conquer challenges that would resist the application of a single mode alone. This is why scientists sketch visual models along with their logical formulas; why musical composers often work with a color, a picture, or a tale in mind; and why business leaders like to see flipcharts and graphics along with verbal presentations. High achievement in any area breaks the boundaries of a single, rigid mode of thought. It relies on integration and synthesis of diverse inputs.

In order to foster young children's use and integration of multiple modes of intelligence, parents and teachers can ask children to write down what they have observed on screen; they can encourage children to act out stories that they have read or listened to on radio; they can give children familiar materials to use as symbolic props in reenactments of the stories; they can encourage young children to sing and dance along with a TV or radio show; they can ask children to draw a scene from a movie that they have seen or from a music recording that they have heard; they can show children how to write a song or a poem about a scene that they have watched; they can show children how to test, try out, and scientifically experiment with ideas that they have seen presented in fictional forms. Methods such as these are limited only by a parent's or teacher's imagination.

3.   *Make it a deep experience for the child.* Unlike the use and integration of multiple modes of intelligence, the deepening of children's experience does not come naturally to modern media presentations. This is one goal that requires people concerned with children's development to work around, rather than with, the formal properties of modern media. In the age of TV, media programming has become too fast-paced and too dominated by abrupt transitions to allow for a full treatment of ideas. In-depth coverage in a modern media presentation is the exception rather than the rule, and market forces will always resist any significant changes on this score.

With conscious and organized effort, citizens can exert some market forces of their own. They can, for example, boycott particularly superficial shows and selectively patronize the more satisfying ones. In addition, there are immediate things that a child's parents and teachers can do to provide the child with more than junk food for thought. They can add information and context to the media stories that young people see; comment critically about lightweight treatments of complex ideas; help children explore the background of a media story that has interested them; discuss the human element in a fast action story, the deeper meaning underlying the headlines, the truth in an account distorted by a superficial treatment; steer children away from the most egregious cases of mindless entertainment; and steer children toward shows that reveal a bit of life's complexity.

For example, a child transfixed by cartoon accounts of rocket ships and space travel could learn about the egoism and vulnerability of space heroes by reading Tom Wolfe's *The Right Stuff* or by seeing *Apollo 13*. A child captivated by televised feats of derring-do would gain an appreciation of the effort and preparation that goes into such feats by reading the biographies of trapeze artists and circus performers. Such biographies also convey the possible pitfalls of dangerous feats, the courage and skill required, and the fears of even the boldest performer. A child who loves war stories could gain a more accurate understanding by reading books about the history and consequences of the wars portrayed in the media presentation. A parent or teacher could fill in the child's knowledge with their own accounts, opening the way to conversations about how and why people fight with one another, about why people act the way that they do during difficult times, about the meaning of war and peace, victory and defeat, reconciliation and peace. A superficial entertainment episode is thus transformed into a valuable learning occasion.

4.   *Make it into a social experience for children.* This is a goal that comes naturally to modern media. It is not difficult to find ways of making a child's experiences with television, radio, movies, and music into a social event. The social participation can bring with it many developmental benefits for the child, although there are some limits to these benefits if the sociality is allowed to detract from the child's independent work.

Parents should seize the opportunity to watch and discuss media shows with their children, but parents and teachers also should be careful to balance children's mass media exposure with independent reading, problem solving, and other activities that demand individual work from children. The balance between the social and the individual is not an either-or matter. For example, a parent or teacher can get children to read the print version of stories that they have recently watched with friends. In this way, the same narrative material can become a bridge between children's social and private worlds, and the child's communication skills and personal insights may be brought to bear on one another, to the betterment of both.

5.   *Make it available in electronic form.* I am hardly the first person to promote children's use of computers, yet it is so important that it bears saying again: all children today deserve access to computers and the extended powers of intelligence that they bring. Through computers, children gain unmatched control of mass media. They can find information, select and modify their entertainment, manipulate symbols, communicate instantly across vast distances, and create their own flow of ideas and images. Nothing like this has ever been possible in the history of childhood. The thinking of all those who experience these new powers when young will be transformed in ways that we now can only imagine.

Cognitive scientists have argued about the nature of this transformation, and (as in any science) there are serious disagreements on the matter. Some believe that the transformation will be a leap unlike any that has preceded it; others believe that it will be pretty much the same kind of cognitive advance that new cultural tools always make possible, whether the new tool is a pencil, a printing press, or a slide rule. This is a debate that I am in no position to resolve. There is only one point that I wish to make here, and I believe that the point is both incontestable and portentous:

computers introduce children to a form of modern mass media that is always interactive. The child at the keyboard must do something in order for something else to happen. What is more, it turns out that in most cases children do quite a bit to make something happen on a computer, and much of what they do is social in nature: sending e-mail messages, writing a document with a friend, sharing a game with someone in cyberspace, showing a younger sibling (or an older parent!) how to tap into a database.

It is true that most education software now on the market for children is trivial (though there are signs that the craft of writing educational software may be gradually improving). In any case, this pertains to what I have referred to as media content. Insofar as the nature of the medium is concerned, computers and the Internet constitute an educational experience par excellence for children. They introduce children to fertile modes of exploration and inquiry. These new media offer children limitless chances to express and test ideas, extend their knowledge and understanding, and discover intellectual possibilities that they have never imagined. The excitement of all this is readily apparent to children; a child's motivation to learn is rarely a problem when computers are the medium of choice. Computer access should be treated as the intellectual birthright of every child in today's world—much like schooling has been for decades—and our communities should ensure that no child is denied access to this mind-enhancing resource because of economic disadvantage.

8

ENABLING A DISABLING SOCIETY

A person lives not only his own life as an individual but also the life of his epoch. . . . All sorts of personal aims, ends, hopes and prospects pass before the eyes of the individual, and out of these he derives the impulse to ambition and achievement. Now, if the life about him, his own time, seems to be at its core empty of food for aspirations; if he privately recognizes it to be hopeless, decrepit, meaningless . . . then, in such a case, a certain crippling of the personality is bound to occur.

THOMAS MANN, *The Magic Mountain*

The modern world in many ways is a wonderful place for a young person to grow up in. Medical science has cured almost all the feared diseases that once ravaged legions of children. Agricultural advances and nutritional knowledge have given most of today's young a balanced diet superior to that which even the wealthiest enjoyed a mere century ago. A great many youngsters have access to clothing and shelter that are wildly luxurious in comparison to those available to previous generations of children. Because of the improvements in medicine, nutrition, and shelter, young people's life expectancies are rising with each new generation.

Nor are the blessings of modern living limited to the physical and material. New horizons in travel, education, entertainment, and employment are opening daily as technology rapidly brings our world ever closer together. Communication with anybody anywhere is only a push of the dial tone or a flip of the computer switch away. All of these changes have made the world a more manageable place for young people with the energy and will to tackle it.

Indeed, many of today's young are doing brilliantly, fulfilling their aspirations, having fun, and flourishing in all regards. But the world also is full of youngsters who are not thriving, as they should, from the benefits of modern living.

Every epoch poses its own risks and challenges for young people. Past generations of youth have been decimated by war, disease, and civil turmoil. Although such tribulations have by no means vanished from the earth, they are not the most common perils endangering young people growing up now. Hazards of this particular cultural moment are less palpable. They center on a condition of the spirit, a condition that I have called demoralization in my writings.[1] I mean the term in both of its original meanings: a loss of aspiration and a cynical attitude toward moral belief. I have seen the signs of demoralization among many young people from virtually all economic strata and cultural backgrounds. In my view, demoralization among the young is a direct consequence of the low standards and expectations that they see in the eyes of the adults around them. It grows in the absence of the kind of inspiring guidance that could be provided by a community with a strong sense of purpose, as embodied in a youth charter.

The Demoralizing Culture and the Disabling Society That Hosts It

During the past half-century or so, our society has changed dramatically with respect to its beliefs and practices regarding children. Some changes have been for the good: children's physical health and material advantages have improved, more attention has been paid to their special needs, and more efforts have been directed at protecting them from dangers and abuse. But some other changes have not been for the good. In homes and schools, standards for children's behavior have fallen markedly for well over a generation.[2] Expectations for their achievement has progressively diminished as well. One of the most striking features of this expectational change is that children now are often treated as disabled when they are simply acting like children.

One of the themes in this chapter, as in the rest of the book, is that children quickly pick up messages from everything in society that affects them. They are acute observers of the social world, continually interpreting the events that concern them. Practices that convey the belief that children are helpless invalids in a threatening world can shape children's views of themselves and their futures in negative ways that can override any beneficial effects that the practice might have.

For example, a policy to classify a child as disabled and medicate him at the first sign of disruptive emotion has the direct effect of calming the child and the indirect effect of conveying to the child a message that he requires outside help—that he would not be able to calm himself down without treatment. The indirect message can leave a more long-lasting influence on the child than the direct treatment. Moreover, children who are categorized as disabled in order to get them more attention and other privileges carry around the burden of a label that eventually may erode their self-confidence. The damaging effects of the label can outweigh the benefits of the additional privileges that they receive.

The prevailing beliefs and practices of a society, and especially those that focus on children, play a key role in shaping a young person's sense of purpose. Inspiring beliefs and practices can nourish young people's aspirations and expand their sense of what they can accomplish and contribute to the world beyond themselves. Disabling beliefs and practices can demoralize young people, starve their aspirations, and ultimately diminish their potentials for accomplishment and service.

In the following section, I discuss a set of societal beliefs and practices that unnecessarily disable many children by the very practice of mislabeling them as disabled. These beliefs and practices are currently so powerful that even individual parents who have doubts about them find it impossible to resist them. The disability dragnet that is sweeping up so many young children has become a major obstacle to our essential task of imparting high standards across the generations. It is impossible to expect much of a child whom everyone, including the child, believes to be incapacitated.

My hope is that as the information that I present below becomes better known and understood by the public, parents will join together with other citizens, in youth charter fashion, to challenge the established diagnostic and treatment practices that are taking so many children in the wrong direction. A parent alone always will have difficulty determining whether her judgment is clouded by bias. (For example, a parent may run the risk of resisting a legitimate diagnosis out of denial or misdirected pride in her child.) But when a parent can communicate freely with fellow parents, teachers, counselors, clergy, coaches, and others who know children well, the parent can find a balanced perspective on this emotionally charged matter. At that point, parents will be able to join in a collaborative relationship with teachers and specialists to act wisely on behalf of their children.

Some of the beliefs that I discuss next have resulted in the choice to medicate large numbers of children for diagnosed learning disabilities such as attention deficit disorder. I wish to state unequivocally that a qualified physician is the only person who is in a proper position to make a judgment about whether a particular child requires medication. Parents who have questions about whether their own child should start or stop taking any medication should always consult their child's pediatrician.

As a matter of general policy, however, medical experts do not always agree among themselves as to the wisest solution for the burgeoning numbers of children who are now diagnosed as learning disabled. Some have expressed concerns that we may be overprescribing medication to populations of youngsters (particularly boys) who may be simply acting unruly or are bored. Such youngsters may be in need of better behavioral and educational guidance, either in conjunction with medication or in lieu of it.

This is a sort of discussion that I believe citizens should participate in—a discussion among parents, teachers, pediatricians, and others who work with young people, reflecting on the kinds of solutions that will best serve children in the long run. In such a discussion, citizens can share information about children's learning disabilities and medication (what is known, and what do the experts advise?), and they can help one another place the problem in perspective and avoid dangerous excesses. A youth charter meeting can create a forum for such a discussion, opening up a confusing and worrisome issue for joint analysis and sound judgment.

Disability and Ability

Our society treats large numbers of its young people as disabled. Physical disabilities, of course, are nothing new. In any society, there are always some young people who are afflicted by blindness, deafness, paralysis, and so on. Fortunately, modern medicine has reduced the numbers of young people with physical disabilities, through prevention, treatment, or prosthetic devices. Moreover, the field of physical therapy has moved in the enlightened direction of urging young people who do have physical disabilities to tackle in whatever way possible all the challenges of a normal life—in other words, to resist succumbing to the belief that such conditions are handicaps.

Yet as the negative significance of physical disabilities has declined, new and less tangible ones have risen to take their place. Now there are psychological syndromes such as the attentional and learning "disabilities" that go under acronyms such as ADD (attention deficit disorder) and ADHD (attention deficit/hyperactivity disorder). There are psychiatric syndromes such as childhood depression, obsessive-compulsive disorder, conduct disorder, eating disorder, and bipolar (manic-depressive) disorder. In addition, there are emotional syndromes that are tagged as phobias or anxieties of one sort or another (for example, "school phobia" or "test anxiety").

The symptoms of such disorders are almost always behavioral: wandering attention, poor self-regulation, disorganization, easy excitability, emotional outbursts, susceptibility to extended states of boredom and frustration, and disruptive social conduct. In a very small minority of cases, a child with such symptoms may have a history of neurological damage or some other physical trauma, but by and large, the behavioral "disabilities" show up as nonphysical, nonspecific disorders, such as learning problems, disruptive conduct, or emotional dysfunctions.

The variety of these complaints is so wide and so idiosyncratic that clinical categories are notoriously fuzzy, often merging into one another. Even within diagnostic categories, symptoms are loosely connected, often sharing little resemblance among themselves. As a result, there is a great deal of error in the diagnosis of young people's behavioral problems.

Some who have studied this problem believe that the sloppiness of the clinical categories has led to a widespread overdiagnosis of syndromes such as ADHD and the other learning disabilities. A 1996 blue ribbon Carnegie task force concluded, "Students identified as having specific learning disabilities account for slightly more than half of all those in special education. There is growing evidence that many of these children may not belong in special education at all. Some are referred by well-intentioned teachers who believe that a special education placement is the only way to get extra help for students running into academic trouble."[3]

A large proportion of claims under the Americans with Disabilities Act stem from diagnoses of learning and attentional disabilities. Over 2 million American children (out of a population of 38 million) are now treated for ADHD with regular doses of methylphenidate (the best-known brand of which is Ritalin). In 1995, 350 million doses of methylphenidate were consumed by children in the United States alone. Because boys are usually more restless in class than girls, they are more likely to be diagnosed with learning attentional disorders. As a consequence, over 12 percent of the young male population between the ages of six and fourteen is now being given methylphenidate.[4] This has prompted one genetics scholar to comment, "I'm quite convinced little boys are getting put on it because they're little boys."[5]

These numbers have grown fourfold since 1990, in a steadily increasing trend that continues. If these trends are extrapolated out for only three more years, over a quarter of our young male population will be taking regular doses of methylphenidate by the turn of the century.

Among mental health professionals, the most common explanation for this rapid rise is that we are finally able to diagnose a long-standing, disabling neurological condition. According to the conventional wisdom in the field, the condition lies deep within the brain. Not too long ago, in fact, ADD was commonly referred to as "minimal brain damage." That term went out of use because, for the vast majority of "learning-disabled" youth, there are no signs of brain cells that are actually injured. Nevertheless, the neurological view was buttressed by a well-known 1990 psychiatric study that found, among ADD patients, low rates of chemical activity in areas of the brain that control attention and motor skills.[6] This finding led to the widely accepted conclusion that ADD is a physiological brain problem requiring chemical treatment.

Often citing the results of the 1990 study, mental health professionals generally have ruled out the idea that ADD might be a behavioral problem with a behavioral solution. For example, one leader in the field has said, "This shows that it is clearly a neurological problem, not just something that comes from poor habits or not being raised right."[7] Among the public, the neurological interpretation has met with little resistance, in part because the hard science evidence seems convincing and in part because so many distinguished authorities in the mental health field support the view.

In addition, society has made it rewarding for parents to believe in physiological roots of this newly diagnosed "brain disorder." Parents find that they and their children have a much easier road if their children are considered to be disabled by a deep-seated neurological affliction than if they are simply considered to be poorly behaved in ways that could be corrected by better guidance. One strong incentive is that a disability diagnosis opens the door for special privileges. In many school districts, children who are put into a learning disabled category receive more personalized instructional time than other children. Such incentives can have a powerful effect on parents with difficult children. Also, older students benefit from extra time on tests, including on vocational and college entrance exams that may be critical for the future. Such incentives can have a powerful effect on the children themselves.

An incentive for parents on public assistance is that families whose children are diagnosed as disabled are eligible for additional payments. This financial increment has led many parents, against their own better judgment, to seek learning disabled classifications for their children.[8] One news account quotes a mother of an eight-year-old boy as saying that, despite her misgivings, she allowed her son to be classified as disabled because "we need the money." "He isn't really disabled," the mother said. "He just wants things his way. I just think he needs help in terms of his attitude."[9]

It also may provide emotional comfort for some to think that children are acting up because of unavoidable brain disorders. Some may think that if a child's problems are behavioral or attitudinal in nature, the parent must be to blame. In fact, this would be a faulty inference. Although it is true that a child's behavior and attitudes are influenced by adults, it is certainly *not* true that the parents are to blame whenever a child acts badly or has trouble learning. There are many other influences on children's behavior and attitudes—influences that parents can do little about. Most parents realize this, but the emotional relief of attributing children's problems to deep-seated physiological causes may provide yet another incentive for believing the neurological explanation.

Finally, drugs such as methylphenidate often do seem to work, at least in a limited, short-term way. They can succeed in calming difficult children. They can help children attend to their tasks in school and elsewhere, particularly if the tasks are simple and repetitive. They can offer some temporary balm for parents and teachers whose children are driving them crazy. They can prevent the disruption of group activities by children who cannot or will not be controlled by other means. For children who truly need such medication, such drugs have been shown to have value. In the cases of children who do have verified brain damage (a small minority of the children who are now diagnosed ADD or ADHD), medical treatments prescribed by qualified physicians are entirely appropriate.

But the limits of the medication need to be understood. Methylphenidate has been described as a short-acting drug that wears off after four hours or so. Unless medicated again, children may return quickly to their disruptive behavior and impulsive attitudes. Over a relatively short period of time (perhaps months), children may habituate to the medication.

The most serious limitation is that methylphenidate seems to facilitate only a narrow spectrum of intellectual effort. It helps some distractable children stay on task longer than they otherwise would, but there is no evidence that medicated children learn to take a particularly thoughtful or skillful approach to those tasks, or that the medication leads to improvements in children's higher-order thinking.[10] The drug's positive effects seem limited to children's performances on tasks that require little serious thought. This is hardly the royal road to intellectual growth.

When medication is properly prescribed, there are real benefits for some children. Yet none of these benefits implies that we should label healthy young people as neurologically disabled and then conclude that only drugs can solve their learning difficulties. By so doing, we are robbing children of the capacity to regulate their own internal states. We are undermining their confidence in their own internal control mechanisms; we are removing opportunities for learning how to cope with frustration and challenge; we are communicating the message that they are not responsible for their own behavior and attitudes; and we are placing them in a drugged state where they may be unable to use their highest intellectual facilities. All these effects may create a sense of dependence on the medication and a sense of distrust in the child's own capacities. Acquiring a drug dependence is harmful for anyone. During the formative years, it can be psychologically deadly.

Only a small minority of children suffers the kinds of neurological damage (tumors, concussions, cell loss from oxygen deprivation and other traumata) that can be found through X rays or other types of brain scan. For most children diagnosed with ADD, there are no signs of physiological impairment, in either the brain or anywhere else in the central nervous system.

In general, the scientific evidence for neurological causation is far weaker than many in the mental health field have claimed. Simply showing low chemical activity in selected spots of the brain does not mean that there is any physical damage or deficit there. In fact, it may well be that the low brain activity is caused by the child's erratic behavior rather than being the source of it. The more we know about the brain and behavior, the more we realize how difficult it is to determine causal directions between the two—especially where, as with ADD, there are rarely signs of physical damage. The *New England Journal of Medicine*, which published the influential 1990 study, took the unusual step of accompanying the study with an editorial that expressed similar reservations.

The special privileges that young people receive from being designated as impaired are not worth the price that these young people are paying for those privileges. I am referring here to the psychological price of being told that one's own inner states and social behavior are beyond one's control. No temporary periods of calm can justify the enduring emotional dependence that could result from this disabling belief.

A research assistant of mine reported that on one typical morning just before school began, she was observing a group of elementary schoolchildren running around their classroom hopelessly out of their teacher's control. My assistant stopped one of the boys to ask why they were acting so wild. "You're just getting us before our medication," the boy replied. "Of course, we're going to be climbing the walls." I have heard many versions of this same story. The children have become convinced that bad behavior is not their fault, and that a chemical treatment is the only answer. They are learning to take drugs rather than to take responsibility for their actions.

Members of the medical and scientific communities have expressed their own concern. A pediatric neurologist warned of the danger inherent in having "these children believe that they have something wrong with their brains that makes it impossible for them to control themselves without using a pill, [and] having the most important adults in their lives, their parents and teachers, believe this as well."[11] A study by psychiatrist Peter S. Jensen was summarized in the following manner:

"Stimulant medication is seen as a 'magic bullet' by most children and their parents. . . . If a youngster's behavior does not improve, parents assume that the medication dose should be increased. . . . Children often disavowed any responsibility for their behavior and claimed they needed a 'good pill' to control themselves."[12]

Medication for children can be prescribed quickly and capriciously, for a host of ever-expanding reasons. I learned of one girl who was given methylphenidate because she complained of feeling different from her closest friends, most of whom had been on the drug for several months. When I heard of this, I assumed that it was an extreme case, but teachers have told me that they have heard of even more far-fetched reasons.

Methylphenidate is only one of the psychoactive or psychostimulant drugs that doctors are prescribing for young people these days. Some children are given dexadrine, a true amphetamine, for ADHD symptoms. (Drugs that stimulate adults have the effect of calming children, although it frequently is a short-term effect only.) Antidepressants like imipramine are given for youth depression and eating disorders. Prozac and Zoloft are prescribed for obsessive-compulsive disorders (extreme messiness or compulsive neatness, lack of concentration, general disorganization). Although none of these drugs is as frequently used as methylphenidate, together they substantially add to the total number of young people who are taking medication for psychological problems.

The dependence that an overly drug-based approach creates can be contagious. It can spread to the way that children respond to other kinds of physical and psychological problems. Teachers and school nurses have told me that their students now consume vast quantities of cold medicines and other over-the-counter drugs at the slightest discomfort.

There is also a real concern that chemical dependence of any kind can lead to substance abuse with alcohol, tobacco, and illegal drugs. Methylphenidate is a powerful, amphetamine-like drug that some young people consider to be a "high." The International Narcotics Control Board of the United Nations has reported that worldwide, many young people now are illegally trafficking in methylphenidate. It seems obvious that this is a route that could begin with a legal prescription for ADHD and end with illegal use of harder and deadlier drugs.

A society that treats so many young people as disabled is well on the way to disabling itself. A society that gives parents rewards for labeling their children as disabled corrupts parents' natural desires to raise strong and vibrant children. A society that gives children drugs rather than guidance for their behavioral problems abandons children's developmental needs in favor of a short-term fix.

For the minority of children with certifiable brain damage, medical treatment under the guidance of a qualified physician is warranted. For most children, however, the slower route is the surer one: teaching them how to manage their feelings, take responsibility for their actions, control themselves, and stick with tasks until they have completed them.

The first step along this route is to convince children that they *can* do all these things. When a respected adult gives a child the message that only a drug can do these things for him, the adult has taken the child a giant step backward along this essential route. To get us back in the right direction, I propose the following guidelines, which can be implemented in any community through youth charter discussions:

1.   *Avoid the terms* disability *and* disabled *as much as possible.* I do not mean this proposal as an exercise in denial or as some "rhetorically correct" euphemism. The real fact is that no living child is ever wholly and permanently disabled. There are always useful and self-fulfilling things that any child can learn to do, whatever the child's condition. Encouraging the child to make the effort will expand the range of what the child will learn to do. Discouraging the child by calling the child "disabled" restricts the range of the child's possibilities. The former is the path to hope and satisfaction, the latter the path to defeatism and demoralization.

2.   *Keep diagnostic categories closely linked to specific symptoms and behavior.* A heterogeneous grab-bag such as ADD or ADHD is too inclusive and too imprecise to be of much use. In fact, such categories always become misused. The tent is so large and so open that everyone finds a way to get in. This leads to sloppy and capricious treatment programs, such as the overmedication of large numbers of children. The best basis for clinical categories is a sign of physiological damage. Failing that, reliable perceptual-motor tests should be used, and results directly linked to the diagnosis. Under no circumstances should clinical diagnoses be made on the basis of children's self-reports, or on the sole basis of speculations by parents, teachers, guidance counselors, and other laypeople.

3.   *Medication should be a last resort rather than a first resort. When needed, it should be combined with guidance, and its use should be ended as soon as a physi-*

cian deems it possible. A drug such as methylphenidate can help manage a child's difficult behavior in the short run. If all else fails, it can serve a useful purpose when administered under the direction of a physician. But no drug can provide the child with the skills that the child needs for the long run. In fact, drug treatments can retard the acquisition of such skills by convincing the child that the skills are unattainable or unnecessary, or by placing the child in a medicated condition that actually retards higher-order learning. The priority should be to provide the child with guidance and real learning opportunities. Medication should be used only where it is needed to serve these priorities, and only for as long as it is needed. This said, *no medication should ever be discontinued unless and until a physician so prescribes.* Methylphenidate is a serious drug, and every aspect of its use, including its cessation, must be monitored by a medical doctor.

4.   *Diminish the incentives that force parents to categorize their children as disabled.* No educational system should be allowed to make a learning disabled track the only, easiest, or best route for a child to receive personalized instruction. No competitive testing system should force students to claim falsely psychological disorders in order to get an even break. No public assistance program should reward parents for labeling their children as neurologically impaired when the parent knows that the child is simply acting up. These are all distortions of public policy that seriously harm the intended recipients of the supposed benefits.

5.   *When children are struggling with learning problems or other mental "disabilities," make the serious effort required to improve learning skills.* This should be the first resort. It is the only genuine solution to children's learning problems and can be accomplished only in the child's home and the school. Policymakers should support such training efforts and ensure that nothing they do interferes with them.

Attention can be cultivated, much like any other intellectual and emotional skill. It is part of the general capacity of learning how to learn that all children must master if they are to succeed. Adults can provide any child with the instruction and experiences that the child needs in order to learn how to learn.

Parents and teachers must work closely with a child who is having learning difficulties, in order to help the child acquire the motivation and personal discipline that make sustained attention possible. This is a child-rearing effort similar to any other. It requires patience, support, encouragement, and honest feedback to the child. Above all, it requires a long-term commitment to guide the child toward activities that will engage the child's abilities, rather than choosing the easier solution of medicating the child and chalking the child off as disabled. The commitment is worth the effort. There is no chemical treatment that can substitute for the kind of parental and teacher guidance that I discuss in Chapters 4 and 5, and I am sure that there never will be.

Treating capable children as disabled is only one part—albeit a dramatic one—of a longer story of lowered expectations for our society's young, a story that has been playing itself out for at least half a century. The lowering of expectations has been well intended, but that does not make it any less harmful to children's future prospects. There can be no effective youth charters in a society with low expectations for its children.

In our society's collective consciousness, children are often cast as victims of a stressful world. Perhaps understandably—given the very real hazards of modern living—we worry that their neighborhoods are unsafe, the airwaves are full of events that disturb them, both parents are working, their families may be breaking up, they are faced with too much pressure and not enough support in school, their lives are over-programmed, and they cannot handle any of it.

Well-meaning people have responded to such concerns with solutions that seem perfectly sensible on their face. In response to concerns about stress, many have "let up" on children by lowering standards for children's responsibilities in the home, their performance in school, and their conduct in the community. Lowering standards is indeed a response of sorts. After all, the most direct means of reducing a child's anxiety over a challenge is to remove the challenge. The problem is that children require challenges in order to develop effective skills. They require expectations of responsibility in order to develop character. They require opportunities for service in order to develop a sense of purpose.

Other responses to the concerns also have seemed reasonable on the surface, but none has accomplished its mission. Indeed, some are backfiring badly. Self-esteem boosting has replaced rigorous academic instruction in early education. Public schools have created a special education apparatus so large that it now accounts for the largest single instructional line in many town budgets. Teachers in some public schools routinely disallow any educational activities that could create competition and invidious comparisons among students, including extra expressions of student interest that might lead to outstanding achievement. As part of the effort to protect the feelings of less motivated students, we have gutted programs for the gifted.

Some of these responses may be necessary in some particular cases. My purpose here is not to contest each of them; rather it is to question the overall direction that these and similar responses are leading us toward. As a whole, the responses reflect a pessimistic societal view of children that portrays them as helpless, fragile, incompetent, and unreliable creatures who need protection above all else: protection from challenges, competition, responsibility, and anything else that might cause them frustration or injure their self-esteem. Responses of this sort exacerbate the problems rather than solving them, because they lead children toward self-defeating orientations such as negativity. Overall, such responses send a discouraging message that young people inevitably will find demoralizing.

We have tended to dwell on the predicaments that we assume young people are in: the pressures and obstacles that they face, their disadvantages, their disabilities. We have tended to overlook their positive aspirations, their ambitions, the possibilities that they all have to forge brilliant futures for themselves and their societies. We are too quick to feel sorry for the young for no good reason. We are not quick enough to help them make the most of their magnificent potentials—potentials that, tragically, can and will atrophy when left unexercised.

A society needs good sense in its approach to raising children, and it is not sensible to send messages of pity, dejection, and condescension to young people who are forming their initial attitudes about themselves and discovering their prospects in life. The psychological fruits of such messages will be self-pity, pessimism, and learned helplessness. These are deadly fruits at any age, and all the more so for young people who are just constructing their self-identities.

Any society worth living in communicates hope, confidence, and lofty expectations to its young. These are messages that bear the fruits of optimism and aspiration and produce hope rather than fear, courage rather than timidity, inspiration rather than cynicism. These are messages that promote success in life during childhood and beyond.

No society can solve its "youth problems" by dwelling on how hard it is to be a child in the society. The only productive response to these problems is to dwell on the opportunities that young people have. We know that some children will survive—and thrive—in the bleakest of circumstances. These are children with a strong sense of purpose—children who move forward toward their goals without letting hardships deter them. This is the capacity that we must help all children acquire. As in other real-world endeavors, a good offense makes the best defense.

Composing a Divided Society

Modern society has changed in another way that profoundly affects children. As many social historians have noted, it has become more oriented toward the individual and less toward communities as a whole. Modernism has elevated choice over tradition, rights over responsibilities, and liberty over solidarity.[13] The positive appeal of this shift has been its promise to enhance personal happiness. Its negative consequences has been its weakening of the bonds that enable people to live harmoniously together in a civilized society.

The orientation toward individualism has contributed to an air of divisiveness among people. It has fueled a general breakdown in the capacity of people to identify with one another across personal and subgroup differences. In turn, this has contributed to the lowering of expectations for children, because common standards are difficult to come by in an age of extreme individualism. If adults cannot agree on what they believe in, how can we expect children to follow a coherent direction or develop a sustaining sense of purpose?

Societal individualism and fragmentation contribute to low expectations for children by making it impossible for communities to develop shared standards for the behavior of the young. Without a set of standards that are widely accepted across the community, parents and teachers have little basis for deciding how, and in what direction, to guide a child. They have no yardstick by which to gauge a child's progress, and they have no common language that they can use to tell a child how to improve.

The vacuum of shared standards leaves parents and teachers all the more vulnerable to claims that their children are impaired or "disabled" in some mysterious way. Without an agreed-on sense of what to

expect from children at different ages, arbitrary and capricious judgments may be made about children who seem out of line by nebulous,
little-understood criteria. In the absence of widely shared standards,
how can a parent (especially a new parent) know if her son is simply
"acting like a boy" instead of acting like a child with brain damage? How
can a parent know what to expect from her child, what sort of guidance
to provide, and to what end?

And there is yet another side to the relationship between low expectations and individualism. Low expectations, by disabling children, contribute to the most extreme forms of individualism that have decimated
our communities. Children who never learn to control their own emotions, learn to solve their problems by taking medication or externaliz-
ing their problems rather than working on their social and intellectual
skills, and lose confidence in their own capacities have little to offer a
community. Instead, they dwell in a state of self-absorption and self-pity.
In the most disruptive cases, they remain a divisive force as they grow
older. The influence of this approach is showing up in soaring rates of
maladjustment among youth, in substance abuse, isolation, excessive
feelings of entitlement, underachievement, social deviance, and non-
participation in social and political institutions.[14] In this manner, so-
called disabled children will disable the society that disabled them—a
rough justice of sorts, although not one that should give those who care
about the society any satisfaction.

In the past few years, social scientists have rallied around the cause
of tempering our extreme individualism and restoring our sense of
community. One of the clarion calls was *Habits of the Heart,* published in
1985 by Robert Bellah and his colleagues.[15] Bellah made the point that
individualism without community participation leads to personal dis-
content, a loss of meaning in life, and an eventual disintegration of the
society itself.[16] There are many others signs of this disintegration.
Participation in social clubs, political organizations, civic associations,
the Red Cross, the Boy Scouts, and other organizations is declining.
What will bind together our social lives—indeed, what will provide
people with a fundamental sense of social responsibility—if we no
longer bother to engage in any collective activities with one another?

There are now many social scientists who have expressed these concerns. Bellah, Putnam, James Coleman, Amitai Etzioni, Peter Berger,
and Jean Eshtain are among the most prominent. These writers, most of
them sociologists or economists, see the big picture of macrosocial

trends, and they deserve credit for alerting us to a condition that threatens the future of our society. But they do not often look for the reasons that cause individual people to create, or at least to go along with, these macro societal trends. In order to understand the decline in social participation, we must understand why people no longer bother to do it. In order to understand the disintegration of our community life, we must understand why people have allowed this to occur. In order to propose solutions for both, we must find out what will make people willing and able to work together for a common purpose once again.

This brings us back to the problem that I address in this chapter and throughout this book. It is primarily a problem in human development. How can we foster in our young the capacity and desire to create a civilized social life for themselves and their society?

In many historical epochs, this developmental goal would not be seen as a problem. It would come naturally from strong societal traditions that themselves provide community solidarity and convey a sense of direction, meaning, and purpose to the younger generation. We are not living in such an epoch. Traditions and common values have been supplanted by critical questioning. Meaning and purpose have become endangered by rampant personal skepticism. Community solidarity has been decimated by a massive breakdown in people's abilities to identify with one another.

It does not need to be this way. Children raised with a sense of social responsibility will seek occasions to contribute to a collective life. They will find communities or create them where they do not already exist. They will identify with others despite surface differences. They will join with others to uphold shared standards and accomplish common purposes.

But children who are raised with low expectations, who are raised to think of themselves as disabled, who become dependent on external stimulation such as drugs and medication, who lose confidence in their own abilities to control themselves, and who spend their youth focusing on their own inner states will never be able to develop a strong sense of social responsibility. They will flounder in a state of self-absorption rather than moving beyond themselves to a larger societal goal.

If we wish to revitalize our society and ensure its future, we must make sure that its younger members have the capacity and desire to work together constructively. We can do this by communicating high common standards to every young person in our society. We must not be deterred by differences among ourselves or among individual children. All young people thrive on high standards, and all of them need a sense of common purpose if they are to create a satisfying collective life.

Communicating high common standards to the younger generation is the youth charter's primary mission. The work must be done everywhere in the home, the school, society, and all the agencies that concern themselves with young people's behavior. In this chapter I have focused on our society's conception of young people as beleaguered and its treatment of young people as disabled. I have rejected this pessimistic approach and proposed a more positive one that aims to build inspiration rather than resignation in the young. In the following chapter, I focus on how our legal system could be used to support, rather than hinder, the youth charter mission of conveying high common standards to all youth.

What about poverty and its role in unjustly cutting down the dreams of talented young people all over the world? When I give lectures about the youth charter in academic circles, fellow scholars from fields such as sociology inevitably protest that the youth charter's emphasis on standards and expectations gives short shrift to the macroeconomic conditions—in particular, poverty—that are really at the heart of the problem. As I have noted on several occasions in this book, a community youth charter should play a role in making opportunities available to disadvantaged youth. Economic justice and charity are essential principles in any community worth preserving, and they are entirely consistent with the message of a youth charter.

Still, I do not deny that the main focus of the youth charter approach is on beliefs rather than material conditions, because a hard look at the facts reveals that poverty, however wrong it is in itself, is not the only risk of today's young. The facts are as follows: Many children who have been raised in poverty, now and in the past, have done as well as any other children on the planet. In fact, during times of severe economic deprivation—the Great Depression, the famines and forced immigrations of the nineteenth century—records show that many young people thrived.[17] Conversely, we know that many children of the wealthy fall into swamps of self-indulgence, become immobilized, and sink into despair. High standards and a sense of purpose are better predictors of youth success than affluence. These essential ingredients are in short supply today. Of course we must do everything in our power to combat poverty wherever it exists. But we cannot stop there. We must work to raise the intellectual and moral standards, as well as the living standards, of all our children.

Like every one of us, young people need a sense of purpose to bind their lives and move them forward. A sense of purpose requires something outside the self to believe in: a goal, a mission, a devotion to others, a faith, a dedication to a larger cause. It can only be fostered in a climate of high standards and expectations. In today's cultural climate, it has become difficult for many young people to find something to believe in. The predominant cultural messages that we give our children encourage them to turn inward rather than to develop their talents and search for an inspiring purpose to dedicate their energies to.

Unfortunately, most current social policy efforts on behalf of young people wholly ignore the standards and expectations that our society imparts to young people. Many of these efforts unintentionally impart counterproductive messages by suggesting that young people's destinies are beyond their own control. They externalize every youth problem by suggesting that antisocial behavior, underachievement, and self-destructive actions stem from poverty rather than from the young person's own choices. Not only is this an entirely demoralizing message, but it also fails to provide children with any way to avoid trouble or improve their chances in life. Only high standards and a sense of purpose can do that. Hence my advocacy of a youth charter approach.

9

GOVERNMENT:
ITS PROPER ROLE

A friend asked me why I would include a chapter on government in a book about how parents, teachers, and other community members can work together on behalf of the young. The government is so far away, she commented; its actions and policies seem many steps removed from the kinds of youth charter discussions that people could have about standards for children's behavior; and, in any case, government is not something that people in local communities could do much about.

My friend's questions exemplify the reasons that I needed to write this chapter. There is a feeling among many citizens that government is just one more external force that is beyond their control. About all they can expect, if they are lucky, is that they may manage to steer clear of it, except maybe around tax time or if they ever reach the age of social security. Aside from this attitude's implications for our sense of citizenship in a democracy—after all, *we* are the government, or at least that is the way it was supposed to be—it conveys a naiveté about the ways that government power can shape our most intimate family practices. In modern times, governmental power increasingly has been wielded in the name of children.

Virtually all government action on behalf of youth is directed toward worthy goals—in particular, the support, protection, and education of children who need or can benefit from such services. Without governmental support of these and other essential services, children would suffer. At the same time, government does not always act in a way that promotes high standards and positive expectations among young people. Nor does it always act in a way that promotes family relations or community solidarity. When this happens, the principles behind a community youth charter can be eroded. Fortunately, in a democracy, citizens can do something about it, but first they must become aware of the problem. This chapter highlights some key areas where government action should be improved if it is to contribute to, rather than detract from, a community's efforts to build an effective youth charter.

Government Intrusion into Family Matters

On March 26, 1997, the following story appeared in the *Boston Globe*. Dr. Bobbie Sweitzer, an anesthesiologist and mother of two children, was cited for neglect by the Massachusetts Department of Social Services (DSS). An anonymous telephone call had informed the department that Dr. Sweitzer had briefly left her children in her car while she dropped off film at a local store: "She was gone less than two minutes, activated the remote alarm and opened the windows a crack before she left, and watched the car as she walked into the all-glass entryway of the store." The department never spoke with Dr. Sweitzer. Instead, it sent her a form letter saying that "the state had found reasonable cause to support the allegation(s)." A spokesperson for the state said, "It's wrong to leave your kids in a car for any length of time." Dr. Sweitzer waged a lengthy legal process to clear her name. After spending $15,000 in fees for psychologists and lawyers, she managed to obtain a reversal of the ruling on grounds of due process. But she pointed out that most parents could not afford to get such relief: "If you don't have the ability to spend thousands of dollars to fight, you end up getting lost in the system." Indeed, a story in the next day's *Globe* revealed that it had become standard operating procedure for the department to cite parents without speaking with them or, for that matter, with any other people connected with the child who is considered to be at risk.

This is no small operation: the Massachusetts DSS issues about twenty-five thousand citations for neglect and abuse a year, in a state with a population of little over 4 million. Moreover, my impression from visiting other parts of North America is that this is neither an extreme nor an unusual case.

During my talks to parents' groups, this issue often comes up when I discuss the subject of disciplinary practices in the home. My position is that discipline of a nonviolent sort is essential for communicating and enforcing standards. I do not believe that discipline should mean spanking or other forms of corporal punishment. Disciplinary practices such as withholding privileges offer parents a safe, calm, and effective means of getting their point across. When I speak with parents' groups, I usually offer examples of how parents might withhold privileges from a child who has misbehaved. For a young child, the loss of dessert for a night or two can send a memorable message. For an older child, a TV set can be turned off, or the youngster can be grounded for a while.

Some of the responses that I get to these rather mild suggestions always surprise me. The general theme can be stated as, "Oh, I could never get away with something like that." "Why not?" I ask. "Because my child would object too strongly." "Well, why not hold the line and tough it out?" "He [she] would start complaining about it to everyone, about how unfair we are to him [her]. The school guidance counselor or psychologist could get involved. We could get visits from the social worker. It would lead to a big mess."

At first I had a hard time taking this sort of response seriously. My first reaction was that this was a ridiculous worry. If the child did complain to a social worker, surely the parent could explain what was going on and the matter would be immediately resolved. What kind of a counselor or social worker would intervene in a nonviolent parental disciplinary practice?

Yet nothing that I say seems to reassure the parents who raise these concerns, and these parents come from all strata of society. Now I take these concerns seriously, because in and of themselves the concerns seem to be undermining the parents' abilities to discipline their children effectively. Whatever the realities of the matter, the perception of outside interference is preventing these parents from acting responsibly in their own homes. The perception is widespread and compelling. We are reaching the point where many parents feel constrained in their child-rearing responsibilities by the representatives of government-supported agencies.

Defenders of an active government role in youth and family policy argue that interference is often needed because so many parents are incompetent or negligent. This is rather like saying that the Grand Inquisition was needed because small groups of heretics raided a few churches and stole some chalices. A government response to a problem should be specific, limited, and highly constrained, and it should work collaboratively with parents and not around them. Otherwise, a government can do more harm than good by assuming too much power and wielding it arrogantly. Imagine how a parent must feel when she receives a government citation about a child-rearing matter that she has never had the opportunity to discuss with anyone. What purpose could such an invasive action possibly serve? In all but the most stubborn cases of parental irresponsibility, the child would benefit far more from an open conversation between concerned adults.

There is no question that many parents today perceive modern government as arrogant, pernicious, distant, and frightening. To make matters worse, children sometimes recognize and exploit the breach between their parents and the government. In my meetings with parents, I have heard stories of young people who threaten to lodge complaints against their parents whenever the parents do not give them their way. I realize that many of these threats may be spurious, but the parents often do not view them as such, and that is the real damage. Perceptions of this sort, if not allayed, can erode the foundations of any community youth charter. Except in highly extreme cases, government should be seen as supporting rather than controlling parents in their child-rearing efforts.

This brings us to the matter of parents' rights. The virtue of a democracy is that people may take collective action to correct an errant governmental trend. In the area of parents' rights, this corrective action is now beginning. During 1996, twenty-eight of the fifty states were considering or had already enacted legislation to protect parents from governmental interference in the area of child-rearing. Such legislation can bolster a community youth charter if it advances the following principles:

1.   *Parents have the right to be informed of all actions taken with or on behalf of their children.* Parents should have full knowledge of any counseling, medical care, instruction, or professional advice given to their children. They should be informed ahead of time of any surveys or questionnaires that anyone may give concerning their child's personal or family life. Parents should be informed of any drug, alcohol, or sexual counseling that their child is given, including any discussions that their child may have with professionals concerning contraception, abortion, or medication of any sort.

In the long run, it is self-defeating for youth service agencies to operate any other way. Without the parents' understanding and support, the agency will be powerless to do anything beyond providing a quick fix for a short-term problem. A young person in trouble needs coordinated help that begins in the home and uses service agencies as allies. In some cases, help may not be available in the home. But even then all efforts must be made to keep parents informed and supportive. The worst thing for a child in trouble is a conflict between adults who should be joining together to help.

2.   *Parents have a right to review all educational materials that schools use with their children.* School professionals cannot act as if parents are busybodies who know nothing about schooling and will only get in the way if allowed access to the school. A school is part of a community, and it receives both its mandate and its effectiveness from that community. Without support on the home front, schools have little power to reach the hearts and minds of the young. In fact, school professionals do not have all the answers about how to educate children, even though often they act as if they do. Parents have a right to know everything that goes on at their child's school, and they have a right to make their voices heard.

3.   *Parents have a right to determine how, where, and by what standards their children are raised.* Parents should have primary authority to define the manner in which their family is organized. They should not be made to live in fear of arbitrary investigations, and they should be protected against the interference of government agencies unless there is clear and compelling cause. If an agency believes that a parent's child-rearing practices place a child at risk, it should inform the parent of this and offer the parent voluntary counseling and other resources. Except when a parent's actions clearly threaten the physical safety of a child and the parent shows no willingness or ability to guarantee the child's safety, it is inappropriate for an agency to intervene through legal sanctions. Government agencies should

work with parents rather than around or in opposition to them. Unless there is convincing, objective evidence that a parent is actually harming a child, government agencies, as a matter of policy, should support the parents' authority.

The Proper Role of Government in Youth and Family Affairs

There is no question that we live in an age of ambivalence about the role and value of government in our lives. Either explicitly or implicitly, most people today are aware of both the virtues and vices of government. Many recognize government's essential role in establishing order, guarding the populace against harm, helping those in need, and supporting education and other social services. Yet many also worry that government may slip into a mode of oppression, corruption, or just plain bungling. Many admit they depend on the benefits that government provides while at the same time complaining loudly about how their government is so intrusive that it has made their lives unbearable.

Perhaps such ambivalence is inevitable. It may be a realistic appraisal of an ancient historical tension between the protective and intrusive sides of governing. After all, government is about power, and humans have always had a capacity to use power for either beneficent or oppressive ends.

In one area of human affairs, however, this ancient tension is not so ancient. In fact, it made its first appearance only recently by historical standards. In the parlance of government, this area is called youth policy. It pertains to fundamental decisions about how young people should be raised, how they should be protected, and how they should be treated when they have done something wrong.

The reason that the tension is more recent in the area of youth policy is that the idea of government intervention in child rearing is a thoroughly modern one. In ancient times, a family had a virtual monopoly on policy regarding its own children. Parents made the basic decisions about how their children were raised and how they spent their time. Education was largely done in the home, with occasional help from the sacred texts, the church, the workplace, the farm, and the streets. Government had no role in schooling—or, for that matter, in anything else to do with youth (except, perhaps, when an army needed to be raised). The possibility that a government could be the source of either support or conflict with regard to one's children would have been unthinkable.

Today, everyone who brings up a child is deeply affected by government programs, policies, and laws. Government provides support for a host of agencies that serve families and children, including hospitals, schools, libraries, and police departments. Government passes laws that regulate much of a child's life. Government legal policy shapes the behavior of every child in society, no matter how remote the family's dwelling or how much it tries to distance itself from the modern world.

Many of the laws are protective in nature. There are laws against child abuse and neglect, laws regulating nutritional products for children, laws shielding young children from exposure to lead paint, laws against putting young children in cars without seat belts, laws that prevent children from drinking, smoking, and driving without a license, laws that ensure child support when families break up, and laws that mandate schooling until children have reached midadolescence. Other laws are meant to protect potential victims of the young. To this end, youth behavior is regulated by a host of juvenile justice statutes, school codes, and community ordinances.

With respect to the well-being of both children and society, there have been invaluable gains resulting from the increased presence of government in youth affairs. Many children have been protected by the responsible actions of public agencies, and many youngsters have been stopped from doing harm to themselves or others. My purpose here is not to argue against the presence of government in all matters related to children but rather to argue that government should always be responsive to the wisdom of the family and the community.

Insensitive government action, such as the DSS case that I described, usually is caused by some combination of lofty intentions, a failure in common sense, expediency, and arrogant stubbornness. Public agencies usually begin with the noble goal of protecting people from harm—harm caused to young people by others, harm caused by young people to themselves or others. Often the agencies do succeed in their mission. At other times they end up adding to the harm rather than preventing or alleviating it. The wrong kinds of government intervention create severe conflict within the child's community. When a government action collides with a parental action, a sense of division is created that undermines the child's respect for authority. The conflict and confusion that such government action creates can limit the ability of parent and community to pass on standards to the child. Together, the divisiveness and low standards make an unholy combination, reinforcing each other's adverse effects. Both will undermine the foundation of any youth charter.

Community divisiveness of this sort was unknown in earlier times. It is ironic that some of the forces that have contributed to divisions between government and communities today developed in the wake of some welcome changes in the extent to which children are valued by the leaders of our government.

Children have become a center of political influence in the United States. This happened so quickly that many in the public may be unaware of it. Yet there have been signs of the shift in every circle of government leadership. When I say that children have gained political status, I do not mean that any individual children have assumed personal decision-making power. Rather, I mean that key political decisions now are being made—or at least justified—with direct reference to children's needs—in other words, young people as a class have shifted from the margins to the center of social influence.

Children have always been the beneficiaries of their parents' hopes and dreams, love and affections, worries and fears. But now children as a social group also have acquired the power and influence that comes with the recognition that they are primary objects of our attention and concern. Never before have so many major social policies of the day been framed on children's behalf or justified in their name. Never before have so many adults molded so many key life decisions—what kinds of laws to pass and enforce, how to structure the tax code, where and when to work, where and how to live—with an eye toward children's welfare. At the same time, social critics continue to argue that we need to do much more to protect children's interests. Protests such as this show how deeply the shift has affected our attitudes toward children.

The signs of the shift are everywhere. Politicians, consciously and with full fanfare, fight to position themselves as the guardians and saviors of youth, competing for the claim that it is their programs that best serve children. This contest draws contenders from a wide range of ideological positions, all vying for this valuable political currency. From the right side of the political spectrum, Pat Buchanan, the staunchest conservative among the 1996 U.S. presidential candidates, proclaimed that "the future of America belongs to our children." His campaign's TV advertisement showed him (a tough, self-proclaimed culture warrior) sitting benignly among a multitude of beaming children. Meanwhile, fiscal conservatives for some years had been promoting their balanced budget policies with the refrain that we should not "mortgage our children's futures." A leading conservative congressman portrayed himself as a champion of children's rights in order to make his case in the key political debate of the day: "Nothing is crueler to our children today than the present welfare status quo."

Later in the presidential campaign, the Republican presidential nominee declared, "The state is now more involved than it ever has been in the raising of children." He then went on to use large portions of his nomination address, the major speech in his campaign, to present his views about children and families. If there has ever before been a time in American history (or, for that matter, in any other country's history) when presidential campaigns have been waged around the issue of child rearing, I am unaware of it.

From the left, a coalition of liberal groups announced a "new tactic" of "stressing potential harm to children."[1] From now on, they have declared, whenever they go public with one of their causes, they will do so in the name of children. The reasons behind this strategy are instructive. Retreating from the electorate's rejection of large-scale government, the liberal groups said that they had determined that the only way to save their programs was to place a child's face on them. Henceforth any arguments for public expenditures must be put forth in terms of children's welfare. In keeping with this strategy, one prominent welfare advocate advised, "When the American people voted for change, and for less government, I don't believe they voted to hurt millions of children, or to take them away from their families."[2]

Another political sign of the shift was the 1996 U.S. State of the Union address, a document that will provide abundant material for social historians of the twenty-first century. The State of the Union address is the president's constitutionally mandated statement about the nation's well-being and future priorities. In 1996, President Clinton determined that the country's number one challenge was to "cherish our children." He went on to say, "It is hard to be a parent today, but it is even harder to be a kid." The president organized the address around the perspective of a threatened child growing up in a hazardous world.

In one prominent journalist's count, the president referred *forty-four times* to "children" or "the child."[3] This is an unprecedented choice of reference, especially by the head of the world's undisputed superpower in the major policy speech of state.

In a line from the speech, the president uttered a sigh of relief about one of the rare things in the world that has become less hazardous for children: "For the first time, since the dawn of the nuclear age, there are no Russian missiles pointed at American children." Of course, as the sharp-eyed journalist noted, Russian missiles were actually pointed at all of us—and mostly at military or economic targets. Military strategists of the cold war era perhaps considered children to be unavoidable "collateral" damage. Not even Russians (the "evil empire" notwithstanding) actually aimed at kids. Now, in presidential hindsight, children were the prime targets at center stage. It is not that he meant this literally. It was just his way of saying that children are (or should be) at center stage in our thoughts.

This is a good indication of a worthy social priority. But center stage in what role? In presidential rhetoric, children have been cast as targeted victims of a murderous onslaught. Is this an accidental characterization, emanating from the president's personal rhetorical style? Or does it emanate instead from a robust worldview that has become deeply embedded within our society? I am convinced that this was not a random flight of fanciful rhetoric by President Clinton. Rather, it reflects a powerful contemporary vision that portrays today's children as constantly besieged by threatening forces beyond their control—and as wholly incompetent to do anything about it.

Shortly after the president's speech, Hillary Rodham Clinton wrote her own book about children. The First Lady described the situation in the following manner: "Everywhere we look, children are under assault: from violence and neglect, from the breakup of families, from the temptations of alcohol, sex, and drug abuse, from greed, materialism, and spiritual emptiness. These problems are not new, but in our time they have skyrocketed."[4]

I agree with every concern in Mrs. Clinton's statement. She is correct in her facts and in her conclusions about the gravity of the situation. Moreover, her book contains valuable recommendations about how children need guidance and a cohesive community to grow up in. But it is also important to note the manner in which the book's language (a reflection of our contemporary culture) characterizes the predicament of today's children. Statements such as the one that I have just quoted characterize children as helpless victims of forces that are entirely out of their control. "Children," the book states, "are under assault"—not only from events that they can do little about, such as their families breaking up, but also by "temptations" such as alcohol, drugs, sex, and greed.[5] Such now-common statements remove from children all traces of volition and active control, *even over their own inner temptations.* Swept away are traditional notions such as active will and personal responsibility. Also swept away are a host of scientific findings showing that very young children are capable of learning moral standards, acting responsibly, and showing self-control.[6] The vision of helpless children floundering in a threatening and bewildering world has become so compelling that it overrides ancient wisdom and modern science alike.

As a citizen, I am glad that powerful and concerned people in government have taken up the cause of children. I am gratified at the prospect that increased political influence may bring children more of society's resources for their education, well-being, and protection. But if greater governmental concern is to translate into true benefits for children, it must be applied in the right direction. The "right" direction that I am referring to is a positive one that builds on children's inherent virtues, inspires their hopes, and offers them higher standards and greater expectations.

It is also one that must draw on the most important resources in children's lives: their families and their communities. Government cannot substitute for parents, teachers, friends, or churches. It should not be a divisive force that separates and immobilizes these crucial resources. Policy and laws must be used to strengthen rather than weaken children's capabilities, and they must be used to support rather than to tear apart communities.

It is hard to be wholly sanguine about the increased role of government in children's lives, despite the immense resources that an active government can bestow on families and schools. As I have just noted, the public rhetoric of political leaders too often plays on the helplessness of young people rather than on their promise. Government agents too often weaken parents and their authority rather than support them. As for supporting community, the recent history of government action is mixed at best. Even with the best of intentions, governmental power can divide communities unless it is wielded carefully and wisely.

We need to bring our government's actions in line with principles of the youth charter. We must see to it that our government supports secure and authoritative parenting, community mentoring, and the high standards and positive aspirations that parents and communities hold for their children. We must also see to it that government supports rather than undermines family and community solidarity. When the people who hold powerful political offices work on behalf of these youth charter principles, government leaders will be able to express their growing concern in ways that improve rather than diminish children's prospects. No citizen alone will be able to secure this kind of benign government presence for an entire community, but citizens in a democracy can take collective action in many ways: through polls, letters, and telephone calls to political leaders, and local forums such as youth charter meetings. In this way, new lines of communication are opened up, and government becomes an informed collaborator to its citizens' efforts.

PART FOUR

The Method

10

GUIDELINES FOR BUILDING A COMMUNITY YOUTH CHARTER

This chapter sets out the procedures that my research staff and I have designed for helping communities build their own youth charters. The procedures are neither final nor definitive; there can be many other legitimate ways to go about the process. We developed our procedures in the course of preliminary pilot work in a few northeastern towns and suburbs. The community that has made the most progress in building a youth charter and using the process toward productive ends is Wellesley, Massachusetts. I have appended the most recent version of the Wellesley youth charter, as of June 1997, to the end of the book.

Following are descriptions and guidelines that we send to communities interested in launching their own youth charter initiatives. We encourage communities to modify the guidelines in ways that make sense to them, experiment with their own ideas, and in general make

This chapter was prepared with the assistance of Anne Gregory.

use of the guidelines in whatever way best serves their needs. We see the set of guidelines as a jumping-off point, a way to get some important community conversations and activities started. It is not a scientific methodology, certified through formal testing, that must be followed step by step. The guidelines reflect our own experience with group meetings and our convictions about the conditions that make these meetings work best. We could imagine how other arrangements might better suit other settings.

One of our convictions is that a youth charter process works best when it starts off as a conversation among adults. Once the adults have had a chance to identify their core standards and expectations for the community's young people, it is important to bring the young people in as active participants in the process. The reason for this sequence is that, in our experience, the presence of young people at too early a stage shifts the focus from standards and expectations to the legitimacy of adult authority. Certainly this is an excellent issue to discuss with youngsters, but it is not a useful one to bring up before the adults have defined for themselves their shared goals for the younger generation, for it is these shared goals that, in the end, provide the best answer to the question of why young people should look to their elders for guidance.

The shared goals reveal the direction of guidance that the adults will offer the young people, and they demonstrate, in a specific and compelling manner, why the guidance is in the youngsters' best interests. Adults need some time to work out their shared goals before they try to explicate them to youngsters (who, if they are as lively and intelligent as young people often are, will be somewhat—to say the least!—skeptical and challenging). Some colleagues of ours who have expressed interest in the youth charter approach have disagreed with the sequence we propose because they believe that young people should be included from the beginning, on principle. We understand and respect this opinion, but our guidelines represent our own experience in the matter.

Definition of a Community Youth Charter

A youth charter is a set of standards and expectations, written or unwritten, that are shared among adults who are in positions to influence the community's young people. A youth charter addresses the core issues of character and competence that young people need to become responsible citizens. It also includes plans for communicating high standards and expectations to young people. How a youth charter is developed depends on the needs and resources of each community.

Setting Up the Charter

The Process

A youth charter begins with an initial town meeting in which as many members of a community as possible gather for a presentation of ideas, problems and opportunities regarding youth development. In order to introduce some ideas for discussion, an invited speaker may give a short presentation on problems and opportunities that young people and their communities face today.

After the opening presentation, the town meeting breaks into small focus discussions in which community members define clear standards and high expectations for youth. Each small group should include a representative cross section of the community: parents, teachers, police officers, religious leaders, youth employers, athletic coaches, local media, librarians, and other individuals who influence the community's young people. Each small group has a facilitator to guide the meeting and a recorder to document the agreed-upon standards and expectations.

The large group then reconvenes to hear summaries of the small-group discussions as presented by the facilitator and recorders. Task forces and established routes of communication are developed to do follow-up work, deal with youth crises that may arise periodically, and create new opportunities for youth development in the community. Meetings are scheduled to discuss the standards and expectations with young people from the community, and the task forces invite young people to participate.

The youth charter should be renewed periodically, at least yearly, to adapt to the changing needs of the community.

Time Line For The Process

I. Planning Stage for the Townwide Forum (months 1–6)

    A. Core group meeting of committed organizers to plan publicity, discuss goals, and set tentative deadlines for the townwide forum.

    B. Coalition building of representatives from community organizations. This could later become the governing group of the youth charter initiative.

    C. Meeting among core group members to determine possible topics for small-group discussion during the forum and to draft a letter to potential facilitators from the community. Reassessment and revision of goals and deadlines, if necessary.

    D. Meeting between core group and other interested parties, for example, potential facilitators, individuals willing to help with publicity and registration, town and school officials whose input or permission is required for the town forum.

    E. Meeting between the larger group of volunteer organizers to outline the agenda for the town forum and to ground group members securely in the theory behind the youth charter.

    F. Final meeting(s) among core group to finalize details: scheduling, location, publicity, and so on.

II. Initiation Stage (months 7 and 8)

    A. Townwide forum (3–4 hours, usually on the weekend)

        1. Facilitators meet the day before or morning of the town forum to organize small group discussion topics and review facilitation skills.

        2. Registration: Volunteers at registration tables greet meeting participants who sign in on appropriate affiliation sheets.

        3. A speaker introduces the concept and purpose of a community-wide youth charter.

    4. Facilitators announce the members of their small groups and the location of their individual meetings.

    5. Small-group meetings occur.

    6. Everyone returns to the large group to share issues and ideas discussed in small groups and to develop task forces that address specific concerns.

    7. Participants break into their chosen task force. Task force participants are willing to commit volunteer time to the task force.

B. Follow-up task force meetings to articulate statements or visions concerning the mission of the youth charter, as relates to their specific task force focus. Each task force will be contributing to a larger written document or a vision of the youth charter, which will be presented to the larger community for feedback. Communication between the leaders of the task forces is essential.

III. Community Outreach (months 9 and 10)

A. One or two townwide forums to shape the youth charter.

    1. Present the collected work of each task force. This collected work will be the foundation of the youth charter but must be presented as work in progress.

    2. Gather feedback on the work in progress and redirect the charter in response to suggestions.

    3. Garner more support and commitment from community members and institutions.

    4. Establish new task forces or add new members to existing task forces.

    5. Solidify a governing body for the youth charter and determine the decision-making process.

 B. Meetings with youth and youth participation in task forces.

IV. Implementation of Action Plans (months 11 through 20)

 A. Action plans are developed and implemented by task force groups.

 B. Action plans address specific community concerns.

V. Updating the Youth Charter

An Annual Townwide Forum to Encourage Reflection on the Implementation and Overall Goals of the Youth Charter (months 21–24)

 A. Assess progress.

 B. Identify community concerns not being addressed thus far.

 C. Reflect on the relevancy of the charter's mission and its targeting of specific concerns.

 D. Consider future directions and revise the charter as deemed necessary.

This time line and plan will now be explained in greater detail. Detailed agendas for meetings, suggestions of publicity, and a plan to engage youth are provided.

Publicity

Publicizing youth charter meetings will boost community awareness and participation. The forms and amount of publicity used depend on the resource constraints and communication infrastructure unique to the community. There are several effective channels for publicizing youth charter meetings.

Newspapers.   Announcements in local newspapers should give the date, time, and location of upcoming meetings. Newspaper announcements also provide space for a brief explanation of youth charters and possible goals to achieve at meetings.

Radio.   Many radio stations must run a certain number of public service announcements on the air and would surely be amenable to announcing youth charter meeting times and other relevant information.

Banners.   A banner announcing the meeting date, time, and location hung in the center of town or at some other prominent location will ensure that community members are provided with the necessary information.

Flyers and Posters.   Flyers containing pertinent information can be distributed to community members in their mailboxes, at the grocery store, through the schools, and at town council meetings or any other heavily attended town gathering. Flyers or more elaborate posters can be tacked to telephone poles or bulletin boards.

The meeting can be billed variously—for example, a catchy title for the youth charter meeting flyers with a short description of the main issues, prominent banners and posters, and word of mouth. Organizers should be creative.

The Role of Small Groups in a Townwide Forum

Constructing Small Groups

It is essential for the success of the youth charter that community members representing a range of interests and organizations have an opportunity to express their concerns and jointly offer solutions. Each small discussion group should have representation from all different sectors of the larger group. A simple way to handle this task is to identify at the start of a meeting which individuals represent which interest groups. Name tags can then be color coded to indicate what sector of the community an individual represents.

When people begin filtering into a meeting, they can be greeted by volunteers at two to three registration tables and be asked to register. Each registration table should be equipped with name tags and perhaps seven or ten sign-in lists, each corresponding to a different community affiliation—for example, school staff, parents, town officials, youth leaders, religious leaders, and concerned community members.

The volunteers staffing the tables should have each individual sign the appropriate sign-in sheet and list the affiliation that he or she feels most comfortable with. The rationale behind asking for affiliation is to facilitate small-group discussions later.

After everyone has registered and the meeting has begun, the volunteers (perhaps during the invited speaker's talk) put together the small discussion groups, remembering that the goal is to have many different viewpoints and community sectors represented in each small group.

Once the groups have been determined and it is time to break up for discussion, each facilitator can announce the meeting place and the names of the individuals in her or his small group.

Small Group Discussions

The small-group discussions are an opportunity for community members to have an honest dialogue about their own standards and expectations for young people as well as their specific concerns about young people. These groups give participants the opportunity to discuss possible solutions, propose entirely new approaches to problems, or draw on the resources already in the community. We see the small-group discussions as covering the following topics:

1. Identify needs and concerns for youth and the community and ways to address those needs.

2. Attempt to identify expectations and standards for youth that are not being met as exemplified by the concerns generated by the group.

3. Identify standards and expectations that connect to the group's concerns for young people and could be the basis of developing community-wide action plans.

4. Brainstorm possible solutions, future task forces, and community strengths that have been underutilized but could be invaluable if put to proper use.

Sample Outline for Seventy-Minute Small-Group Discussions

   I. Introduction (10 minutes)

        A. Facilitator explains the outline of the small-group discussion and the attempt to have a range of interests and organizations represented in each group.

        B. Participants give their names and affiliation (e.g., "parent of a middle school child," "police officer," "high school administrator," "concerned community member").

  II. Brainstorm: What Are Your Concerns for Your Community and the Young People here? (20 minutes)

        A. Put the lists in thematic categories (e.g., problems with lack of supervision, lack of communication between school, parents, youth and police). (*Purpose:* List the concrete concerns that the group can use to ground a discussion of issues of morality, character, standards, and expectations. This list will also be used to develop an action plan.)

 III. Brainstorm: Standards and Expectations in Relation to Listed Concerns (20 minutes)

        A. How do these concerns relate to the standards and expectations you hold for young people? Participants can generate a list of various expectations and standards they hold for young people that specifically relate to the concerns they listed.

        B. What standards and expectations will help young people and the community? Discuss the possibility of building consensus around standards and higher expectations that could help address the list of concerns. How can the community as a whole be responsible to its young people? (*Purpose:* To discuss concrete concerns about young people in terms of standards and expectations. For example, if a concern is raised that young people are drinking at unsupervised parties, what does such behavior mean for healthy development of young people? What issues of character or morality underlie such behavior? Another purpose is to discuss what participants feel are important elements in fostering a supportive environment for the healthy development of young people. Focus should be placed on areas of agreement.)

IV. Action Plans (20 minutes)

A. What vision of the future do you have for your community?

B. How can you and the community clearly articulate certain standards and expectations that will support the healthy growth of young people? How can the community work together across organizations and draw on each other's strengths?

C. What time and resources can be drawn on? What strengths in your community are not being utilized to their fullest?

D. What actions need to be taken to address some of the listed concerns? What can realistically be accomplished? What is our next step? (*Purpose:* To end the discussion with a list of possible actions that will uphold certain standards and expectations the group has for young people. This list needs to be concrete and realistic.)

E. Make available sign-up forms for participants to indicate if they are interested in pursuing future involvement in organizing and volunteering.

Recording of Small-Group Sessions

Each group will have a notebook in which a recorder will write up the ideas generated in the group. A volunteer can serve the role as recorder. The selected recorder or facilitator from each group reports back to the larger community meeting. The notebooks from each group are saved for future meetings, for summary of ideas, and for evaluation of that community meeting.

Facilitators

Facilitators' Responsibilities

Facilitators for the youth charter meetings should be designated in advance, preferably by having interested individuals volunteer. The facilitators should meet with each other before the main town meeting—early enough before the meeting that there is time to discuss all issues but not so far in advance that what has been discussed will be forgotten. A few hours or a day before the town meeting generally works. At the facilitators' meeting the topics for discussion should include a review of basic facilitation skills and responsibilities as well as a discussion of the agenda for the small-group meetings that follow. During the town meeting, the facilitators' main responsibilities will be to guide the small-group discussions over a variety of concerns and topics.

Useful Hints For Facilitators

During the small-group discussions, it is essential that the facilitators remember that their role is outside the discussion. Facilitators must remain objective about all the viewpoints expressed by members of the small group and therefore cannot get caught up in any debate themselves. The facilitator's main role is to focus the discussion and redirect group members to the task at hand when discussion strays from the original topic or question.

Here are some hints for facilitators to keep in mind as they conduct group discussions:

- Designate someone in the group to serve as a scribe, so that the group's ideas can be recorded. It is difficult to both facilitate and take notes, so it is important to have a group member other than the facilitator serve as scribe.
- Reinforce the need for confidentiality before any discussion begins. Group members should be reminded that much of what is said should remain among them once the meeting has ended.
- Designate an informal queue, to ensure that each individual has a chance to speak in turn. The queue should be informal enough to

allow for immediate responses to issues or statements as they are
made but structured enough that everyone who has something to
say has the opportunity to be heard.

- Work to keep the peace when differences of opinion or arguments
arise. Should group members become argumentative or hostile, it
is up to the facilitator to interrupt and remind them that in an
open discussion all opinions are welcome.

- Toward the end of the time allotted for small-group discussions,
provide a summary of the discussion, noting what was accomplished and what issues were raised.

- Volunteer to be the spokesperson for the small group when all of
these groups get back together.

Task Forces

After the townwide forum, task forces that address specific issues or
concerns raised during the forum will begin meeting. Each task force
will need a leader who can help bring focus to the issues, move the
group toward consensus, and help the group reach clear goals. The task
force leaders need good organizational and facilitation skills, which
they will call on often in their efforts to maintain morale, encourage
honest discourse, and include diverse perspectives. It is important that
leaders not take strong ideological positions that alienate volunteers
and distract the group from their common cause.

Task forces should set clear and achievable goals. To prevent burn-
out and encourage involvement, it is advisable that task forces meet for
sixty to ninety days. At the end of this period, the volunteers can
determine whether their task force should continue and whether they
themselves have the time and energy to extend their volunteer commitment—or whether it would be better to recruit new task force members and leaders.

First Follow-Up Task Force Meeting (One Hour)

1. (5 minutes) The leader introduces himself or herself and presents the goals for this meeting. The leader gives a two-minute summary of what issues were raised specifically concerning this task force. A posted time chart that breaks down the meeting into time slots may help give people a better sense of how the meeting will proceed.

2. (10 minutes) Brief (very brief) introductions. Each person in the group gives his or her name and a sentence or two about why he or she is attending this particular task force.

3. (20 minutes) As a group, select two action plans and discuss the viability of implementing each of them.
    Questions to keep in mind on a theoretical level:
    - What message are we conveying with this action plan? Are there certain expectations and standards that we are upholding with this plan?
    - How will the larger community respond to this?
    - How does this action plan fit in with what other organizations are doing?
    Questions to keep in mind on a logistical level:
    - Is this possible to complete in sixty to ninety days?
    - What resources can we put toward it?
    - How much time will each member of the task force need to commit?
    - Can we break down our larger goal into smaller, achievable subgoals?
    - What will be our markers of success and failure?

4. (15 minutes) Publicity and getting more people involved. Each task force should consider the role that youth can play in their task force. How can the needs and voices of young people be heard in your group? Each task force may need a few members to volunteer to take charge of integrating youth into their planning process. This may mean that they recruit two to five young people to join the task force. It may mean that they meet with youth groups or classes. Or it even may mean setting up a panel to hear a group of young people present their opinions.

5.   (10 minutes) Since each task force endures for sixty to ninety days, the leaders must plot out specific goals to be reached by certain dates. Have a posterboard calendar so the group can fill in goals that need to be met before certain dates. Each goal should have one or two names of task force members written underneath it. Clarifying who is responsible for completing the task (even if it is making a few calls to inquire about something) will help ensure that tasks get completed before the next meeting. The dates when the next meetings will be held should also be discussed and printed on the calendar.

Community Outreach

A process of moving forward and stepping back for reflection and evaluation is essential. After the task forces have reached their goals within sixty to ninety days, it is time to go back to the larger community and gather feedback. Opening avenues for community-wide dialogue around youth-related concerns will keep the youth charter process on a grassroots level. To expand participation continually, task forces and leaders should always look to involve more community members.

Depending on the resources, modes of communication, and access to the media, communities will encourage dialogue in different ways. Some suggestions for increasing dialogue and participation follow:

1.   *The Internet and e-mail.* Set up a Web page that is periodically updated and includes news about the youth charter and the actions of the task forces. The youth charter Web page could be set up to include conferencing or forums, which would allow community members to read other people's thoughts and write in their own. The Web page can also be linked to other Web sites that inform people about a range of issues, such as local news, parenting skills, after-school activities, and school events.

2.   *Local media.* Work closely with a local newspaper and request that it periodically publish updates about the charter. Newsletters can also be distributed to disseminate important information.

3. *Phone tree.* Create a telephone list that facilitates volunteers' calling community members not yet involved in the charter so that they can encourage participation and gather feedback.

4. *Community walks.* Reach out to neighbors, and introduce the youth charter ideas.

5. *Questionnaires.* Distribute a questionnaire to youth and adults in the community. Respondents can give their opinions about specific proposals.

Youth Involvement in the Charter

Youth involvement is essential to the successful creation, implementation, and updating of the youth charter. From the beginning, of course, adults must be the leaders of this initiative so that they can honestly reflect on their community's young people and their own concerns, standards, and expectation for young people. However, after the initial discussions between adults in a community, young people's perspectives, needs, and concerns must be solicited and integrated into the ongoing work.

Without youth involvement in the three ongoing stages of the youth charter—creation, implementation, and update—then young people's investment in the ambitious project will be low and success less likely. The youth charter would become yet another program handed down to them—another program that may or may not address their own needs and concerns. The adults and the young people of a community must establish a trusting give-and-take relationship that welcomes involvement and values contribution. Ideally, each group would take each other's concerns seriously. While developing mechanisms to solicit young people's perspectives, adults must also clearly maintain leadership roles that can be so often lacking on a community-wide level. Communities must strive for open and honest communication while at the same time explicitly revealing decision-making processes. It is important to make it very clear which governing body has the ultimate decision-making power and how much authority young people have in influencing final decisions.

Just as organizers will strive to involve adults who represent a range of constituencies and organizations, they should also strive to capture the diverse perspectives of young people. Some strategies for involving a diverse group of young people follow:

- Each institution that offers youth-related activities nominates one or two young people to get involved in the townwide initiative. This process would ensure the involvement of youth oriented toward a range of activities: sports, academic clubs, school government, community service, and arts programs.
- Adult participants go to areas where young people congregate and informally present the youth charter ideas. This tactic would engage young people who may not be officially involved in school or extracurricular activities.
- Bringing the youth charter proposal into the school could potentially involve large numbers of students who participate in a range of activities.
- If resources are available, hiring young people to organize and lead the youth involvement component would open up opportunities for those who must earn money outside of school.

Youth can be involved in the three components of the youth charter: creation, implementation, and update. Such a categorization, however, may be misleading in that we envision a circular process more than three distinct stages. Ideally, a community could set up the mechanisms to engage large numbers of citizens in a process of moving ahead, stepping back, reflecting and changing direction, and moving ahead again. Youth would be integrally involved in this circular process, whereby a young person would not solely be involved, for example, in the implementation of an action plan, but also involved in shaping the plan and assessing its purpose and effectiveness.

Creation of the Youth Charter

After the initial drafting or envisioning of the charter, young people should be asked to reflect on the initiative and to offer their thoughts and ideas. The young people's input needs to be carefully considered and given the authority it deserves. Their ideas will most likely help move the charter in a more effective direction.

How thoroughly adult organizers reach out to young people depends on time, resources, and their own commitment to youth involvement. Adult organizers may want to hand out their written charter as a work in progress in the schools and hold a large meeting to solicit feedback. Panel discussions comprising both young people and adults may also deepen the level of engagement. On a more comprehensive level, adult organizers may conduct a survey to engage large numbers of young people in a process of reflection on the proposal.

After gathering feedback, adult organizers need to respond. This response can take on many forms. Perhaps the governing group would integrate young people's suggestions in the youth charter. Perhaps it would release a response to the feedback while maintaining the original document or vision. Developing a strategy to maintain dialogue with young people and to demonstrate the importance of such a dialogue would have to be made a priority.

Implementation

Adult community members need to come to some agreement about the level of youth involvement. We recommend a genuine commitment to include youth at all levels of decision making. There are several routes a community may take to reach this goal. Four such routes are suggested below:

1.   All the institutions involved in the charter could recruit young people to serve on their own governing boards. Adult representatives of those institutions could then bring issues discussed during youth charter meetings back to their home institutions for discussion. The youth perspective would be represented in each institution involved in making decisions concerning the charter. Thus, through an institutional representative, a young person could have his or her opinions aired.

2.   A more direct voicing of young people's opinions would be to have them serve as active members of the youth charter governing group. These young people would be part of a cadre of youth leaders who would be trained in leadership skills. They would run meetings, lead discussions, and

recruit youth volunteers. In addition to participating in youth charter meetings, they would be responsible for bringing in young people to participate on task forces and action plans. In a sense, this cadre of youth leaders would be the liaisons with young community members.

3.   A community could develop a youth council, a more formal governing body of young people. This council could work alongside a parallel adult organization and make formal recommendations to the task forces and the charter's governing group.

4.   Each task force could construct its own plan to involve youth. The specificity of each plan would address the individual needs of each task force, each of which may require different levels of youth involvement. For example, a sports task force could engage youth in their specific issue by organizing a panel on sports and youth. The youth panel would discuss the role of sports in their lives, including competition, scheduling conflicts, and sportsmanship. Afterward, some of the youth from the panel could join the task force.

Updating the Charter

Just as adult community members will go through a process of reflecting on the youth charter, so too should young people. An annual forum to examine the progress, outdated concerns, and future directions of the charter would ensure that it is in sync with the times.

Appendix

TASK FORCE REPORTS
FROM THE WELLESLEY YOUTH
CHARTER INITIATIVE

The four task force reports from Wellesley were produced by groups of citizens and students working together voluntarily. Neither the task force reports nor the youth charter meetings in Wellesley were officially sponsored or endorsed by the Town of Wellesley. The reports reflect only the opinions of people who have participated in the process thus far, and do not speak in any way for townspeople who have not participated.

A. Synopses of Task Force Reports

Youth Activities

The citizens of Wellesley respect the needs, challenges and interests of our youth. We see ourselves as a community of parents and adult friends, having a desire to create diversified youth activities while maintaining a safe environment for all. We believe in a system that continually strives for high standards and expectations for our Wellesley children. Our young people are a valuable community resource and asset. They are the future of Wellesley. Therefore, our goal is to listen and understand their needs so that we may help them meet their continuing challenges while channeling their enthusiasms in positive directions.

As a result of our research, we are in favor of advocating for Wellesley to establish a Youth Commission. A review of our Youth Commission Initiative is available.

STATEMENT FROM THE YOUNGER MEMBERS
OF THE TASK FORCE

Kids need support and things to do in their own town.

Kids need to be respected and recognized as an important voice.

Kids need a program and space provided as we already do for our nursery-aged children and our senior citizens.

Sports

We believe that organized sports are created to allow children to have fun. We believe that children should participate in a milieu that fosters good sportsmanship, personal growth in physical skills and self-esteem, and a sense of community involvement and allegiance. We believe that in youth athletics it is truly not "whether you win or lose but how you play the game." Sports provide children with age-appropriate opportunities to mentor younger and less experienced players and to learn how to win graciously and to lose with dignity. In short, athletic competition not only provides enjoyment for the participants but also provides real-life lessons: how to cooperate with others, how to compete, and how to deal with authority figures.

We recommend:

1. Adoption of a townwide statement of sportsmanship to be signed by coaches, parents/spectators, and players.
2. A commitment, to the extent possible, to avoid scheduling games and practices during times of known religious observances.
3. Polling of the parents of the players by the coaches prior to scheduling holiday games and tournaments.

4. The establishment of a formal mentoring program involving all sports leagues.

Drug and Alcohol Use

Wellesley is a community that cares about the development, health and safety of its youth. This task force was formed to address a serious issue concerning our youth—the illegal use by minors of alcohol and drugs. Unfortunately, there are no easy answers.

As a result of our preliminary work in this area, the task force recommends the following:

- *Ensure understanding of the law and how it will be enforced.* In that the possession and/or use of alcohol and drugs by minors is illegal in Massachusetts, it is the role of the Police Department and parents to educate our youth regarding the law and the enforcement policy of the Wellesley Police Department.
- *Provide substance-free recreational environments.* It is recommended that the community make a commitment and invest substantial resources to provide more substance-free recreational environments for teens and that they encourage teens to socialize within these environments.
- *Create student leadership opportunities.* High school students should be encouraged to play an active role in this area with their peers and younger students.
- *Ensure availability of information, resources, and support.* Develop resource information, utilize local resources, reestablish a youth commission.
- *Promote and facilitate dialogue for parents and teens.* Promote discussion, survey the community, distribute DAPAC [Drug and Alcohol Policy Advisory Coalition] party guidelines and pamphlet.

If we are to work toward solutions to the problems of drug and alcohol use by minors, all elements of our community, including our teenagers, will need to work together. This task force views its work as a beginning. There is much work to be done. Progress will require that our community commit time, resources, and financial support in the future.

Spirituality

The behavioral and ethical standards about which we seek agreement in this youth charter are based on the expression of such spiritual qualities as kindness, compassion, goodness, unselfishness, honesty, trustworthiness, self-control, responsibility.

To the degree that these qualities are lived, they result in the following actions:

1. Acknowledging the rights of others
2. Following the maxim that one should behave toward others as one would have others behave toward oneself
3. Behaving in an honest and trustworthy manner
4. Striving to learn and practice spiritual discipline
5. Maintaining high standards for one's own behavior by being morally responsible and resisting inappropriate peer pressure.
6. Anticipating the consequences of one's own behavior and accepting responsibility for it
7. Reaching out in service to others, caring especially to touch those particularly vulnerable

While other actions certainly could be included, the task force feels these important points provide a basic set of common expectations from which to begin townwide discussion and consensus building. We encourage the youth of Wellesley to join us in discovering how a vital community can reach consensus on moral and ethical standards of behavior and how we can work to gain townwide acceptance of such standards. *(Synopses executed by Lisa Stone.)*

B. Complete Task Force Reports

The Youth Activities Task Force

Who

Urge the Town of Wellesley to hire a *youth commissioner* who reports to a volunteer board composed of interested citizens and youth serving as a *youth commission.*

Suggested areas of interest under the direction of youth commissioner include:

   Youth advocate to serve as a liaison to town officials

   Biannual seminars (self-defense, youth issues, etc.)

   Scheduled youth meetings (like town meetings)

   Youth representation on town boards and advocacy at annual town
      meeting

   Youth job referral sources (includes baby-sitting, clerking, etc.)

   Townwide community serve-a-thon in addition to a community service referral source

   Tutoring Big Brother/Sister mentors, buddies

   Tutoring from local college students

   Youth recognition awards

   Creation of an informational booklet designed for kids regarding
      Wellesley Youth Commission

   Youth-designed newspaper column as regular feature in local newspapers

   Movie theater/arcade

   Outdoor summer concerts for middle school and high school-aged
      youth

   Community pool

   Available space for pickup sporting games and tournaments

   Local college athletic facilities made available

   Skateboarding, rollerblading, and biking areas established

   Advocate for retail store choices—like Army/Navy type for clothing

   Coordination of teen center and *Nite Shift* [a coffeehouse].

What

An office and a reliable space for meetings and events.

Where

Youth Commission is to be housed at town hall, with e-mail, informational library, telephones available.

Youth activities spaces could tie in with the Recreation Building.

When

To begin ASAP.

How

Funded by town general budget; supported by private, corporate, and civic contributions; perhaps town cable vision subsidy.

Why

Kids need support systems and things to do in their own town. Kids need to be respected and recognized as an important voice. They need a program and space provided as we already do for our nursery-aged children and our senior citizens.

The citizens of Wellesley respect the needs, challenges and interests of our youth. We see ourselves as a community of parents and adult friends, having a desire to create diversified youth activities while maintaining a safe environment for all.

We believe in a system that continually strives for high standards and expectations of our Wellesley children.

Our young people are a valuable community resource and asset. They are the future of Wellesley. Therefore, our goal is to listen and understand their needs so that we may help them meet their continuing challenges while channeling their enthusiasms in positive directions.

The majority of Wellesley students attend the Wellesley public schools, while a smaller proportion attends private schools. We believe it is important for all of Wellesley's youth to have opportunities provided under the sponsorship of our town, to enable them to be accountable for their behavior, to learn and to grow together, socially and in partnership with their community.

Presently there are a handful of self-supporting programs offered by volunteer parents and the Recreation Department for our middle school and high school-aged students. Their continuation of these programs depends on donations and volunteer support.

In order to understand further and learn more about other youth programs, a task force implemented a telephone inquiry, designed a questionnaire, and interviewed fifteen neighboring recreation departments and youth commissioners. In addition, a focus group was conducted involving high school, middle school, and one private school representative. As a result of our research, we are in favor of advocating for Wellesley to establish a youth commission. A review of our youth commission initiative is available.

The following task force members contributed to the preparation of this report:

Rita M. Allen, Chair; Rainy Wilkins, Malva J. Crothers, Pat Piper-Smyer, Connie Smith, Timothy Hansen. Students: Wes Enicks, Daniel R. Crothers, Heather Mullen, Meghan Cavaliero, and Joan S. Cook.

The Sports Task Force

When I was growing up, sports was just something we did. After school, weekends, whenever . . . a regular group of friends—all boys in those days—would get together for a pickup game of whatever sport was in season at the time. There were no referees in attendance and there certainly were no parents observing. Sportsmanship was the tacit acceptance of the rules of the game. Anyone who didn't abide by the rules wasn't invited back for the next game. If there were disputes, then a "do over" was in order. I don't recall any "hot-dogging," and "trash talk" hadn't been invented.

And now, thirty-five years later, I find myself, as a parent of six children, directing a task force addressing issues of sports for our community's children. I suspect that if we left the kids to their own devices, as were we as children, a task force or other such adult intervention would be unnecessary. Once children's sports became organized and supervised by adults, it was inevitable that adults would become concerned about issues in sports that the children themselves were ignorant of.

Last November, at the first meeting devoted to a youth charter, participants discussed the place and significance of sports in our children's lives. Parents were concerned that the importance placed on sports slighted other activities available to children. The impact of sports scheduling on family life was bemoaned. And, beyond sports as play, parents discussed the goals and expectations of sports and the character development to be derived from participation in organized sports.

Our task force heard these concerns from the parents of Wellesley and turned our attention to three areas of interest.

All of us have been involved with children's athletics, as spectators and coaches. We all could recount incidents of bad sportsmanship on the part of players, coaches, and spectators. Thus, we sought to create a statement of sportsmanship for the various leagues in town. It is our hope that this statement will be adopted by all of the sports leagues in Wellesley, that all of the participating players will become familiar with it, and that this statement will ultimately be a positive influence on amateur athletics in Wellesley.

That sports themselves can have a positive influence on children is obvious, but concerns have been raised that sports scheduling can too often interfere with other activities in children's lives. Most specifically, many parents have been distressed by the conflict of many sports activities with other family commitments, notably religious observation and education. We recognize that to a great extent scheduling of games is beyond the control of town sports directors, who must accede to the dictates of intertown leagues. Parents can and must make decisions that reflect their own values and priorities. That is, if, for example, hockey practice conflicts with Sunday religious observation, parents must decide whether to let their child play, if to do so will mean missing Sunday school or Sunday morning mass. However, we would urge local league officials to do all they can, especially, for younger children, to preserve Sunday and Saturday mornings for family time.

An equally strong case can be made for coaches to avoid scheduling games and tournaments during holiday weekends without consulting parents beforehand. Joining a team is often the first time young children commit themselves to an organization outside their immediate family. Parents should support this commitment by encouraging children to attend as many games and practices as possible. However, holiday games and tournaments present a challenge to parents who must balance such a team commitment against special family time. Thus, we would ask coaches to poll their team families at the beginning of seasons before signing teams up for holiday play.

Our final area of interest was what we came to call "mentoring." We believe that sports provide an excellent opportunity for older children to interact with and teach younger children. The older children derive the pleasure and pride that comes with volunteering one's time and energy to help others, and the younger children benefit from contact with older children as role models.

Many of the town leagues do, in fact, already include older children in their coaching staffs. We would propose establishment of a formal mentoring program involving all sports leagues. Such a program should involve public and private school students, who could fulfill community service commitments by signing on to assistant-coach a sports team. We believe such a program will be well received by the leagues, the schools, and, most important, by the children themselves.

Those of us who have worked on this task force did so, I sense, because of our love of our children and because we genuinely believe that sports can exert valuable influence on children and on the adults who coach them.

By participating in organized sports, children can achieve personal growth in physical skills and self-esteem. They can develop a sense of community involvement and allegiance. And they can learn to compete and excel in a nurturing environment.

For parents, participation as coaches and spectators permits shared activities and interests with our children. It provides opportunities to teach children how to win and to lose in fair play, how to deal with authority figures, and how to cooperate with others in achieving a common goal.

We don't have to tell the children that sports provide all these benefits. We merely have to tell them to have fun.

The following task force participants contributed to the preparation of this report: Dan Vogel, leader, Paul Epstein, David McAvoy, Mark Erhartic, Tom Beaton, Lise Woodard, Paul Cremonini, Peter Stone, and Sally Frese.

Town of Wellesley Amateur Athletics Sportmanship Statement

We believe that organized sports are created to allow children to have fun. We believe that children should participate in a milieu that fosters good sportsmanship, personal growth in physical skills and self-esteem, and a sense of community involvement and allegiance. We believe that in amateur athletics at this level it truly is not "whether you win or lose but how you play the game." Sports provide children with age-appropriate opportunities to mentor younger and less experienced players and to learn how to win graciously and to lose with dignity. In short, if the adults who organize and coach town sports encourage it, athletic competition for children not only provides enjoyment for the participants but provides for the children real-life lessons: how to cooperate with others, how to compete, how to deal with authority figures.

In this context, we, as a community, hold to the following:

For Players
- Treat teammates and opponents alike with respect and kindness.
- Play hard to win but within the rules of the game.
- Respect and abide by the decisions of the officials.
- Win with dignity, lose with grace.
- Represent your team, your family, and your community with pride.
- Take every opportunity to encourage teammates to succeed.

For Coaches:
- Always be an example of good sportsmanship to your players.
- Accept the decisions of officials in a respectful manner.
- Teach your players through positive reinforcement, not by demeaning them.
- Remember it is an honor to be called a "coach"; do not abuse it.
- Remember that opposing players are, like your players, only children.
- Foster in your players a love of the game, not a lust for winning.

For Parents/Spectators

- Remember you are watching children, no matter the color of their jersey.
- Children learn from your behavior; be an example of good sportsmanship.
- Leave the coaching to the coaches and the officiating to the officials.
- Recognize and applaud good play on both sides.
- Support your child by attending his/her games.
- Encourage your child's commitment to his/her team.

Wellesley Youth Sports Player Contract

I, _____, wish to participate in _____, sponsored by _____.

My parents and I have read and understand the Wellesley Sportsmanship Statement. As player and spectators we agree to abide by the spirit of that statement.

I pledge to support my teammates, practice good sportsmanship, and have fun.

Date _____

Player signature _____

Parent/guardian signature _____

Drug and Alcohol Task Force

Wellesley is a community that cares about the development, health and safety of our youth. This task force was formed to address a serious issue concerning our youth—the illegal use by minors of alcohol and drugs. Unfortunately, there are no easy answers.

To understand the problems and devise potential solutions, we initiated dialogue with parents, community leaders and the Wellesley Police

Department. The task force looked at ways that parents, community groups, schools, town officials and police could work with teenagers to focus attention, energy and resources in this area. We also did an initial survey of neighboring communities to gather information and ideas as to how they were dealing with these problems.

As a result of our preliminary work in this area, the task force recommends the following:

Ensure understanding of the law and how it will be enforced. In that the possession and/or use of alcohol and drugs by minors is illegal Massachusetts, it is the role of the police department and parents to educate our youth regarding the law and the enforcement policy of the Wellesley Police Department.

- Policy communications: The Police Department's "General Policy Concerning Youth and Alcohol" should be reviewed for clarity. For example, the term "possession" should be defined as it is enforced, citing specific examples where helpful. The phrase "community service as determined by the Wellesley Police Department" appearing on page 1 of the policy should be clarified. A list of potential community service assignments should be included, along with some explanation as to how the assignments are determined. The use of "diversion programs" referred to in the policy needs specific explanation. The community and police should work together to review the policy to make certain that its guidelines can be clearly understood. This updated policy should be distributed to all Wellesley families.

- Police information: A representative of the Wellesley Police Department should meet annually with parents to promote understanding and communication about the law and Wellesley's enforcement policy. Parents should review this policy with their children so that Wellesley minors may understand and abide by it.

- Police and school interactions: The interaction between the police and school department in handling infractions should be clarified. See, for example, the Memorandum of Understanding from Newton and Westwood's student handbook.

- Police resources: Information about resources available to youths and parents through the police, such as diversion and substance abuse programs, should be outlined.

- Youth officer: Designate a youth officer as the vocal and visible point person on all matters related to youth, drinking and drugs. This officer should be able to relate easily to youth, parents and teachers. The better the connection among these groups, the better the communication will be. Wellesley should contact other towns to learn about possible expansion of the role of youth officer in the area of prevention and support.

Provide substance-free recreational environments. It is recommended that the community make a commitment and invest substantial resources to provide more substance-free recreational environments for teens, and that they encourage teens to socialize within these environments.

- Additional youth activities: Support development of additional youth activities that offer alcohol and drug-free environments, such as the NiteShift coffee house.
- Post-prom parties: Support for post-prom parties. Based on the popularity of the current all-night graduation party at the high school, this should be well received. It would alleviate risks of many post-prom activities. The task force has information on such initiatives from the towns of Newton and Norwood.
- Substance-free household program: The town should generate and maintain a list of parents of teens who will commit to providing a household where guests of their son or daughter will be allowed to socialize in an environment where alcohol and drugs are not readily available. The school PTSO packet sent home in August could serve as the vehicle for gathering consent of parents interested in participating in such a program. The town newspapers could provide private school families the opportunity to learn of this effort and to participate as well. We call this program the "Substance-Free Household Program." Similar programs under different names are already in place in other communities throughout the Commonwealth. We have attached a form that could be used to compile such a list [not included in this Appendix].
- Financial support: Ensure that the teen center already in place for middle school students be financially secure and that the coffee house pilot program for junior and senior high school students receive annual financial support by the town. We encourage the town to look at additional efforts by other towns in this area.

Create student leadership opportunities. Beginning with the 1997–98 academic year, high school students should be encouraged to play an active leadership role in this area with their peers and younger students.

- Student advisory board: We encourage the town and the high school to work together to invite students to establish a student advisory board to accomplish this purpose. It is our hope that this student board will become knowledgeable on the subject and a role model and resource for other students. A sample sign-up sheet for students is attached for the convenience of the high school. Private school students should be encouraged to participate in this initiative.

- Tips for teens from students: We suggest that as an initiative of this student advisory board, a tips for teens advice sheet be prepared for students not yet at the high school. This advice to young teens would assist them in making sound decisions in their school and social environments and help them cope with peer pressure.

- Utilize students as a resource: We further encourage adult committees charged with responsibility in this area to utilize this group as an important resource and as a vehicle to increase dialogue on this subject.

Ensure availability of information, resources, and support.
- Develop resource information: We recommend that the town develop literature and resource lists on the subject of the health and safety risks of the use of alcohol and drugs by minors, and make it readily available to residents through the libraries, schools, community center and other facilities. Counseling centers and facilities for families in need of services in this area should be included.

- Utilize local resources: Wellesley should make use of the surrounding prevention centers for access to resources and up-to-date educational information. The compilation of a list of speakers and programs is encouraged to promote regular education on this subject by the town.

- Youth commission: We urge the town to reestablish a youth commission to oversee the interests of youth. While there are groups in town that currently attempt to address youth concerns, it is imperative that the town designate one visible department to advocate for youth needs and coordinate information and efforts on their behalf. Several surrounding towns currently have effective youth commissioners and youth advisory boards.

Promote and facilitate dialogue for parents and teens.
- Promote discussion: It is recommended that the community takes steps to provide opportunities for parents to participate in meaningful discussion with one another on this subject on a regular basis throughout the year and for students to do the same. Guest speakers, community and school programs should be used to increase dialogue on this subject and to generate creative means to solve the serious issues associated with these problems. Efforts should be made on an ongoing basis to continue networking with surrounding towns to learn of their efforts in this area. Parents are encouraged to renew discussions and increase communication with their teens on this subject.
- Survey community: A parent questionnaire on the subject of minor use of alcohol and drugs could be distributed through the middle and high school newsletters, with inclusion in the local - newspapers for parents of private school children. This would, hopefully, provide us with valuable feedback from the community. Attached is a survey drafted by the task force [not included in this Appendix].
- Party guidelines: Ensure annual distribution of Wellesley Drug and Alcohol Policy Advisory Coalition (DAPAC) party guidelines to all middle and high school families and publish the same in the local newspapers for community awareness.

If we are to work toward solutions to the problems of alcohol and drug use by minors, all elements of our community, including our teenagers, will need to work together. This task force views its work as a beginning. There is much work to be done. Progress will require that our community commit time, resources and financial support in the future.

The following task force participants contributed to the preparation of this report: Fran L. Whyman, co-chair; John S. Whyman, co-chair; Mark Erhartic, Diane D. Hollister, Thomas J. Hollister, Nancy Lindsey, Cheryl D. Mullen, Nancy Mutrie, Laura Nalesnik, Lynne Stanton, Kathleen Vogel, and Daniel H. Vogel.

Task Force on Spirituality

This youth charter envisions a shared view of sound moral standards and ethical values by which parents, teachers, public servants, and others in the community can teach children the difference between right and wrong and guide them into responsible and loving adulthood. Most would agree that these standards and values are built upon the foundation of our religious and ethical traditions. While civil and criminal laws represent the baseline of our standards, we aspire to achieve and maintain in Wellesley a level of behavior and interpersonal relationships much above that base level.

Today young people in our community often receive conflicting messages concerning standards of behavior they should meet and expectations they are capable of fulfilling. These contradictory messages come from many different sectors of our community, in addition to the broader influences of the popular culture, and create a confusing framework for their guidance. If we wish to help our young people develop sound moral character and to gain a sense of purpose in life, then it behooves us to identify our community's core values and standards and to communicate these clearly above the hubbub of contrary voices and agendas.

We believe it is possible to create a positive environment in Wellesley which has multiple sources of spiritual guidance, fosters mutual respect for others and their property, values interdependence within the community, encourages open communication and nonjudgmental listening, and does not tolerate violence of any kind.

While words are important, we believe that adult actions deliver the clearest messages to youth. Appropriate adult behavior, exemplified consistently in word and deed, is essential in raising children. Modeling the behavior that is sought enables youth to make a successful and smooth transition into adulthood.

In our society today, there is a growing awareness that spirituality is a vital element of a meaningful life. The term "spirituality" has a variety of meanings. In its most fundamental sense, it is knowing that a greater power exists which influences, shapes, and guides us. It may also be defined as the consciousness of spirit, not of material things. This consciousness helps us make choices that have a positive impact on our

relationships with family, community and the environment. Thus, spirituality results in the expression of good.

Capacity for spirituality is inherent in each individual, but the development of one's spiritual identity is an ongoing life process. Spiritual nourishment is essential to everyone. Children and young adults need it to enable them to mature in ways that will lead to constructive, fulfilling, and enriching lives. Adults require ongoing spiritual nourishment to enhance the spiritual environment in homes, schools, houses of worship, and throughout the community.

The behavioral and ethical standards about which we seek agreement in this youth charter are based on the expression of such spiritual qualities as kindness, compassion, goodness, unselfishness, honesty, trustworthiness, self-control, responsibility. To the degree that these qualities are lived, they result in the following actions:

1. Acknowledging the rights of all others
2. Following the maxim that one should behave toward others as one would have others behave toward oneself
3. Behaving in an honest and trustworthy manner
4. Striving to learn and practice spiritual discipline
5. Maintaining high standards for one's own behavior by being morally responsible and resisting inappropriate peer pressure
6. Anticipating the consequences of one's own behavior and accepting responsibility for it
7. Reaching out in service to others, being careful to touch those particularly vulnerable

While other actions certainly could be included, the task force feels these important points provide a basic set of common expectations from which to begin townwide discussion and consensus building. Any or all can foster spiritual growth and nurture discernment of life's deeper meaning.

It is our belief that individual and collective spirituality is fundamental to the living of these standards. Some people may be aided in their spiritual development primarily through organized religion, for religious institutions historically are teachers of moral and spiritual law. For some it may occur as a result of service to others, or from experiences with nature, or perhaps through involvement with music and the arts. Many people are aided, no doubt, through a combination of these and other pursuits. Participating in one's own religious community as well as interfaith activity are means of bringing the people of Wellesley together and fostering our collective spiritual growth.

Residents of all ages have the opportunity to reach out to those in need and to offer help, for serving others is one way in which we gain a greater sense of spirituality in our lives. A variety of service programs already exist in Wellesley which provide such help. But we see the need for a mechanism to coordinate and publicize the programs already in place as well as new programs that may develop.

We encourage the youth of Wellesley to join with us in discovering how a vital community can reach a consensus on moral and ethical standards of behavior, and how we can work to gain townwide acceptance of such standards.

The following task force members contributed to the preparation of this report: Frederic Livezey, chair; Carolyn Bernstein, Richard Carls, Katherine M. Cramer, Susan Cummings, Kimberly N. Dziama, Carol R. Galginaitis, Jay and Sally Hammerness, Evelyn Howard, Rebecca Taylor, Tricia Epstein, and Elizabeth King.

Notes

PREFACE

1.   F. Ianni, *The Search for Structure: A Report on American Youth Today* (New York: Free Press, 1989).

CHAPTER 1: WINDSOR, 1997/1998

1.   These are actual quotations from articles in the *Boston Globe,* December 5, 1993 ("Suburban Kids 'Bomb' Graffiti Scene"), August 7, 1995 ("Art with an Urban Edge"). What are the effects of publicly condoning graffiti? A kind of "natural experiment" on this question was unwittingly conducted by a news team in Los Angeles a few years ago. I quote from a report by Jon Keller in the *Boston Globe* (July 7, 1996, p. 19): "Graffiti reports jumped upwards of 100 percent after a Los Angeles TV station aired a five-part series glorifying taggers."

CHAPTER 3: YOUTH CHARTERS

1.   F. Ianni, *The Search for Structure: A Report on American Youth Today* (New York: Free Press, 1989) pp. 354, 247.

CHAPTER 4: GUIDANCE ON THE HOME FRONT

1.   See my critique of popular child-rearing advice: W. Damon, *Greater Expectations* (New York: Free Press, 1995). In *Greater Expectations,* I explain how much of the

advice that parents are now receiving is child-centered to the extreme. Such advice has encouraged parents to give in to their children's every whim, shield children from challenges necessary for their growth, and indulge children with lavish material goods, unearned praise, and limitless autonomy. Overly child-centered practices produce and encourage children to become self-centered and self-absorbed and to acquire an unrealistic state of entitlement. The overly indulgent child-rearing practices have contributed to a lowering of standards that is depriving children of the guidance that they need to develop their full potentials of competence and character.

2.   M. Csikszentmihalyi, K. Rathunde, and S. Whalen, *Talented Teenagers: The Roots of Success and Failure* (New York: Cambridge University Press, 1993), p. 244.

3.   See Damon, *Greater Expectations*.

4.   P. Leach, *Your Baby and Child from Birth to Age Five* (New York: Knopf, 1989), pp. 316–317.

5.   See Damon, *Greater Expectations*, pp. 115–118, 176–182.

6.   T. Phelan, *1–2–3 Magic: Effective Discipline for Children 2–12* (Glen Ellyn, Ill.: Child Management, 1995).

7.   See W. Damon, *The Moral Child* (New York: Free Press, 1990); Damon, *Greater Expectations*.

CHAPTER 5: SCHOOL SUCCESS

1.   D. Goleman, *Emotional Intelligence* (New York: Random House, 1996).

2.   W. Damon, "Learning and Resistance: When Developmental Theory Meets Educational Practice," in E. Amsel and A. Renninger, *Change and Development* (Hillsdale, N.J.: Erlbaum, forthcoming).

3.   G. C. Massey, M. V. Scott, and S. M. Dornbusch, "Racism Without Racists: Institutional Racism in Urban Schools," *Black Scholar* 7 (1975): 18.

4.   A. Powell, E. Farrar, and D. Cohen, *The Shopping Mall High School: Winners and Losers in the Education Marketplace* (Boston: Houghton Mifflin, 1985); T. Sizer, *Horace's Compromise: The Dilemma of the American High School* (Boston: Houghton Mifflin, 1984); R. Kramer, *Ed School Follies: The Miseducation of America's Teachers* (New York: Free Press, 1991); C. Sykes, *Dumbing Down Our Kids: Why America's Children Feel Good About Themselves But Can't Read, Write or Add* (New York: St. Martin's Press, 1995); C. Finn, *We Must Take Charge: Our Schools and Our Future* (New York: Free Press, 1991); T. Sowell (1993), *Inside American Education: The Decline, the Deception and the Dogmas* (New York: Free Press, 1993); A. Wynne and K. Ryan, *Reclaiming Our Schools: A Handbook on Teaching Character, Academics and Discipline* (New York: Merrill, 1993); J. P. Comer, *School Power: Implications of an Intervention Project* (New York: Free Press, 1993); D. N. Perkins, *Smart Schools: Better Thinking and Learning for Every Child* (New York, Free Press, 1995); H. Gardner, *The Unschooled Mind: How Children Think and How Schools Should Teach* (New York: Basic Books, 1991).

CHAPTER 6: BEYOND HOME AND SCHOOL

1.   H. Gardner, *The Unschooled Mind* (New York: Basic Books, 1991).

2.   C. Branta and J. Goodway, "Facilitating Social skills in Urban School Children Through Physical Education," *Journal of Peace Psychology* 2 (Special issue).

3.   Ibid., p. 308.

4.   C. Taylor, "Sports and Recreation: Community Anchor and Counterweight to Conflict," *Journal of Peace Psychology* 2 (Special Issue): p. 342.

5.   Patricia Lynn Stern, "Teen Sexuality Among Inner-City White Youth: Becoming an Adult in Milton," in J. Garrison, M. Smith, and D. Besharov (eds.), *Sexuality, Poverty, and the Inner City* (Menlo Park, Calif.: Henry J. Kaiser Family Foundation, 1994), p. 45.

6.   Elijah Anderson, "Sex Codes Among Inner-City Youth," in Garrison, Smith, and Besharov, *Sexuality, Poverty, and the Inner City,* pp. 22–23.

7.   F. Furstenberg, "How Families Manage Risk and Opportunity in Dangerous Neighborhoods," in W. J. Wilson (ed.), *Sociology and the Public Agenda* (Newbury Park, Calif.: Sage, 1993).

8.   N. Garmezy, "Stressors of Childhood," in N. Garmezy and M. Rutten (eds.), *Stress, Coping, and Development in Children* (New York: McGraw-Hill, 1983), pp. 43–84.

CHAPTER 7: THE MASS MEDIA

1.   Amy B. Jordan, *Children's Educational Television Regulations and the Local Broadcaster: Impact and Implementation* (Philadelphia: Annenberg Public Policy Center, University of Pennsylvania, 1997), p. 4.

2.   Marie-Louise Mares, "Positive Effects of Television on Social Behavior: A Meta-analysis," (Philadelphia: Annenberg Public Policy Center, 1990), A. Huston and J. Wright, (1997). "Mass Media and Children's Development," in W. Damon (ed.), *Handbook of Child Psychology, Vol. 4: Child Psychology in Practice* (5th ed.) (New York: Wiley, forthcoming).

3.   Mares, *Positive Effects.*

4.   See Huston and Wright, "Mass Media."

5.   R. T. Truglio, "Sex in the 90s: What Are the Lessons from Prime-Time TV?" (Paper presented at the meeting of the Society for Research in Child Development, New Orleans, 1993).

6.   Huston and Wright, "Mass Media."

7.   Ibid.

8.   Mares, *Positive Effects.*

9.   Ibid.

10.   W. Damon, *The Moral Child* (New York: Free Press, 1990).

11.   J. L. Singer and D. G. Singer, *Television, Imagination, and Aggression: A Study of Preschoolers* (Hillsdale, NJ: Erlbaum, 1981).

12.   Huston and Wright, "Mass Media."

13.   Ibid.

14.   Ibid.

15.   Amy Jordan, *The State of Children's Television: An Examination of Quantity, Quality, and Industry Beliefs* (Philadelphia: Annenberg Public Policy Center, University of Pennsylvania, 1996).

CHAPTER 8: ENABLING A DISABLING SOCIETY

1.   W. Damon, *Greater Expectations* (New York: Free Press, 1995).

2.   Ibid.

3.   *Years of Promise: A Comprehensive Learning Strategy for America's Children* (New York: Carnegie Corporation of New York, 1996), p. 13.

4.   International Narcotics Control Board survey, cited in "Agency Sees Risk in Drug to Temper Child Behavior," *New York Times,* February 29, 1996.

5.   Anne Moir, quoted in *Forbes,* August 12, 1996, p. 151.

6.   A. J. Zametkin, et al., "Cerebral Glucose Metabolism in Adults with Hyperactivity of Childhood Onset," *New England Journal of Medicine* 323 (1990): 1361–1366.

7. Dr. Jerry M. Wiener, chair of psychiatry at George Washington School of Medicine, quoted in "Children Who Can't Sit Still," *New York Times,* August 4, 1991.

8. "Disability Grants for Children Fuel Welfare Debate." *Boston Globe,* May 12, 1994.

9. Ibid., p. 28.

10. J. M. Swanson et al., "Effect of Stimulant Medication on Children with Attention Deficit Disorder: A 'Review of Reviews,'" *Exceptional Children* 60 (1993): 154–162.

11. Pediatric neurologist Fred Baughman, cited in *USA Today Magazine,* January 14, 1995, p. 85.

12. *Science News,* May 27, 1989, p. 332.

13. D. Bell, *The Cultural Contradictions of Capitalism* (New York: Basic Books, 1976).

14. W. Damon, *Greater Expectations.*

15. R. Bellah, R. Madsen, W. Sullivan, A. Swidler, and S. Tipton, *Habits of the Heart: Individualism and Commitment in American Society* (Berkeley: University of California Press, 1985).

16. For a further analysis and a vision of a better alternative, see R. Bellah, R. Madsen, W. Sullivan, A. Swidler, and S. Tipton, *The Good Society* (New York: Harper & Row, 1992).

17. G. Elder, *Children of the Great Depression* (Chicago: University of Chicago Press, 1975).

CHAPTER 9: GOVERNMENT

1. *New York Times,* January 13, 1995.

2. Ibid.

3. Maureen Dowd, "Playing the Kid Card," *New York Times,* February 5, 1996.

4. H. R. Clinton, *It Takes a Village to Raise a Child* (New York: Simon & Schuster, 1996).

5. Ibid.

6. W. Damon, *The Moral Child* (New York: Free Press, 1990).

Index